Alvaro Dickinson Field

Worthies and Workers, Both Ministers and Laymen of the Rock River Conference

Alvaro Dickinson Field

Worthies and Workers, Both Ministers and Laymen of the Rock River Conference

ISBN/EAN: 9783337232221

Printed in Europe, USA, Canada, Australia, Japan

Cover: Foto ©Lupo / pixelio.de

More available books at **www.hansebooks.com**

WORTHIES AND WORKERS,

BOTH

MINISTERS AND LAYMEN,

OF THE

ROCK RIVER CONFERENCE.

BY

REV. A. D. FIELD,
OF THE
ROCK RIVER CONFERENCE.

CINCINNATI: CRANSTON & CURTS.
PRINTED FOR THE AUTHOR.
On sale by Cranston & Curts, 57 Washington Street, Chicago.
1896.

COPYRIGHT
BY A. D. FIELD,
1896.

PREFACE.

WHEN I undertook to write the History of the Rock River Conference, which was published in 1886, the plan was, in the proper place, to give a full sketch of the workers as they appeared on the scene. But when the work was ready for the printer, it was found impossible to crowd all the matter into one volume. The best thing that could be done was to take out the "Lives" of the actors. Ever since that work was published, I have been waiting the time when this volume could be published. A full account of several chief actors in Rock River history is given in the volume already published, and will not be repeated here. If the reader wishes to read some quite interesting sketches, he will find in the HISTORY lives of Dr. Dempster, the founder of Biblical schools; W. M. D. Ryan, and others.

In a third volume, the author will try and gather up all that have been left out.

INDEX.

Large CAPITALS are Ministers; small CAPITALS are Laymen.

	PAGE.
PREFACE,	3
CHICAGO,	9
METHODIST PREACHERS,	30
FIRST ROCK RIVER CONFERENCE,	47
OLDEST APPOINTMENTS,	49
GENERAL CONFERENCE DELEGATES,	51
JESSE WALKER,	53
WILLIAM SEE,	107
S. R. BEGGS,	115
JOHN SINCLAIR,	119
PETER R. BOREIN,	124
HOOPER CREWS,	135
A. E. PHELPS,	150
JOHN CLARK,	162
B. H. CARTWRIGHT,	165
HENRY WHITEHEAD,	171
S. F. DENNING,	174
R. A. BLANCHARD,	190
MILTON BOURNE,	193
SIAS BOLLES,	197
J. W. AGARD,	200
J. R. GOODRICH,	203
GEORGE DAVISON,	204
J. F. CHAFFEE,	205
EUNICE BUSH,	206
LUTHER BEAL,	207

CONTENTS.

	PAGE.
BENJAMIN BOWMAN,	209
ELIAS CRARY,	212
MRS. LUCY WENTWORTH,	212
ZEBIAH WENTWORTH ESTES,	214
THOMAS FREEK,	216
J. W. FLOWERS,	217
N. P. CUNNINGHAM,	219
DAVID CASSEDAY,	220
JOHN DEW,	222
M. DECKER,	225
CHESTER HOISINGTON,	226
S. A. W. JEWETT,	228
ALVA GAFFIN,	229
J. G. GIBSON,	231
WILLIAM GADDIS,	231
WILLIAM ROYAL,	233
M. L. REED,	234
ANDREW NEWCOMER,	236
A. S. W. McCAUSLAND,	238
JAMES McKEAN,	238
J. T. MITCHELL,	240
W. W. MITCHELL,	246
ELISHA B. LANE,	249
S. G. LATHROP,	249
GEORGE LOVESEE,	252
MARTIN KRINBILL,	254
L. S. WALKER,	255
WARREN TAPLIN,	258
W. D. SKELTON,	259
MARSHALL SHERMAN,	261
ELIHU SPRINGER,	261
ISAAC SCARRITT,	264
MRS. WILLIAM WHEELER,	268

	PAGE.
A. WOOLISCROFT,	269
JOSIAH W. WHIPPLE,	271
D. M. BRADLEY,	272
JOEL MANNING,	274
SAMUEL McCARTY,	279
OTIS HARDY,	282
GEORGE C. COOK,	286
E. Q. FULLER,	290
PHILO JUDSON,	303
ELIZA H. JUDSON,	306
LUKE HITCHCOCK,	307
ELIZA GARRETT,	312
GRANT GOODRICH,	317
ORRINGTON LUNT,	320
GEORGE F. FOSTER,	326
A. R. SCRANTON,	332
A. D. FIELD,	338
O. H. TIFFANY,	351

WORTHIES AND WORKERS

OF THE

ROCK RIVER CONFERENCE.

CHICAGO.

IF the reader will look upon a map, he will see that Lake Michigan lies in a position almost north and south, sixty miles wide and three hundred miles long. About fifty miles north of Chicago, near the Wisconsin line, a sluggish stream, a mere ditch, about five rods wide, takes its origin, and flows nearly south on a line with the lake, keeping nearly ten miles from it. This is the Des Plaines River. At its beginning it is perhaps thirty feet above the level of the lake; but on reaching a point southwest of Chicago it falls to a level with the lake. The Chicago River sends its south branch away in a southwest course towards the Des Plaines. The two streams, in the locality just named, are mere sluggish ponds. The land for ten miles west of the city lies only five to eight feet above the sluggish waters. The south branch of the Chicago River ends in sloughs and marshes, that in times of ordinary water connect it with the Des Plaines. The waters from many of these marshes part and run both to the Gulf of Mexico and to the Gulf of St.

Lawrence. Often, at times when the Des Plaines is choked with ice, the floods pour over through the Chicago River, and create great havoc. One of these overflows, in 1849, swept the shipping from the harbor. The lakelets along this course have been used for over two hundred years as passage-ways for the boats of alternating prospectors. At all times of the year, except winter, there was a free route for heavily-laden canoes from Lake Michigan on into the Illinois River and down to the Mississippi. To this circumstance we owe the early fur-trading French and Indian village, and the beginning of the present great city. It was the mania for fur-trading that planted the first colony, and the suggestion of a connecting canal that founded the city. It was this marshy passage that made Chicago the great entrepot between the north and the south from the ages before Columbus until it was made insignificant by the network of modern railways, that have made the canal nearly obsolete, or at best a great sewer, to carry away the sewerage of the city.

The towns of Kaskaskia and Cahokia, in Illinois, were founded over two hundred years ago by French priests and adventurers, who found their way from Canada around the lakes, down this passage from the Chicago River to the Des Plaines, and into the Mississippi. In the notes of these early voyagers there are accounts of the river, of Indians, and of the country. The name Chicago is found in the earliest records. In an old document, dating in the French occupation days, now in the archives of France, a chief, Chicaugo by name, is mentioned. Chegaug is the Indian name both for skunk and a wild onion. So that, from the earliest day, the traveler has had his choice of naming the place Skunktown or Oniontown, either one of which is full as savory as the earliest settlers of the place. It is proper to say, however, that a few years ago a document was found deeding a tract of country in Northern Illinois, wherein Chicago River is spoken of as Onion River, and that probably gives us the true origin of the name.

In looking over the annals of two hundred years we find frequent mention of voyagers who tarried for a time on the banks of Chicago River; but it is best for the purposes of these pages to begin at a point so tangible that history may drive its stakes to remain.

The history and influence of the American fur-trade needs to be written. Two impulses served to settle the great West. The fur-trade from 1800 till 1840 opened up the States of the Northwest and Oregon. Gold and silver mines took up the work in 1849, and from that day they have been the alluring motives that have made the valleys and the mountains of the Western States teem with human life. And it may be said, in an aside, that some of the great families—notably the Astors of New York, and the Kinzies of Chicago—derived their foundation from the fur-trade.

In 1804 the Government built a fort at the mouth of the Chicago River. In 1812, when General Hull surrendered to the British at Detroit, he sent an order to Captain Heald, commanding at Fort Dearborn, to evacuate the post and to march his company to Fort Wayne. In obeying these orders, Captain Heald set out with his command in August, 1812. When one and a half miles on his way, along the lake-shore, the Indians, who were under British influence, closed in upon the band and killed or scattered them. This event is known in history as the Chicago massacre. It is a touching tale, but it does not serve our purpose to speak more fully of it here.

The fort was rebuilt in 1816, and from that time until the autumn of 1836 a company of soldiers was quartered there. At the time last named the soldiers were removed, and Fort Dearborn remained a striking monument of the past until about 1865, when "Business," that greedy monster that swallows up or wipes out the most sacred mementos, crowded the last vestiges of the old fort out of existence.

The first real settlement of Chicago by the white people began with the building of the fort in 1804. In that year John Kinzie settled, with his family, on the north side of the river, near the lake. Mr. Kinzie came from Detroit. For years before he had been a fur-trader, and for years after he was a leading trader, Indian agent, interpreter, etc., in the West. From that time members of the Kinzie family were the chief actors in all the most prominent matters of the new country.

Until 1830 there was nothing at Chicago, besides the soldiers, but John Kinzie and his assistants. Most of these last were Canadian Frenchmen, who had married Indian women. Their names are yet preserved in towns and villages. The place which drew the attention of the white man had drawn the attention of the Indian for centuries, and still in 1830 it was a great gathering place for the surrounding tribes. It continued to be the favorite home of the Indians until as late as 1840, when the last of the once powerful races disappeared over the Mississippi.

The real beginning of Chicago must be set down as occurring in 1830. A traveler may stop in Chicago to-day and remain for a week, and never hear of the canal or see a canal-boat; but there is a canal, connecting the south branch of the Chicago River with the Illinois River, along the marshes spoken of in the commencement of this article. Though it has so far dropped out of sight that the traveler will never see or hear anything of it, that canal made Chicago. From 1830 to 1850 it was the one great dependence for the success of the place. In 1850 there was nothing in the whole city so prominent.

For fifty years previous to 1830 there had been growing communities in Southern Illinois and in Missouri, around St. Louis, and there were forts and trading posts at Detroit and other places along the lakes. As early as 1825, and before, small flatboats, laden with provisions for the forts at Chicago and Green Bay, made their way up the Illinois River and across into Lake Michigan through the sloughs that connected the Lake with the Des

Plaines River. In 1828 Lewis Cass, then governor of the Territory of Michigan, took a trip across Wisconsin by way of the Wisconsin River down to Rock Island, by way of the Illinois River up to Chicago and Lake Michigan. Excursions of this kind were frequent.

Jefferson Davis was then (1828) a lieutenant at Fort Winnebago, in Wisconsin, and under Government orders he surveyed the lake, and in particular sought for the best place for a harbor. General David Hunter was in charge of the fort at Chicago from 1825 to 1830, and in 1825 married a daughter of John Kinzie, sending a soldier on foot down to Peoria, a hundred and fifty miles, for a marriage license.

It will be seen how these boatmen and adventurers, as they pushed their boats with difficulty through the reeds of the Chicago marshes on their way up and down, would suggest to one another the need of a better channel to connect the north and the south. Besides, it was the day and age of canals. Railways were as yet only an experiment. The Erie Canal had just been opened. Other waters over the then settled States had been connected by excavated water-ways, and, indeed, the canal idea was like a revelation to the country. It was the only great "boom" of that age, as railways have been the "boom" of this age. Nothing, then, could have been more natural than the gradual rise of the idea that some day a canal would open the courses of navigation between the lakes of the North and the great rivers of the South. Canada and New

Orleans might thus clasp hands! It was a great idea; and this idea made Chicago!

Illinois Territory was organized in 1809. The northern line ran due west from the southern point of Lake Michigan, a fact that in the end would have left Chicago in Wisconsin. In 1815 Nathaniel Pope was elected the delegate to Congress. He saw the importance of having a lake front and lake harbors in the future State of Illinois, and procured the passage of an act changing the line to the forty-second parallel, thus throwing the location of the great city into the State in which it now takes a leading position. But it was earlier than this that people began to think of a canal. In *Niles' Register* of August 6, 1814, occurs the following passage:

"By the Illinois River it is probable that Buffalo, in New York, may be united with New Orleans, by inland navigation, through Lakes Erie, Huron, and Michigan, and down to the Mississippi. What a route! How stupendous the idea! How dwindles the importance of the canals of Europe compared to this water communication! If it should ever take place (and it is said the opening may be easily made), the Territory of Illinois will become the seat of an immense commerce, and a market for the commodities of all regions."

What a strange foresight! All west of Ohio was then an unbroken wilderness.

At the first session of the Illinois Legislature, after it had become a State, in 1818, Governor Bond brought the subject of a canal from Lake Michigan to the Illinois River before that body, and Governor Coles renewed the subject in a message in 1822, and in 1823 a Board of Canal Commissioners was appointed, and the same year surveys and estimates were made. All this in an unbroken wilderness! In 1825 an act was passed incorporating the Illinois and Michigan Canal Company. In the meantime the Representatives from Illinois were urging Congress to pass measures in aid of the project. Daniel P. Cook was the leader in this movement. Accordingly, in 1827, Congress granted to Illinois a belt of land along the canal three miles wide. In 1829 the State Legislature passed a bill organizing a Canal Board, and appointing commissioners. These commissioners were empowered to locate the canal, lay out towns, to sell lots, and to apply the proceeds to the construction. In the fall of 1829 the commissioners reached Chicago, and employed James Thomson to survey and lay out a town. This work Thomson accomplished, and his map bore date August 4, 1830. This is the beginning of the city. That map, with other early and precious documents and records, was destroyed by the great fire of 1871.

The history of Chicago as a city begins in 1830. The inhabitants at the time were, besides the officers and soldiers at Fort Dearborn, John Kinzie, Dr. Wolcott, John Miller, William See, James Kinzie, and a few French Canadians, laborers, and boatmen around the trading post. By August of that year there was quite a company of settlers. At an election held in that month thirty voters' names are recorded.

As I came to Chicago early in 1835, when the town was but four years old, I am often asked if there were then any inhabitants at all. People who ask that question forget that our Western cities do not rise with slow and gradual growth, but that they spring into existence in full power. It was thus with Chicago. The prospects of the new canal brought people to the place by hundreds. At the time of my coming there were already about 2,000 inhabitants. It was, however, a shifting, speculating, drinking, floating crowd, drawn there by the visions of the wealth that was to be made out of town-lots and opening trade. But, alas! the people were doomed to wait eighteen years before the canal was able to pass even a canoe across the intervening way. But for the time being—1830 to 1836—everything was on a high tide. Fortunes were made and fortunes were lost for the space of six years with a frenzy wild as a "Black Friday" on Wall Street.

But slowly and surely the work of preparation went on. The canal had land, but no money, and wild lands at $1.25 per acre, even if sold, would not produce the needed thousands. It is not necessary to give in detail here the proceedings of the State Legislature for the five years when it was struggling with the question of finances. It is enough to say that at length measures were adopted that promised the needed funds, and at last the great project was to go on. The canal was to start out from the south branch of the Chicago River at a point three miles from the mouth of the river. From the main river all the way out the river was fringed by woods and thickets. The banks of the river were trimmed up. A plank-walk and tow-path was laid for three miles, to Bridgeport, and on the Fourth of July, 1836, the crowd, five thousand strong (this present writer drifting with the human tide), with wild hurrahs, with flags and drums, and, above all, with plenty of the choicest liquors, floated on the river and tramped on the walks out to the opening place. Boats of all sorts—a steamboat large as a river tug, a schooner gayly bedecked with green boughs, and laden with women and children—steamed and was towed by gangs of men out to the grand rendezvous; and somewhere about noon, with speeches and toasts and hurrahs, the first shovels of earth were thrown out, and at last, after twenty years of waiting, the Illinois Canal was becoming to our seeming a reality. Contracts were made, and the real work of excavation began in earnest. For months all went on well. People flocked to the new Chicago, and town-lots went up into the thousands. Business of all kinds began running at the highest. The canal and its workmen needed provisions, lumber, teams, and the country for a hundred miles around felt the impulses of the new enterprise. The city began to plan for its future. In 1837 it became an incorporated city, with W. B. Ogden as its first mayor.

Six months of this prosperity passed, and then the collapse came! All over the United States, in 1837, there came general failure and bankruptcy.

All credit seemed to vanish from business circles. Money became worthless, and disappointment prevailed over the whole land. Some one ought to write out a history of the dark days that began in 1837. The whole country felt the calamity; how much more Chicago, whose every hope was built upon credit and what *was to be!* The people had come there because the canal was being opened, and every sort of business was started on the idea of trade arising from the canal. When work ceased, and the laborers left the country, and the supplies the canal called for were no longer needed, the reader can imagine the condition the people of Chicago were left in. My father began cutting timber at the head of Lake Michigan for use. When he began, timber was fifty cents a foot; in the end it could not be given away, and it was left in the Calumet River to rot. This was in 1837. It was twelve years before that canal project was resuscitated. Eight years of perfect prostration followed. This brought lots and lands and buildings down to the lowest auction-sale prices, and general bankruptcy prevailed.

I turn back to some matters heretofore omitted.

Chicago is situated about thirty miles north of the most southern point of Lake Michigan. At the point where the city is built there is a deep, sluggish stream, more like a bayou than a river, about two hundred feet wide. Originally its banks were so abrupt vessels could haul up within a plank's length of the shore. This river, beginning at its mouth, runs half a mile directly west, at right angles with the lake, then parts into two branches, which turn in a gentle curve to the northwest and the southwest, until they drain the same marshes that are drained by the Des Plaines. This river formed the natural drainage for the ten miles of low, wet prairie lying west of the lake. Along the lake the winds of centuries had thrown up sand-ridges ten or twenty feet high. The remainder of the land on which Chicago was built rose but five or six feet above the river. Near the river's edge there were a few rods of dry land, but for most of the year the remainder was low, marshy ground. The land alternated with ridges and swales. The ridges were covered with hazel-brush; into the swales in wet times the water gathered in ponds. It is from this circumstance that I, in the early day, either skated or gathered hazelnuts on almost every block of the city. The ponds would be passable only after long summer drouths, as the land was tenacious clay, and there was no drainage. In the winter of 1837 on the West Side there was a sheet of ice for ten miles, over which we school-boys skated. All over the city, as late as 1845, there were wells, in which water could be reached at about five feet. Nearly all the north side of the river in 1836 was covered with timber, and from Madison Street the east side of the south branch was skirted with thickets and groves. Such was the ground on which Chicago was built. The papers of the early day contained frequent jokes, more true than funny, about teams miring in the streets, and there being places where there was no bottom. In those days it was one of the commonest things to see teams stuck in the mud on Lake Street. There was no kind of pavement laid down until 1845, and then, when part of a street was planked, it proved a nuisance, because the slush spurted up between the planks.

When people first began to settle in the place it was difficult to decide where the town would be. Three points struggled for the ascendency, until the city by growth covered the whole area. The first cluster of buildings was on the North Side, near the lake. There, in 1834, the first church was built, and in 1836 the first respectable church. This was the St. James Episcopal, on Rush Street. In the same summer (1836) a stylish hotel, the Lake House, was erected. From its grand northern portico Daniel Webster made a speech in 1837. But by 1836 the main portion of the business was transacted on the South Side, on Dearborn and South Water Streets, with a few scattered stores on Lake Street. At the same time, a half mile away, on the West Side, there were several places of trade. But at length the South Side won; so that in 1843 there was not a place of trade of any sort on the West Side, and only a grocery store on the North Side. The gorgeous *Lake House* had become a rookery, filled with washerwomen and other tenants. Long rows of frame-built stores stood vacant, to be let as tenant houses or for school purposes. The business of the city centered on the South Side for years before the North or West Sides had trading places.

At the time the operations on the canal came to an end, in 1837, the country west of Lake Michigan to the Mississippi was almost entirely unsettled. About that time emigrants began to pour in; but it was a long time before they had produce to sell or means to spend in trade. The city that had depended almost entirely upon the trade that the work on the canal had brought was left almost entirely without patronage. The travelers who were just beginning to make their way to the West were about the only sources of income. A city of 5,000 inhabitants, surrounded by a desert, was very nearly the situation of Chicago at that time. Nearly all the first citizens, that might have become millionaires, lost their property and passed out of sight. Up to 1843, when trade began to revive, almost the universal form of payment was by "orders." There was no money. It was almost impossible to get cash for labor or goods. The laborer was given orders on the merchant, and the merchant gave orders on the meat-market, and the market-man was given orders on the shoeshop; and as these orders were often not backed by the best credit, the men on whom they were drawn were slow in filling them. I once set out to supply myself with a new suit. I received orders on the tailor and the shoemaker; but as the materials out of which my things were to be made were valuable, it was a long time before my new suit came.

But the same impulse that brought citizens to Chicago brought settlers to the country west. By 1840 the country back of the city to the Mississippi was covered by sparse settlements. These settlers, for a hundred miles west, found Chicago their only market and trading-point. There were no railroads or other conveyances for produce. The stage-coach for the traveler and the wagon for the farmer were the only means of travel. Little burgs sprung up at convenient places all over Illinois, but they furnished no markets for produce. For fifteen years on—from 1836 to 1850—the main products of the country were hogs and wheat. The hogs were dressed and taken to Chicago for sale, and the wheat was hauled a hundred miles over the tedious, miry roads. Dressed hogs ranged in Chicago from $1.50 to $2.50 per hundred, and wheat from fifty to sixty cents per bushel. When a farmer took to the city twenty or thirty bushels of wheat, a distance of forty or eighty miles, the reader can figure out the amount of money he would have when he reached home, after a week's absence. By 1845 this trade had become so great that during all the fall months South Water Street, where all the warehouses were located, would be packed with teams, waiting their turn for unloading. From the time that this trade became sufficient to give the people business the city began to rise again.

The revival of credit throughout the country, and the increase of capital, caused the project of completing the canal to be revived, and in 1847 work was renewed. In June, 1848, the city turned out once more in a mass and marched up the same old path by which they went in 1836 to the starting-point of the canal. In 1836, just twelve years before, the crowds went out to witness the first removal of earth; now it was the day of fruition! With music and speeches the crowd greeted the first packets as, with banners and music, they made their way through the completed canal. Chicago has never since seen a day of triumph like that! From that time the city has been the great market-place of the Western World.

The first railroad was built from the city to the Des Plaines River in 1849, and by 1855 there were railways running out from the city in every direction. From that time the noted canal, on which for years the whole being of the city seemed to depend, has been an insignificant thing. It exists, of course, and is continually transporting merchandise out and country produce in, but it cuts a very little figure in the business of the city, and is almost unknown to the traveler.

The building of the railroads is too great a matter to treat upon here. But to show the ideas of the early days, I give the following incident: In 1847 it was proposed to build a railroad west of Chicago to the Mississippi River. That summer I was a student at Mt. Morris, a hundred miles west of Chicago. One day a meeting was called in the seminary chapel to listen to some proposals of J. Y. Scammon, a Chicago lawyer, concerning the proposed railroad. After explaining the proposed plans, he made the following statement: He urged the people to subscribe, and suggested that subscribers to the railroad-building fund could pay their amounts in ties and team-work. He proposed to build a railroad as they then built country meeting-houses—by subscriptions paid in work!

It remains for me to take up a few threads of this history. The churches of a city are silent powers that attract but little public attention; but he that would ignore them forgets factors in civilization greater than commerce.

In 1825, Mr. John Hamlin, of Peoria, Illinois, had contracts to furnish provisions to the forts at Green Bay and Chicago. These supplies he carried to their destination from the lower Illinois River country by means of small flatboats, rowed by five or six men. On one of these trips up the Illinois and Des Plaines Rivers, in the early spring of 1825, Mr. Hamlin was accompanied by Rev. Jesse Walker, a driving Methodist preacher, who will go down in Methodist history as the greatest pioneer preacher of that Church. The boat would tie up to the bank early each evening, as they could not voyage by night. Seated on the logs, with the boat's crew around him, Mr. Walker would "line" out familiar Methodist hymns, which he and the men would sing with a zest that would wake the far-off echoes. Thus hymn after hymn would be sung at the evening encampments. This is the first appearance or record of any minister in the regions of Chicago since Marquette and Joliet were there in 1662. In the spring of 1825 Jesse Walker established a mission among the Indians on Fox River, sixty miles southwest of Chicago. This was continued until 1830. At that time Mr. Walker was appointed to Chicago, to look after the religious interests of the projected town. He had, in 1820, been permitted to organize the first Methodist Church in St. Louis; and now he had to do the same service for Chicago. Among the people who went to the place in 1830 there were several Methodists. Most prominent among these was William See, a local preacher. He was employed by the Government to do blacksmithing for the Indians. Cook County was organized in 1831; and this William See became the first county clerk at Chicago, the county-seat. In July, 1831, Rev. S. R. Beggs, then on a circuit down near Peoria, went up to Chicago, to assist Mr. Walker in holding meetings. One Sunday morning, after preaching in William See's log house on the West Side, Mr. Beggs called for members. Six or seven persons came forward and joined the Church. A Methodist society was organized, it being the first Christian Church of any kind in the city. In 1832 Jesse Walker purchased the log house of Mr. See, and turned it into a meeting-house and school-room. In this room the first Sunday-school was organized. In June, 1833, Rev. Jeremiah Porter, a newly-arrived chaplain at Fort Dearborn, organized a Presbyterian Church in this log church on the West Side. In the fall of the same year, Mr. Freeman organized a Baptist Church. I may add that the three original societies have had a continuous existence. The Catholics built a church on State Street in 1833, the first church in the City after Mr. Walker's log church. The Methodists built a neat frame church on the North Side in 1834, and the same year the Presbyterians built the same same sort of a church on Clark Street, between Randolph and Lake Streets.

Up to the time when Chicago began to be built, all the inhabitants of Illinois had come up from the South, following the course of the rivers. From this cause the schools of the State were at first and for years subscription or private schools. Most of the first settlers of Chicago were from the East; and thus it happened that a free public school, opened in Chicago in the fall of 1834, was the first free public school in the State of Illinois. The first schools were begun in 1832. By the autumn of 1835, when the writer of these pages entered them, there were two schools in the city. Up to 1845 the schools were not much above primary affairs. They were presided over by transient teachers in old forsaken buildings, wherever for the time these could be obtained. In 1835 the South Side school was kept in the Presbyterian Church. In 1837 the West Side school was in an old abandoned hotel, and after that for years in an old dwelling-house on Monroe Street. In 1845 substantial brick buildings were erected, and from that on the schools of Chicago have been famous.

I may add that I was a witness to and a participator in nearly all the transactions narrated in this article. It is a curious experience to have stood by for sixty-one years while this phenomenal city has been having its phenomenal growth. It is an uncommon experience to be a part of a place from the days when it was a village in the desert till it became the second city in the Western Hemisphere.

It is the disposition of Americans to outdo, even if it is to excel in calamity. It is probably the fact that Chicago has been the scene of the greatest calamity on the American Continent. I do not know that it has ever been disputed that the great fire of October, 1871, began on the West Side by the upsetting of a lamp by a cow, which some dullard was milking. The fire began among some old stables and shanties. The wind was furious from the southwest. The flames took a northeast course, crossed the south branch about a half a mile south of the main river; then the fire swept all before it on the South Side, crossing the river to the North Side, on, on, to the northern limits of the city. But little was left between the river and the lake. The desolated territory covered a space about half a mile wide and a mile long. On this ground was all that there had been of the city from 1830 till 1860.

Much has been said since 1871 about the energy that restored the city in greater grandeur than before. It would be pleasant for me to give this credit to citizens of Chicago; but truth will lead us to a somewhat different conclusion. The owners of property were most of them men who had come up, by innate energy and enterprise, from nothing to wealth. They had buildings and blocks; but these were generally greatly involved—built often on credit, the principal to be restored by the proceeds of rents. The fire swept away rents from which incomes came. So much real estate was thrown upon the market, sales were slow and prices down.

The real facts are, that a greater part of the rebuilding was done by new men and by outside capital. Many of the former business men rebuilt, and still remain, while hundreds were swept away by the terrible calamity. One of the most extensive wholesale grocers was obliged to act as an agent for a patent-pill maker. One very energetic man went into a country town, and bought an interest in a mill. Another who was worth his thousands, is a runner for a wholesale house. These business men are found all over the West, trying to make a living. It was too late in life for them to begin at the bottom again. But in the meantime the city has gone up grander than ever.

I have said that the site of Chicago rose but five or six feet above the level of the lake. When the town began to stretch itself to modern dimensions, the matter of sewers became a vexed question. It will be seen that a system of sewers that would drain a large city was impossible. After long debate, the city government adopted the heroic measure of raising the grade of the city eight feet, so that the traveler of to-day treads eight feet above the old paths of the Indian and the fur-trader. To effect this grade the city merely raised up the streets, leaving every land-owner to do as he pleased with his buildings and his lots.

How large is the city of Chicago? I may say, in general terms, twenty miles long and ten miles wide. In 1837 the writer hereof lived sixteen miles from Chicago, in a wild wilderness country. In 1891 I revisited the old place. Two miles beyond the old home, eighteen miles from the Chicago Court-house, I found a Chicago policeman treading his beat.

The idea of locating a town where Chicago is arose from the convenient waterway from Lake Michigan to the Mississippi. The canal was the main stay of the city from 1830 till 1850; but from that time the railroads have made the city. It lives and grows because it has at the back of it all the country to the Pacific Coast. Its great enlargement arises also from the fact that it has so much country around it for suburbs. The greatest business item of Chicago to-day is its suburbs. By this means, the city is reaching out for twenty miles in every direction. When this enlarging process will cease none can tell; but electric cars and suburbs may, before many years, make a city forty miles square.

METHODIST PREACHERS.

It has been my portion to mingle with all sorts of men as classes, but among them all I have found none as a class so genial in spirit, so companionable in life, as Methodist preachers. For some reason, I do not quite understand, the Methodist preachers, who have been the most zealous workers in the spreading of the gospel of any, have been the least solemn. There is little of sour godliness among them. If occasionally you find one of the sour sort, it is one, generally, that has set himself up as a separatist, who announces himself as more pious than his brethren. One of this sort once got the noble, the devout Hooper Crews down to the mourners'-bench at a camp-meeting.

I never read the life of that majestic Abraham Lincoln but I am reminded of Methodist preachers, particularly in the story-telling propensity. Like him, nearly every preacher I have known intimately has in social life been given to telling stories to illustrate any subject in hand. No men see so much of the varied phases of life as these preachers. Living amid hardships, amid all sorts of people, amid all sorts of scenes, their memories become stored with rare events and stirring experiences, and when once in congenial companionship this fountain is opened, it flows with narrative abundant. I am sorry to say that there creep into the ministry now and then those who bring the coarse, sometimes the smutty with them. These are few, and they are sure to go off the track in time. I have met now and then preachers that have reminded me of an event. In the old stirring temperance days of 1842-45, a rough, coarse lake captain, who had been a drunkard, became a temperance man, and when on shore often spoke at temperance-meetings. At a meeting at the Bethel, on the North Side, in 1844, the captain, while speaking, began to pour hot shot into what he deemed were false temperance people. He clearly indicated Colonel R. J. Hamilton. This brought R. J. to his feet, when an altercation ensued. The closing shot of the colonel was: "You have come up from the ditch, and have brought the slime of the ditch with you." I have seen preachers that reminded me of that saying; but from all such characteristics the great, nobler portion have turned away. One never heard coarse, vulgar stories from the lips of Vincent, or Fuller, or Crews, or Hitchcock, or Axtel, or Quereau, or William Aug. Smith. And you never heard one of these men making silly after-dinner speeches! This pureness of speech was one peculiarity of Dr. E. Q. Fuller. He loved children, he loved flowers, he loved all that was grand in nature, and by these his whole converse was inspired. He was an inveterate storyteller; but his stories, like Lincoln's, always had a purpose, and aroused you to the importance of the aim for which the story was told. In all my intercourse with him for years, during which time I spent days and days in social converse, I never knew him, save once, to utter a coarse or low sentiment, and then the cause was so urgent we all pardoned him. We were at Conference. On Sunday morning Bishop Simpson preached one of his overwhelming sermons; in the afternoon Dr. Dempster preached as he had never preached in the West before. But in the evening a "star" preacher took the pulpit. He was one of those evanescent men who go from one Conference to another seeking the highest places. This man's manner that evening made us pronounce him a "blow." The whole thing was weak and flat, with attempts at bluster. E. Q. Fuller and a lot of us were seated in a corner. Fuller wrote on a slip of paper and passed around among our "set" these words: "Soul for breakfast, brains for dinner, and g—ts for supper."

The pleasantry of different men was peculiar. Dr. Eddy in hours of relaxation was not a child, or a boy, but more like a clever, winsome girl. I never heard him crack jokes or tell stories, and yet there was always a playful, genial pleasantry about him that can not be described in print. I may, perhaps, give a hint of it in the following: While he was editor at "66 Washington Street," I had occasion to go to the city for some literary purpose, and was one forenoon at work in Dr. Eddy's office, in the third story. There was a call at the speaking-tube. Dr. Vincent was hunting me; and be it said that, in those days, J. H. Vincent had a sort of city lisp to his speech. He asked if I was in the office. I could not hear the voice of Vincent but could, of course, hear the answer of Eddy. The Doctor answered: "His illustrious excelsissimo is here." This was uttered in so perfect a Vincent lisp I knew at once who was asking for me.

These preachers, when greatly tempted, are often as mischievous as boys. At one Conference a noble, able doctor, whose name I always utter with affection, was on the Conference program for a speech on education. Some one had broken the laws of the equities by putting up a racy speaker before the elaborate doctor. This had a tendency to make the last speaker tedious. He had spent days preparing his discourse. He went quietly at work in making his speech, and took up the progress of education in the Church during each century. He spoke of the first century, then the second, then the third, and so on. One could see that if every century received the attention a few of the early ones received, we would not go home till morning. Dr. Vincent was sitting in the pulpit. He wrote on a slip of paper, and sent down to Dr. Eddy, who sat among a group of us near the pulpit, these words: "Dr. Eddy, I am going to sleep; when we reach the nineteenth century, please black my boots and wake me up."

One of the occasions of conflict in the Rock River Conference was the meeting of Eastern and Southern types of Methodism. The modes were often so different you would hardly know they were of the same Church. The East favored choirs, rented seats, etc.; the South opposed. But I intended to refer here to only one feature, and that the greater emotional development of the Southerners. About 1866, the Rock River Conference was almost entirely made up of preachers of the Eastern type. The three Conferences in Illinois, south of Rock River, were composed of preachers of the Southern type. These peculiarities were never so fully brought in contrast as at a grand reunion of the four Conferences in 1866, at Bloomington, in the centenary year. It was the first and only time the Illinois Conferences have met together since the first separation in 1840. On the day appointed, one of the grandest meetings I ever attended was held in a hall holding one or two thousand people. Each Conference was seated by itself with a sea of lay people packed between the preachers. As the day wore on, and the inspiring addresses were being uttered, a tumult of responses rose up often from the three Southern Conferences, while Rock River men sat staid and silent. They sat with intent gaze, drinking in the thrilling sentiments of the occasion while but few words escaped them; the others rang the house with responses. Knowing the men well on each side the line as I did, for all this difference I had reason to have as great confidence in the piety of the preachers from the North side as in that of those from the South side. One afternoon at the Conference at Elgin, in 1870, C. H. Fowler was preaching the Missionary Sermon. It was a superb effort, one of the loftiest endeavors of that rising man. The house was crowded. All eyes were intent on the preacher, but yet it was as still as evening. I left my busy desk, and went into the vestibule for rest, and stood in the door listening to the preacher. One of Rock River's favorite men, then not long from Indiana, standing at my side said: "Look at those preachers. How silent! Why, if that sermon was being preached to my old Indiana Conference, the preachers would raise the shout of hallelujah, and bear the preacher on a tumult of praise to the very skies."

Perhaps an exception was the preaching of Bishop Ames at the Conference at St. Charles in 1852. E. R. Ames had been elected bishop in May, and this was his first visit to Rock River Conference in the capacity of a bishop. He preached on Sunday. I have talked with several prominent men since then, who have agreed with me that it was the greatest sermon we ever heard. The effect was peculiar. I do not remember anything just like it. There were few words uttered, but everywhere strong men were weeping like children. People were sobbing aloud. Such men as Philo Judson and Luke Hitchcock sat in and around the pulpit convulsed with weeping. O, it was a strange, weird power the bishop had over us that day! But I must add that I never heard the bishop come up to that height again.

Very much has been said concerning the ignorance of the early preachers. The real fact will reveal a different view. The early preachers were young men called from among the people. These young men, as I have had ample occasion to know, were the most sprightly and intelligent of the young men—those who had naturally studious habits. It has always been a difficult thing for dullards to get into a Methodist Conference. They sometimes apply, and sometimes, through the pressure of ardent friends, get in; but as a rule, they find no welcome, but sour-spirited, they float away to *certain* other Churches, where they live for awhile on the strength of the support given new recruits. These most intelligent young men who succeeded received the best education there was to be had; and if it was meager, they were at least the most advanced of any of their circle; and if their education was little, they always preached to people who had less. With hardly an exception they were lovers of knowledge, and at once began reading the best books in their reach. They read up carefully upon the subjects that most interested them. While they may not have been adepts in any of the higher branches, there was little on the great religious themes of controversy of which they were ignorant. They knew everything that could be known concerning baptism, Calvinism, Universalism, the doctrines of Alexander Campbell, or anything else that was rife. There is another thing that is to be borne in mind: from the earliest day, while often the public schools were poor, there were seminaries and academies in all parts of the land, and most of the young preachers of fifty years ago attended some one of these at least a year or two. This was the case with such men as J. T. Mitchell, Peter Borein, Silas Bolles, R. A. Blanchard, Milton Bourne, John Clark, and others. Whenever ignorant and unworthy men crept by chance into any of the Conferences, they soon "went West," there to be crowded either into the blank Church or into oblivion!

It will perhaps be noticed that in the sketches of men in this book I have said very little about the piety of the subjects. The reasons are many, but chiefly this: A man who found himself, amid the privations and hardships of the early work, without piety, soon found the toil too irksome to bear. Nothing but a pure and ardent devotion to the Master's work and the love of immortal souls would have kept them in the work. I have therefore taken it for granted that they were devout and humble Christians. And any one who knew them well found it difficult to make comparisons. A person is not on very sure ground when he undertakes to say that A is more religious than B. It is not difficult to measure intelligence, preaching capacity, eloquence;

but none but the Master can measure the devoutness of a human soul! I undertook this once, to my confusion. In 1863, circumstances led me to say to a group of preachers that A. B. C. was the most devotedly religious man of any preacher in Rock River Conference. Before a year, the real inwardness of that man could be seen by this incident: From the gospel, he turned to preaching upon all matters. One noted sermon was on The Horse. In this, he said: "If I had the means, I would own the neatest team in this city; and then I would like to see the man that could pass me on Wabash Avenue." He confided to a friend about this time the fact that it took eight pairs of kid-gloves to do him a week! He was already taking his way to the dogs, whither he afterwards went.

Nor can you put much trust in the superior professions of the men themselves. I could tell a tale here were it not for being too severely personal, and that I would not be guilty of a fling at that divine word, holiness. Some of the people I have known, who have used that desecrated word the most, have been lacking in the first principles of honor! So be it understood that Phelps, and Crews, and Mitchell, and Blanchard, and Walker, and Fuller were men devoted to God and his service. This was the inspiration of their noble lives.

The modes of travel forty years ago were peculiar. There were no railroads then, and few stages. The married men who had household goods had an easier time than the young men who had but a single trunk to move. The men of families would hire teams by the day, and make a week of it; but we unmarried men, who rode on horseback, had experiences that seem strange in these days of rail-cars. The first railway in Rock River Conference was laid from Chicago to the Des Plaines in 1849; about 1850 it reached Elgin. In 1853 the Illinois Central reached Kankakee; and it was a long time before roads were running as far as Rock River or the Mississippi. A literal account of my own travels will serve as an illustration. At the Conference at Rockford in 1849 I was appointed junior in Iroquois County. My trunk was at Hennepin, ninety miles away. I borrowed a harness and wagon, and made the trip of one hundred and eighty miles just to get a trunk. In 1850 I went to Hancock County. I traveled two hundred miles on horseback to my circuit; then again borrowed a harness and light wagon, and went seventy miles to Peoria County, whither U. J. Giddings had brought my trunk. In 1851, I went to Kankakee County. Here I borrowed another harness and wagon, and went out two hundred miles and back—a journey of four hundred miles—for my trunk. This is a fair specimen of the way we all did; and it was the only way we could do.

On going to my first circuit at Hennepin, on the Illinois River, in 1848, I immediately ordered a package of books from the Book Concern at Cincinnati. That was our nearest and only source of supply in the West. There was no express; there were no railways. This package was to contain the books I needed for use in the course of study; and I was, of course, very anxious to receive them, as well as others I wished to read and to sell. The preachers sold books in those days; it was a part of their business. I waited for those books until winter set in, then gave them up. One day, the next April, I happened to pass along the river shore, and there I saw standing by itself a box directed to me. It proved to be the long-looked-for treasure, just dumped on shore by a passing steamboat. It had lain in a warehouse at St. Louis all winter.

I will note another thing that may seem strange to the moderns. In the days of forty years ago there was a premium on unmarried men. The country was new, and the "quarterage" was small; so that many efficient married men were obliged, from year to year, to locate for want of means to support their increasing families. This being the case, a whip, so to speak, was held over the young preachers' heads forbidding them to marry; and whenever any of our number dared to take to himself a wife, he felt that the first thing to be endured was the censure of the older members. As late as 1849, when the case of a young man was up who had just finished his two years' probation, and the elder informed the Conference that the young man had been so indiscreet as to marry, Bishop Janes very severely uttered the sentiment that no young man had a right to marry until he had gained a standing in the Conference. The only thing that seemed to save the head of the young brother was the assurance that he had married a very superior young lady.

METHODIST PREACHERS.

The preacher's pay of forty years ago was not calculated to make us very vain. A man received $100; his wife $100; and then for the married man's family there was estimated his "table expenses." The unmarried man was allowed $100, and left, like old-time school-teachers, to "board round." For three years I never had a place where I remained more than one night at a time. The young preacher was never at home, but always a visitor; and ever when he came the fat chicken had to be dressed; so that with chicken three hundred and sixty-five times a year it is no wonder I came to detest the universal delicacy. My total receipts the first year was $86; the second, $80; the third, $55. My first year after marriage we received, counting "donation" and everything else, $88. I think the whole salary of the Chicago preachers about 1840 was about $500 per year, and most of that in "store pay;" for there was no money in Chicago in those years. Everybody paid everybody in orders. The grocery-man got his boots and shoes on credit, and the shoe-man paid his bills in orders on the grocer, and the preacher was glad to get his share of the "orders." It is said the Baptist preacher one time found in his receipts—put in by mistake—an order on the saloon!

In the whole fifty years of the Rock River Conference's history there has been but one trial for heresy, and Dr. H. W. Thomas has the honor of that supreme distinction! The heretics of fifty years ago can all be numbered on the fingers of one hand. Two of these had the honor to withdraw from the

Conference before any pressure whatever was brought to bear upon them. There have been several instances where very strict examining committees have felt constrained to report Conference candidates as being a little crooked on some points, and in a few instances men have been sent before special committees; but there the matters have ended. If any one shall ask how it comes that with these hundreds of men there has been such unanimity, I answer, there has never been, can not be expected to be, an entire unity of view. The preachers are united on the great themes of salvation; but it were too much to ask that every man should be just like every other man. If the Conference were at any time brought to a test, for instance, as to the nature of the resurrection body, and made to comply with Watson's Institutes, there would be a flinching, and that, too, among many men who have been General Conference officers. Upon such points they are silent, because they have arrived at no positive views. It is enough for them to read, "It doth not yet appear what we shall be," and for themselves trust to the revealments of the great day; and they have had the good sense not to distract their congregations with abstract points on which they themselves have no positive opinions. It is probable every preacher may have his pet heresy; and so long as it does not distract and divide a congregation, there may be no special harm in it. The one great motive in pressing Dr. Thomas to an issue was in this: Had Dr. Thomas had an independent Church, like Ward Beecher, the whole world would have said, Thomas and his people for it. But he each year occupied churches built for and dedicated to the use of societies that were to be continued Methodists forever. Soon men of true views were to follow the Doctor, only to find themselves appointed to factious charges. Some of the noblest men in the Conference followed Dr. Thomas, only to make years of failure from causes named. Had the Doctor held any of his views as pet theories and preached the old doctrines of the Cross, no man would have bothered him; but his crude, adolescent notions became his supreme message, and, with gentle ways and rare eloquence, by the time his term of service on a charge was over, the Churches were made inharmonious, and whoever followed him came to Churches disaffected toward the old Methodist gospel. It would be almost as clear a case of unfitness as if a Methodist preacher should be appointed to a Universalist Church. Societies that had been planted by the money, and labors, and prayers, and tears of true men, in a year were warped from their old standing on to unliberal ground. And spite of all entreaty and pressure, Dr. Thomas persisted in doing this destructive work from year to year. Who is there that will say to old Rock River preachers it were wisest to let that thing go on? While touching upon this matter, I think that truth demands the statement of a fact that is not generally known. All parties, in public, have given Dr. Thomas credit for sincerity and honesty. I was not sufficiently intimate with him to know his motives. I know very well that in other cases like his the men were not honest men. But this I know, that while he was stationed in Chicago, as early as 1872—ten years before his final departure—the Doctor told a mutual friend of his and mine that his greatest wish was an independent congregation in Chicago, like that of Mr. Beecher in Brooklyn; and I think that all the evidence goes to show that for ten years Dr. Thomas was working for that end, and that he allowed matters to take the form of persecution for the purpose of rallying to himself a congregation led by sympathy. That, I believe, was the end aimed at; that was the result.

When I joined the old Clark Street Church in 1842, there were many English among the prominent members; and as a consequence, many English customs prevailed. Among these was the use of love-feast tickets. These continued in use in that Church till 1844, when they passed out of fashion. L. Hitchcock was pastor in 1843. His health failed in the spring of 1844, and H. Crews, the presiding elder of the district, supplied his place. As pastor, I think Mr. Crews issued the last ticket ever used at Clark Street. The love-feasts were always held with closed doors, and none were admitted who could not show tickets. The following is a copy of one issued by Luke Hitchcock:

ALVARO FIELD.

"I, even I, am the Lord, and beside me there is no Savior."—Isa. xliii, 11.

L. HITCHCOCK.

SEPTEMBER 12, 1843.

The following is one of the last ever issued at Clark Street:

ALVARO FIELD.

"In thee, O Lord, do I put my trust; let me never be ashamed; deliver me in thy righteousness."—Psa. xxxi, 1.

FOURTH QUARTER, JULY, 1844.

H. CREWS.

I spent the winter of 1848 among the English mining people at Mineral Point. There the love-feast ticket was in full use. The ticket was a sort of receipt for "quarterage," and there were many elder people who would not pay their "quarterage" until they had received their tickets. I have several of these tickets given me at Mineral Point by the pastor, I. M. Leihy. After I became pastor, in 1848, closed doors were sometimes adopted. The last time the practice was followed on any charge of mine was at Yellowhead Church (Grant Park), in 1854. I remember it from the friction it occasioned. The doors were never closed at any Conference love-feast since I began attending. At the Plainfield Conference in 1850, love-feast was given out for nine o'clock. Bishop Hamline came in at the hour, and arose in the pulpit and asked if the doors had been kept closed. Being answered in the negative, he observed: "I can not tell my experience before a promiscuous audience; we will therefore hold a prayer-meeting instead of a love-feast." He took charge of the meeting, and I suspect it was the dryest prayer-meeting on record! That maneuver killed closed doors with the preachers. The last time I ever heard of closed doors was at Waukegan, in 1856, when C. P. Bragdon was pastor. He said that the doors would be closed at nine, and after that they might as well try to open the gates of heaven as that door. The first open love-feast I ever knew was at Clark Street in 1845. We had just moved into the new brick church, out of the old flat frame. William M. D. Ryan, the pastor, gave out, one Sunday, with that supreme flourish natural to him, that on Monday evening there would be an open love-feast. Everybody was invited; and everybody came to see what a love-feast was. When Mr. Ryan got the people there, he modestly asked of them three hundred dollars to finish the basement. And he got it!

Perhaps some of our readers may wonder, on reading of the large circuits of the early days, how so many appointments could be filled. Week-day preaching was the old-time custom. On many circuits there were appointments to be filled every day in the week. These were regularly and well attended. I remember that Ash Grove, in Iroquois County, where was one of the largest Methodist communities in the West in 1849, preferred week-day preaching by the circuit preachers, so that they could have Sunday preaching by the local preachers, and thus get more "meeting." I think a week-day appointment I had at Mount Langum in 1854 was the last regular week-day appointment I ever had. About that time they went out of date in the bounds of the Rock River Conference. After being raised in a city Church, where the congregation numbered a thousand people, to stand up in a private house, among the chairs and tables, and try to preach to a dozen or more people, seemed like child's play around the old home circle.

THE FIRST SESSION OF ROCK RIVER CONFERENCE

Mt. Morris, August 26, 1840. Bishop Waugh, presiding; Benjamin T. Kavanaugh, secretary.

An extract from the address made by President Ridgaway at the session of Rock River Conference, 1891, in which he referred to Bishop Waugh's visit to Illinois at the organization of Rock River Conference in 1840:

"August 16th Bishop Waugh spent in Detroit, Mich., and thence went on to Ann Arbor, and on to Marshall, where he presided over the Michigan Conference. From Marshall he rode across the State to Lake Michigan, going much of the way in an open wagon exposed to the hot sun. On a miserable boat without a redeeming quality, he came to Chicago and lodged with a Mr. Berry, of the attention of whose family he makes grateful mention. 'Although somewhat indisposed I preached (Sunday, August 23d) in the morning in the Methodist Church, and in the evening in the Presbyterian Church. The Methodist meeting-house here is small, but there was apparently an intelligent audience present. Monday, the 24th, we left Chicago at daybreak. This place did not meet my expectation altogether. It had not the business air which I expected. Nevertheless, it is a growing place, and will in time be a city of some note.' He proceeded over the prairies—'Not a tree or a shrub was to be seen within the range of vision. Men, women, and children looking sickly, poorly fed and clothed, and worse lodged in miserable cabins not fit to house cattle in'—until they reached Squire Hitts's in the neighborhood of Mt. Morris. At a camp-meeting in an adjacent grove about a mile away he organized the Rock River Conference, August 26th. The Conference met in a log pen three hundred yards from the encampment. 'I know not that I ever saw a ruder structure. It was about twelve feet by eighteen, built somewhat in the form of a shed. The lower side was five logs high, the upper about seven. The logs were rough and crooked, and where the openings were from eight to ten inches between the logs they were partially closed by putting in a similar log or split timber. There was a large opening for the entrance, but no door to close it after we had entered. Several portions of an old roof were laid over the top, which might scarcely have been called a flat roof, and in this pen, open on all sides and at the top too, as we soon found by the entering rain, we commenced and progressed with the business of the Conference. This will in time be an interesting Conference. The spirit of the brethren is patient and kind. The preachers are very poorly supported on their circuits, but I never heard a single complaint.' What if the good bishop, after the lapse of only fifty-six years, could look upon Chicago with its 1,250,000 population, and the Rock River Conference with its three hundred and fifty preachers! Such were the foundations which the earlier bishops of Methodism assisted in laying. From Mt. Morris, after briefly inspecting the new building of the Conference seminary, he moved southward in company with a Mr. Sinclair, to meet the Illinois Conference at Springfield. As a sample of the accommodations on the way he says of one place: 'They could not be prevailed upon to take anything, saying they were glad that we had called on them. What a combination of Christian kindness and dirtiness was here!' Of his entertainment at Springfield he writes: 'Here I found a good mattress, which was in a neat bedchamber. What luxury to one in very recent circumstances!'

"The Conference session began on September 16th, and closed on the 23d. 'The members of the Conference seemed to be a body of well-disposed men of medium talents, without much literary attainment.' He hoped much, however, from the future influence of McKendree College, which had recently been founded."

The following are the names of the preachers who received appointments from this first Conference. It has always been a matter of regret that Luke Hitchcock's name was not on the list. On account of failing health he had located in the Oneida Conference in 1838. In 1839 he came West to see what a Western climate would do for him. As he was doubtful as to the result, he did not unite with Rock River Conference until 1841. But all this time he was filling appointments as a supply. The names on the Conference list follow:

John T. Mitchell, Hooper Crews, Wm. Gaddis,

John Nason, Silas Bolles, O. A. Walker, Milton Bourne, S. H. Stocking, L. S. Walker, Nathaniel Swift, William Kimball, Caleb Lamb, John Sinclair, Jesse L. Bennett, Elihu Springer, Rufus Lummery, W. Weigley, Wesley Batchellor, Asa White, J. M. Snow, Harvey Hadley, John Clark, A. McMurtry, R. A. Blanchard, Wm. Vallette, C. N. Wager, Philo Judson, J. W. Whipple, E. P. Wood, Samuel Pillsbury, R. Brown, T. S. Hitt, Henry Summers, Isaac I. Stewart, T. M. Kirkpatrick, M. F. Shinn, N. Smith, Joel Arrington, M. H. McMurtry, W. B. Cooley, Nathan Jewett, J. L. Kirkpatrick, B. Weed, G. G. Worthington, Chester Campbell, B. H. Cartwright, John Hodges, P. S. Richardson, H. Hubbard, W. Wilcox, B. T. Kavanaugh, D. King, H. J. Brace, George Copway, H. P. Chase, A. Huddleson, J. Johnson, S. Spates, H. W. Reed, W. Simpson, A. M. Early, J. G. Whitford, J. Ash, S. P. Keyes, Jesse Halsted, H. R. Coleman, Julius Field, John Crummer, L. F. Molthrop, Henry Whitehead, Salmon Stebbins, D. Worthington, James McKean, Sidney Wood, H. W. Frink, Alfred Brunson, Robert Delap, and T. W. Pope.

For a full list of appointments see Field's History of Rock River Conference, page 200.

In 1896 only A. M. Early was left in the conference.

At this first Conference the following were received on trial—N. Swift is the father of P. H. Swift, a prominent member of the Conference in 1896: P. S. Richardson, C. N. Wager, Henry

Hubbard, Nathaniel Swift, L. F. Molthrop, W. B. Cooley, Sidney Wood, Asa White, M. F. Shinn, H. P. Chase, D. Worthington, Henry Whitehead, James Ash, R. A. Blanchard, A. M. Early, E. P. Wood, Chester Campbell, and Philo Judson.

Which is the oldest society in the Conference it is difficult to tell, though some indications point to the supposition that the class at Galena was organized in the spring of 1829, and the class at Plainfield in the fall of 1829. These are the two oldest societies. Other classes were organized as follows: Chicago (July), 1831; Princeton, Ottawa, and Oswego, 1833; Elizabeth, 1834; Joliet and Marengo, 1835; Polo (March 10), Rockford (September 2), Naperville, and Light-house Point, 1836; Byron, Prophetstown, Elgin (June 12), Belvidere (September 24), Roscoe, St. Charles, Durand, Dixon (May), and Chicken Grove, 1837; Mt. Morris, Yorkville, Aurora, Round Prairie, and Earl, 1838; Lockport, Yellow Head (now Grant Park), 1839; Freeport, Albany, Sterling, and Lisbon, 1840; Council Hill and Centenary, Chicago, 1842; Grace Church, Chicago, and Sandwich, 1847; Apple River, 1849; Evanston, Rockton, Rochelle, Dwight, Mendota, and Bristol Station, 1855; Ashton and Amboy, 1856; Harvard and Forreston, 1857.

GENERAL CONFERENCE DELEGATES.

1836—Illinois Conference: Peter Cartwright, Hooper Crews, Simon Peter.

1840—Illinois Conference: Peter Akers, Peter Cartwright, S. H. Thomson, H. Crews, John Clark, J. T. Mitchell.

1844—First Rock River Conference delegates: Bartholomew Weed, John Sinclair, H. W. Reed, J. T. Mitchell.

1848—Henry Summers, Richard Haney, A. E. Phelps, Philo Judson, John Chandler.

1852—A. E. Phelps, Luke Hitchcock, S. P. Keyes, R. Haney, J. Chandler.

1856—G. L. Mulfinger (German delegate), L. Hitchcock, J. Luccock, H. Crews, John Dempster (reserve, in place of S. P. Keyes), H. Summers, R. Haney, John Morey.

1860—L. Hitchcock, G. L. Mulfinger, H. Crews, T. M. Eddy, J. C. Stoughton, J. Dempster.

1864—L. Hitchcock, T. M. Eddy, G. L. Mulfinger, W. T. Harlow (reserve, in place of John Dempster), S. A. W. Jewett, W. F. Stewart.

1868—L. Hitchcock, E. Q. Fuller, R. A. Blanchard, D. P. Kidder, James Baume, T. M. Eddy.

1872—L. Hitchcock, C. H. Fowler, Miner Raymond, S. A. W. Jewett, W. S. Harrington, J. H. More.

1876—C. H. Fowler, Wm. Aug. Smith, S. A. W. Jewett, F. P. Cleveland, L. Hitchcock.

1880—C. H. Fowler, L. Hitchcock, R. M. Hatfield, S. A. W. Jewett, N. H. Axtell.

1884—J. H. Vincent, C. H. Fowler, W. A. Spencer, R. M. Hatfield, F. P. Cleveland.

1888—J. H. Vincent, C. G. Truesdell, Lewis Curts, W. A. Spencer, F. M. Bristol.

1892—F. M. Bristol, Lewis Curts, F. A. Hardin, J. M. Caldwell, H. B. Ridgaway, William H. Burns.

Lay Delegates.

1872—Grant Goodrich, B. F. Sheets.
1876—R. F. Queal, H. Green.
1880—O. H. Horton, E. P. Cook.
1884—Orrington Lunt, Otis Hardy.
1888—Nathan E. Lyman, Frances E. Willard.
1892—William Deering, B. F. Sheets.

JESSE WALKER.

The early Christian battles in the West have been fought. The heroes of the Cross rest quietly on earth, their spirits having gone to their triumphs in heaven. Now the chroniclers are going along the lines of conflict, gathering up the shreds of events, and weaving them into interesting story, to serve as records to be read by the Christian soldiers of the future. Among these early soldiers there was none more brave, none won greater victories, none conquered more lands for the Lord, than Jesse Walker. In the preface of this book I have called him the *pioneer preacher*. It is probable that in the whole history of the Methodist Church in America no man, by actual services, has a better claim to this title. From Tennessee to Missouri, from Southern Illinois to Wisconsin, from 1802 to 1835, he was ever the foremost preacher on the frontiers. He was first to establish the Methodist Church both in St. Louis (1819) and Chicago (1831), those two great metropolitan centers of the West. At almost every intervening point between these two cities he was first to set up the standard of the Cross, and the chroniclers from Tennessee to

Wisconsin find occasion to mention his name and labors. In most of the books on the early times he is one of the chief heroes.

Jesse Walker was born in Buckingham County, Virginia, June 9, 1766. His parents were not professors of religion, but were moral, and taught young Jesse to pray, and to attend church, and to abstain from gross sins. Jesse's school privileges were few, twenty days being the whole of his school life. When but nine years of age he was deeply affected by the sermon of a Baptist preacher, and, beginning alone to seek the Lord, he was soon converted; but since there were few helps to childhood piety, he soon forgot his heavenly blessing, and wandered away, until he became very wicked. At length—in July, 1786, when about twenty years of age—he was brought back to the Savior, and led into the Methodist Church. His future wife was converted at the same time. Young Walker at once exhibited talents, and showed by his zeal that the Great Master had work for him to do. He was almost immediately appointed class-leader, and was often induced to accompany the preachers around their circuits to aid them in their work. He was urged to join the traveling connection, but for sixteen years he held back. His main plea was his reluctance to expose his delicately-reared wife to the hardships of a circuit preacher's life in a day when little provision was made for the support of a preacher's family.

To see fully what the above assertion means we must look back a few years. In the neighborhood of Jesse Walker's early home there lived a rich English gentleman, Webly by name. He, with his family, was a staunch Virginia Episcopalian, and a slaveholder. There were two children—a son and a daughter. About the time the daughter was of age her parents died. Her brother, who had interests in the East India Company, set out for England to attend to business affairs, and on the way was shipwrecked. The daughter became sole heir to the property, which consisted mostly of slaves. She was a gay young lady, dressing in the highest styles of fashion, and engaging in all the sinful amusements of the day. She mingled in all the gayest gatherings of the old Virginia chivalry. And we may add here that she was highly educated—a fact that is to-day influencing her great-grandchildren. In the midst of her gay life, Susannah Webly—probably in the same revival with Jesse Walker—was powerfully converted, and at the same time she joined the Methodist Church. She laid aside her gaudy apparel, her friends making mention even of a large silver back-comb she laid aside; she freed her slaves, keeping two of the girls in the family to aid in the housework, and, to end all, married the poor but zealous young Jesse Walker. She was from the first an ardent Christian worker; but, out of respect to her, her husband hesitated to undertake the work of a Methodist preacher.

Not long after their marriage the young couple, in seeking employment, moved down into North Carolina, then into East Tennessee, and afterwards into West Tennessee, where they settled, near Nashville. During these years Jesse Walker supported his family by dressing furs and preparing deer-hides for the use of the people. To understand what this means we must remember that this was previous to 1800, when all the country west of Virginia was "backwoods" country, and when dressed deerskin was the most common material for clothing. Even Abraham Lincoln, in Illinois, as late as 1830 wore buckskin pantaloons. This trade, then, of Jesse Walker's was not a small, nor an ignoble affair, but a lucrative business.

During all these sixteen years (1786–1802) the preachers and Walker's own convictions were urging him to take up the itinerant work. He was now—in 1802—thirty-four years of age. He had a family of four children, and felt that he had no ability to do the work required. This suggests his modesty, and is one reason, no doubt, why he preferred to preach to the frontier rather than the more settled communities. After long resistance, he yielded to duty under the stroke of affliction. He entered his home one day to find his children very sick. Soon two little boys, who died in two hours of each other, were laid out for the same grave. In this hour himself and his wife yielded to the heavenly call. The wife, the noble Susannah, from that hour bade him go where duty led, and she would care for the home. She never after looked back, but through the thirty years that followed was Jesse Walker's greatest earthly encouraging force. Walker sent up his name, and was in 1802 received into the Western Conference as a laborer. He went to Red River, in Tennessee, and in this, his first year, he gave Peter Cartwright license to exhort. He filled some of the difficult appointments in Tennessee and Kentucky until 1806.

For some reason the preacher appointed to the lone Illinois work in 1805 did not fill out his year. The presiding elder, William McKendree, afterward bishop, in looking for a man to take up the work, selected Jesse Walker, and in the spring of 1806 the two set out on horseback to look over the work, and see what could be done. Between Kentucky and the settlements in Illinois there lay a vast uninhabited wilderness. The two travelers camped in the woods at night, roasted their own meat, the game they killed, and slept on their saddle-blankets, with their saddles for pillows. Their greatest trouble was in crossing the booming streams. It was a time of much rain, and as many as seven times they swam their horses across the rapid currents. By carrying their saddle-bags upon their shoulders, they kept their books and part of their clothing dry. At last they reached the settlements, and were heartily greeted. They remained a few weeks, and formed a "plan" of appointments, and set the work in order. After preaching near a place called Turkey Hill, a gentleman said to McKendree: "I am convinced there is a divine influence in your religion, for though I have resided here some years, and have done all within my power to gain the confidence and good-will of my neighbors, you have already many more friends here than I have."

Jesse Walker returned to his circuit in Kentucky, and preached there until Conference, and then, in 1806, received his appointment to the Illinois Circuit. He reached home from Conference about noon one day, and by ten o'clock the next day was ready to start with his family to his new work, two hundred miles distant. The family consisted of his wife and two daughters—Polly, about eighteen, and Jane, probably sixteen. They all traveled on horseback the same lonely road Walker and McKendree had traveled a few months before. After a tedious journey, in which they suffered much from cold and hunger, storms and high waters, they reached the Turkey Hill Settlement in St. Clair County. Near there Mr. Walker settled his family, at a place where they continued to reside for several years. The home was an old log-cabin belonging to a Brother Scott. It had a plank floor and a stick chimney, with hearth so low the edge of the floor made seats for all the family around the old-fashioned fireplace.

The first preacher to Illinois had been appointed in 1803, so that Jesse Walker was the fourth man appointed to this great State. He entered at once upon his work, and it was not long until souls began to be converted. On New-Year's eve, at the close of 1806, he held a watch-night meeting, probably the first ever held in Illinois. In April, 1807, he held a camp-meeting near the present town of Edwardsville, which is generally thought to be the first Illinois camp-meeting. There were but three preachers present. These were Jesse Walker,

Charles R. Matheny (who had been appointed to the circuit in 1805), and Hosea Rigg. The meeting was a successful one, where many were converted. A young lady of influence, sister-in-law of the judge of the Territory, was so powerfully converted her shouts of joy sent a thrill all over the encampment. This gave a great impetus to the work, and before the meeting adjourned, quoting Jesse Walker's words, "The last stick of timber was used up;" that is, the last sinner was converted. During the summer another meeting was held at a place afterwards called Shiloh, and where the first Conference ever held in Illinois met in 1820. The circuit preacher had the aid of his presiding elder, Wm. McKendree, Abbott Goddard, and James Gwin, besides some local preachers. Mr. McKendree had been holding a camp-meeting with the preacher over in Missouri. On Friday morning of the Shiloh meeting, the horn had been sounded as a signal to arise, and a second sounding of the horn had called the people to the altar for morning prayers. At this solemn hour a hymn was sung, and while singing, suddenly the people heard the sound of voices in song at a distance. It was McKendree and his accompanying preachers. They rode up, and the singing continued, amid hearty hand-shaking, tears, and smiles, for some time before the preachers could alight from their horses. The preachers of to-day know little about the joyous greeting of fellow-preachers in those days when the laborers were so few. The meeting held in the spring, and the one just held across the river in Missouri, awakened a great deal of curiosity and some opposition in the settlements. A certain major raised a company to drive the people from the ground. On Saturday, while James Gwin was preaching, the company rode into the congregation and halted. This produced quite a commotion. Mr. Gwin requested them to leave the ground, and they retired to the spring for a fresh drink of brandy. The major said he had heard of these Methodists before. They disturbed the peace of the neighborhoods by preaching against horse-racing, card-playing, etc., and interfered with their amusements. After a while the company quieted down, and concluded to camp on the ground to prevent the preachers from doing any harm. But at three o'clock, while two of the preachers were singing a hymn, an awful sense of Divine power fell upon the congregation, and the people began to run away. Some fell to the ground. Sunday forenoon McKendree preached, and so won the major he became very friendly, and continued thus ever after.

The whole year on the Illinois Circuit was one of success. During the year the second church in the State was built; this was at Shiloh. The first, called Bethel Church, had been built in Goshen settlement. At one time Jesse Walker visited a neigborhood near the Illinois River, where there was a settlement of some sixty or seventy people. He held meetings for three days, and then read the General Rules, and invited the people to join the Church. The most prominent man among them arose to his feet and said, "I trust we will all unite with you to serve God," then walked forward and gave the preacher his name, while all the rest followed.

At the time Jesse Walker was appointed to Illinois in 1806, John Travis had been appointed to Missouri. This was the first appointment to that State. In 1807 Walker was sent over into Missouri, and a new man appointed to Illinois. But in 1808 he returned to the Illinois side again, to return to Missouri again in 1809. This was to Cape Girardeau Circuit, to which he was returned in 1810. This work he planned out of almost entirely new territory. It had been explored by the preacher on a neighboring circuit the year before, but the country was left for Jesse Walker to work up. He moved his family to the town, which was as unpromising a place as a zealous preacher ever found. It was the boast that the Sabbath had never found its way across the Mississippi. The people were new settlers, who had hardly a way to live themselves, with poor prospects to feed a preacher and his family. While here, Walker held a camp-meeting, a sort of gathering in which he had great confidence. There were five tents on the ground. Sometimes there were as many as two or three hundred people present. There were a few conversions and some additions to the Church. At the sacrament there were eleven communicants. From Cape Girardeau he returned to the Illinois Circuit in 1811.

The Illinois District was organized in 1811, and in 1812 Jesse Walker was made presiding elder of this new district. This he traveled for four full years and then, in 1816, was removed to the Missouri District, on which he remained until 1819. John Scripps, one of his preachers, gives an account of some of Jesse Walker's trips on the Illinois District, which we condense below. Will the reader please remember the sermons to the few when we come to speak of his preaching at Chicago? He commenced his round at Goshen meeting-house, near Edwardsville, on Friday, April 1, 1815. Closing the meeting at Goshen on Monday, he traveled all the week, filling nightly and daily appointments, till he arrived at the Big Spring meeting-house on Friday, the 8th, where his quarterly-meeting lasted till Monday, April 11th. Another week of daily services brought him to the Davis school-house, near the confluence of the Big Muddy River with the Mississippi. At this place there were some conversions, and a class of sixteen persons was formed. Jacob Whitesides was sent from the company of preachers to form the Okaw Circuit. On Monday, the 18th, Jesse Walker, J. Patterson, and John Scripps set out for the Massac camp-meeting, to be held at the rock and cave on the Ohio River. They traveled through an almost uninhabited country, and almost pathless woods to Thomas Standard's, where a congregation awaited their arrival. The meeting was one of thrilling interest, and lasted until midnight. On Friday, April 22d, the company arrived at the camp-ground. The meeting commenced at once and proved very profitable, with many conversions. The meeting closed on Monday with a sermon from Brother Walker, and Monday night found him preaching to a large congregation in Proctor's meeting-house. Crossing the Wabash near its mouth, they ascended the river in Indiana Territory; crossed the Black, Patoka, and White Rivers to Brother Johnson's, twelve miles from Vincennes. On Friday, April 29th, the quarterly-meeting for Vincennes Circuit was held. It was a time of power. A short ride of six or seven miles was made on Monday, and a meeting held at night at Dr. Messick's; the next day a meeting was held at noon at Harrington's tavern, and at night at Anthony Griffin's, on Black River. They recrossed the Wabash, and held a quarterly-meeting, on May 6th, at Brother Hannah's, in a block-house. The next appointment was at New Madrid, one hundred and eighty miles away in Missouri, which our travelers reached so as to commence promptly on May 13th. From thence they rode sixty miles to Cape Girardeau, where the quarterly-meeting commenced May 20th. At both these appointments, and at nearly all others through the summer, camp-meetings were held. This was needful, from the fact that no house in the country could hold Jesse Walker's congregations that, on account of his popularity, came ten and twenty miles from all directions. He spent three months in this round without seeing his family. The faithful "Sukey," as he familiarly styled her, took care of the home in his absence. The roads he traveled were narrow, winding horse-paths, with miles without any path at all. Rains poured, and streams were crossed by swimming the horses. The stopping-places were log huts, which served as meeting-house, kitchen, and bedroom; the fare, corn-bread, fried bacon, and herb-tea.

Jesse Walker made this same round in one of the severest winters of that day. The toils and pains and privations of that journey are on record, but the reader can imagine them as well as to read them in type. Take the travels of the April round, and put them into a winter of sleet and ice and half-frozen streams, and we can see, without narrating it, some of the beauties of the early itinerancy. And but for these very labors, Illinois would have gone to barbarism.

We come now to an event of greatest moment. It is the planting of the Methodist banner in the city of St. Louis. The real work that Jesse Walker accomplished in this was no greater than he performed in many another place. This receives greater prominence only because of its greater consequences.

The Missouri Conference met at McKendree Chapel, in Missouri, in 1819. Jesse Walker had completed seven years in the presiding eldership, and now received an appointment as simply "missionary." He was free to roam where he pleased, his work being to "break up new ground" and look out new fields of labor. The need of this service arose from the fact that to every preacher appointed was given more work than could be well attended to without going into new neighborhoods.

While yet at Conference, Jesse Walker resolved that his first work should be to see if the gospel could not be carried into St. Louis. John Scripps, when on the Coldwater Circuit, a few years before, had taken the city into his bounds, and had preached in an old log building used as a court-house, this being the only public building in the place, except the Catholic cathedral. It was also used as a theater. Mr. Scripps continued to preach there, and in a school-house which was built during the year. But when he left, the place was abandoned. There was no further Methodist preaching there until Jesse Walker re-established an appointment.

Brother Walker formed his plans at Conference. Two young and zealous preachers were engaged to join him in the attempt to gain a foothold in St. Louis. The city at this time was settled chiefly by French, and as far as there was any religion, it was Catholic. But vice of every kind led the people and held sway.

After establishing themselves in their own circuits, the two preachers met Jesse Walker, according to appointment, to join him on his entry into the then Capital City of the West. When they reached St. Louis, the Territorial Legislature was in session, and every public place was full. When it became known who they were, they received ridicule and curses. There seemed to be no opening for meetings, or for even lodgings for the preachers. Hindered at every point, they rode into the public square, and held a consultation on their horses. The young preachers concluded that, had the Master work for them, a door would be opened; and by this token they concluded the Lord had no work for them to do there. Their leader tried to rally them, but in vain. The West had almost everywhere received the preachers with gladness, but here were only insults. They deliberately brushed the dust from their feet, and rode off, leaving the disconsolate Walker sitting on his horse alone. Perhaps that hour had more of despondency than any other Jesse Walker ever suffered. In the midst of his disappointment he said: "I will go to the State of Mississippi, and look up the desolate places there." Turning his horse to the south, he rode away. He rode as far as eighteen miles with anguish of spirit, and yet all the time praying, thus seeking to know the will of the Master. The early itinerants had a wonderful trust in the guiding of Providence. At length he broke into the following soliloquy: "Was I ever defeated before? Never! Did ever any one trust in the Lord Jesus Christ and get confounded? No! And by the grace of God I will go back and take St. Louis!" Turning, he immediately retraced his steps to the city. With some difficulty he found lodging in a tavern, where he paid the highest rates for everything. The next morning he set out to explore the city. He first strove to find some Methodist inhabitant. He heard of a carpenter who professed to be a Methodist. He sought him out, and on inquiry the carpenter took Brother Walker aside, and said privately: "I was a Methodist once, before I came here; but finding no brethren in St. Louis, I never made myself known, and do not now consider myself a member, and do not wish this to become known, lest it injure my business." Walker gave up all such broken reeds.

While passing about the town he found some members of the Legislature who knew him, when the following converse ensued: "Why, Father Walker, what has brought you here?" He answered: "I have come to take St. Louis." They admired his zeal, but thought it a hopeless undertaking, and advised him to abandon the undertaking and return to his family. But to all such suggestions his inward, if not vocal, response was: "I have come to take St. Louis, and by the help of the Lord I will do it."

He obtained permission to preach in a temporary place of worship occupied by a few of what were called "Hardshell" Baptists. At the first appointment there was a small attendance. He obtained leave to preach again; but at the second appointment there were many present, and the interest rose so high the house was after that closed against him. He next found a large, unfinished dwelling-house, which he rented for ten dollars a month. Passing by the public square, he saw a pile of old benches that had just been taken from the court-house, which had been refitted. These he obtained, and, borrowing tools, he fitted up the largest room of his rented house for a place of worship. Here he began preaching, twice on the Sabbath, and frequently on week nights. At the same time he invited in the children of poor parents, and began to teach a free school. He kept house by himself to avoid expenses, and soon returned to his home in Illinois for provisions and bedding.

The chapel was soon filled with hearers, and the school-room with children. Soon some of the better class of citizens desired to send their children to school, and to pay for the privilege. To accommodate them, he hired a young man more competent than himself to assist in teaching. Very soon signs of revival began to appear. Its first subjects were the colored people; then the poorer class of whites began to come in, and finally the interest grew so deep many of the intelligent and influential were converted.

Our preacher had but just entered upon these signs of success, when, by the death of the owner, his building passed into new hands, and he was notified to vacate the place.

At first this seemed a new defeat, but out of it the preacher evolved greater success. Immediately he conceived the plan of building a chapel, and, without knowing where the means were to come from, he put the work under contract. Walker was to furnish the materials. A citizen owning lands across the Mississippi gave Brother Walker leave to take the lumber from his timber, and when the woodmen went over to work, the generous citizen paid their ferriage over the river. Soon the chapel was raised and covered. The ladies furnished the church. The vestrymen of a deserted Episcopal Church gave Walker their Bible and the pews from their church. New friends came to his aid in meeting his contracts. When the chapel was opened the revival received a fresh impulse. As a result of this first year he reported one chapel, a flourishing school, and seventy members in St. Louis. The next year he was regularly appointed to St. Louis. So rapidly did the new Church grow, the Missouri Conference was held there in 1822, and one of the first men in the Conference appointed to the new station.

The reader's attention is called here to an event illustrative of Jesse Walker's perseverance that occurred some time in the years when he was engaged in his work in Missouri. In his wanderings he became acquainted with William S. Tee, a man of large property in the mines at Potosi. He was a man of noble and generous impulses, but profane and wicked. Loving everything heroic, he formed a sincere attachment for Jesse Walker, and had great admiration for his zeal. After his success at St. Louis, our preacher resolved to visit Potosi, a place where Satan held undisputed sway. Brother Walker sent an appointment to the place, but soon received word from the miners that if he came to fill his appointment they would "regulate" him. He sent word that his Master had required him to go, and he should do his duty. Tee heard of the threats, and asked Walker if he really intended to go. When answered in the affirmative he said: "Well, you are a great fool to think you can do those reprobates any good; but if you want to try you shall have a chance. Do n't be afraid; I shall be there, and they shall hear the gospel once in their lives at any rate." On the day appointed Jesse Walker, with rifle on his shoulder, set out on horseback for Potosi. He found assembled three hundred as desperate men as ever congregated, all armed as Missouri and Arkansas men could arm themselves. Tee, with a large party of his men, was there when Mr. Walker rode up. Before preaching began, Tee mounted a stump, and exclaimed: "Mr. Walker is a minister; I do not know anything about his religion. I know he is a brave man, and a clever fellow; and though he was a great fool to think his religion could do you any good, yet he wants to preach, and he shall do so, and you must hear him. And now, the first man that interrupts him goes from this place a dead man." Then turning to the preacher, he said: "Walker, now give them hell-fire and damnation, for they deserve it." Mr. Walker set his rifle down, mounted a stump, sang and prayed, and feeling that God had made the wicked his protection, and having a sense that God was with him, he preached with power. A revival broke out and a great reformation followed, the fruits of which remain to this day.

Several writers have undertaken to describe the appearance and character of Jesse Walker as he appeared in those days, and in this place we halt to condense some of these descriptions. Bishop Morris thus describes his person: "Let the reader suppose a man about five feet six inches high, of rather slender form, with a sallow complexion, light hair, small blue eyes, prominent cheek bones, and pleasant countenance, dressed in drab-colored clothes, made in the plain style peculiar to the early Methodist preachers, his neck secured with a white cravat, and his head covered with a light-colored beaver, nearly as large as a ladies' parasol, and they will see Jesse Walker as if spread out on canvas before them."

An incident here will illustrate what frequently happened when the backwoods preachers of Illinois and Missouri went down into the more cultured regions of Tennessee or Kentucky. The following is from Peter Cartwright: "I think it was in the fall of 1819 our beloved old Brother Walker came over to our Tennessee Conference, which sat at Nashville, to see us. But O how weather-beaten and war-worn was he, almost, if not altogether, without decent apparel to appear among us! We soon made a collection, and had him a decent suit of clothes to put on; and never shall I forget the blushing modesty and thankfulness with which he accepted that suit."

"As to his mental endowments," says Bishop Morris, " he was without education, except the elementary branches of English imperfectly acquired. But favored with a good share of common sense, cultivated by some reading, but much more by practical intercourse with society, and enriched with a vast fund of incidents peculiar to a frontier life, which he communicated with much ease and force, his conversational talent, his tact in narrative, his spicy manner, and almost endless variety of religious anecdotes, rendered him an object of attraction in social life. Unaccustomed to expressing his thoughts on paper, he kept his journal in his mind, by which means his memory, naturally retentive, was much strengthened, and his resources for the entertainment of his friends increased. He introduced himself among strangers with much facility, and so soon as they became acquainted with him, his social habits, good temper, unaffected simplicity, and great ease of manners for a backwoodsman, made them his fast friends. As a pulpit orator he was not above mediocrity, if up to it; but his zeal was ardent, his moral courage firm, his piety exemplary, and his perseverance in whatever he undertook was undaunted. Consequently, by the blessing of God upon his labors, he was enabled in the third of a century to accomplish untold good."

Jesse Walker was to the Church what Daniel Boone was to the early settlers—always first, always ahead of everybody else; preceding all others long enough to be the pilot of the newcomer. His natural vigor was almost beyond measure. He did not seem to require food and rest, as other men. No day's journey was long enough to tire him, no fare too poor for him to live upon. To him, in traveling, roads and paths were useless things. He blazed out his own course. No way was too difficult for him to travel. If his horse could not carry him, he led him; and where his horse could not follow, he would leave him and take it on foot, and if night and a cabin did not come together, he would pass the night alone in the wilderness. Looking up the pioneer settler was his chief delight, and he found his way through woods and brakes by instinct. He was never lost, and, as Bishop McKendree once said of him, "He never complained, and as the Church moved west and north it seemed to bear Walker along. Every time you would hear from him he was still further on; and when the settlements of the white man seemed to take shape and form, he was next heard of among the Indian tribes of the Northwest."

In 1823 Jesse Walker's appointment was as follows: "Missionary to the Missouri Conference, whose attention is particulary directed to the Indians in the bounds of said Conference." This appointment opened up a new era to our hero, and placed him in near connection with Chicago, the great city of the lakes, where, not many years after, he was first to set up the Methodist banner.

A few years before this, John Stewart, a colored man, had gone among the Wyandot Indians in Northern Ohio, and had had the largest success in bringing the Indians to Christ. This inspired the Church everywhere to do something for the Indians. In those days the country from Peoria to the far north was filled with roving tribes. We judge that at first Jesse Walker had no positive ideas as to where was the best chance to begin, and we think it was by actually looking over the Indian population that he finally found himself settling down at his mission on Fox River.

After Conference he set out to look up the Indians, and to see where to begin. On looking for some Indians who generally camped between the Illinois and Mississippi Rivers, he learned that the whole tribe was across the river in Iowa on a hunting expedition. Immediately he resolved to follow them. He procured a sack of corn and an interpreter, and set out in pursuit of them. He crossed the Mississippi in a canoe, and swam his horse beside the boat. After a difficult journey they at length reached one of the Indian camps. When they rode up, an Indian, who knew the interpreter, said: "Who is with you? A Quaker?" "No." "A minister?" "Yes." They all seemed to be pleased. The chief—a tall, dignified man—came out and gave them a welcome reception, and cared for their horses and themselves. They were entertained very cheerfully. The chief, learning that Jesse Walker wished to have a talk with the Indians, sent out and invited the leaders in the neighboring camps to a council. This was held that same evening.

When the company who came were seated, the wife of the chief took a bowl of meat and broth of opossum and venison, and passed it first to her husband, then to the missionary, and after to the company, serving the oldest first. Then the pipe of peace was passed, from which all in turn took a whiff. This done, the chief stuck the blade of his hatchet into the ground, and inquired what was the object of the meeting. Jesse Walker made known his mission; spoke of the Bible, and handed the book to the chief. Then the chief rose, and made answer: "The white children's Father has given them a book, and they will do well to mind what it tells them." But he doubted whether it was intended for his red children. However, as some of their older men were absent, they could not then decide the matter. In a few days they would hold a larger council, and give him an answer. The result of the second council was leave to establish a mission school.

Having settled this matter, our missionary returned to his home to make preparation for his new work. He had not gone a day's journey before a messenger came galloping after him with the message from the chiefs, telling him to be sure to come back in the spring.

Mr. Walker was elected at the Conference of 1823 as one of the delegates of the Missouri Conference to the General Conference which sat in Baltimore; and, in company with Thomas A. Morris, afterwards bishop, who was a delegate from the Kentucky Conference, he rode on horseback from the West to Baltimore. This trip occupied two or three months of the summer of 1824. In passing through Washington, he visited the Secretary of War, and secured permission of the Secretary to open his Indian mission. It is very likely it was at this time the Government promised to pay two-thirds of the expense of the mission-school on which Salem Mission so much depended, and which amount, to the great embarrassment of the mission, was never paid.

For various reasons, and chiefly because of the length of time required for this journey to the General Conference, nothing was done until after Conference. At the Conference of 1824 Jesse Walker was continued as missionary to the Indians. He immediately opened a school at Fort Clark, now Peoria, which continued all winter, in which he had "six Indian children, whose progress was extremely flattering for so short a period." Finding the body of the Pottawatomie Indians were settled further north toward Chicago, in the spring of 1825, with five white families, he proceeded to the mouth of Fox River, where he held a satisfactory council with five chiefs of the tribe. The missionaries immediately built cabins for the accommodation of the families. These were the first houses on the site of Ottawa.

While at Peoria in the spring of 1825, Mr. Walker formed a class at Peoria. Not being satisfied with the location of his mission, in that spring he took a trip with John Hamlin, whose wife was a Methodist, in a Mackinaw boat to Chicago. With a crew of six persons besides Hamlin and Walker, they ascended the Illinois and Des Plaines Rivers. "Walker," says Hamlin, "had prayers with us night and morning; and, as we laid by early every afternoon, the old pioneer would line hymn after hymn, and he and the boys made the woods ring with the old Methodist hymns." We may add that this was the first appearance of a Methodist preacher into Northern Illinois; and from that day to this the reverberations of Methodist songs have never died out in the bounds of the Rock River Conference. This, on the part of Jesse Walker, was a trip of exploration; and at this time he decided to remove his mission station up to Ottawa; but having no one to guide him, he found that Ottawa was not the best location. He was not on Indian lands, and the body of Indians was further north. After building his cabins, he found he had made a mistake; and being in great perplexity as to what course he should follow, he retired, despondent, alone into a grove to pray. While at prayer, he was disturbed by the sound of footsteps, and, looking up, he saw a nobly-formed Indian standing near, with a smile of welcome on his face. This was Shabbonee, the friend of the white man. The chief introduced himself with the expression, "Me Shabbonee," at the same time giving Brother Walker a warm shake of the hand. Jesse Walker could speak no Indian, and Shabbonee little English; so there was little conversation, but enough to give Walker to understand that he had found a friend. Shabbonee soon disappeared. He went to his own camp, about a mile distant, from which he soon returned, bearing on his shoulder a quarter of venison and a wild turkey. He was accompanied by a half-breed, who became interpreter. The next day, under the guidance of Shabbonee and Furkee (or Furque), the missionary explored the country up the east side of Fox River until he came to a beautiful spot twenty miles above the mouth of the river, where was a spring in a beautiful grove. Here Jesse Walker drove his stakes, and established Salem Mission, the first Methodist appointment in the bounds of the Rock River Conference. This location was on Section 15, Township 35, Range 5, now in the town of Mission, in La Salle County.

We may add here that, in all his reports, Jesse Walker speaks of Indian chiefs, but gives no names; but from various other sources we have learned that Shabbonee, Billy Caldwell, or the Sanganash, Alexander Robinson, and even Waubansee, a warlike chief, were Walker's friends and helpers.

In a report given in October, 1825, Jesse Walker thus describes his location: "The place is about one hundred miles above Fort Clark, about twenty miles north of the Illinois River, between it and Fox River. The soil is very good, timber plenty, and the spot well watered." He called the place Salem, and that name is attached to the mission in the appointments of 1827.

Jesse Walker continued to labor with the Indians at Salem Mission from the spring of 1825 till the fall of 1828. In 1825-26 he called to his aid some of his relatives. His brother, Dr. David Walker, came up in 1826, and entered (when the time came) the section of land on which Ottawa now stands. His (David Walker's) son, George E. Walker, became the first sheriff of La Salle County.

As soon as the headquarters of his mission were established, in 1825, he sent for his son-in-law, James Walker, and his wife to come and help him. James Walker came up from Belleville, Illinois, where he had married Jane, Jesse Walker's youngest daughter, in 1819. He brought a horse-mill with him, which was set up at the mission, and which afterward was the first mill at Walker's Grove (Plainfield). James Walker became the general overseer of the mission farm, while his wife became the chief teacher.

James Walker was a son of one of Jesse's brother's, who had gone early to North Carolina, and who afterwards, with his brother Jesse, settled at Nashville, Tennessee. All the readers of United States history ought to be familiar with the campaigns of General Andrew Jackson in the West, in the war with England in 1812. Many of the first young men of Tennessee followed General Jackson in his toilsome marches. Among these was James Walker, who enlisted in the beginning, and served all through to the end. He was in the hottest of the fight behind the ditches at the battle of New Orleans.

We relate a peculiar incident here, because, in all our readings, we have never seen mention of such things. Our story comes direct, and may be relied upon. Among the young men from Tennessee were many zealous Methodists; for by that time the Methodist societies were found in almost every neighborhood of that State. In the haversacks of these were carried their Bibles and hymn-books, and it was their invariable custom to gather for evening prayer-meetings. At last the army was found lying in camp near New Orleans. The near approach of battle increased greatly the fervor of the praying soldiers. They were getting ready to die bravely, if they must. "At times," says James Walker, "I was led to think the portals of heaven were thrown open, and a stream of light and glory was poured out upon our souls." They became, no doubt, a little noisy. At any rate, a very officious young officer made a serious complaint to General

Jackson about the noise, calling it a nuisance. The general asked what they were doing. "Well, they sing, exhort, pray, and shout, and call it a prayer-meeting," was the officer's reply. "Old Hickory" answered thus: "Young man, go back and join the meeting; and tell them to remember me in their prayers. May God forbid that a prayer-meeting should ever be considered a 'nuisance' in my camp!"

When the war was over, in 1815, and James Walker was mustered out of service, he went home and set free the portion of slaves which had fallen to him, and soon set out to join his uncle, Jesse Walker, in Southern Illinois. Here, as stated, he married Jane G. Walker, at Belleville, in 1819. As stated in the early pages of this book, Jesse Walker's wife, Susannah, had been well educated. Being left with the care of her family, she saw that her daughters were well educated also. Her daughter Jane not only had her mother's teachings, but was enabled to attend the best schools in Illinois of that day. While Jesse Walker was out on his campaigns between 1806 and 1825, his family generally found a home in some of the best communities in Southern Illinois. When, then, Jane Walker came to Salem Mission with her husband in 1825, she proved to be one of the most efficient aids Jesse Walker could have in his work. From that time until 1828 she was the main teacher of the school. In the last-named year James Walker took the horse-mill which he had brought to the mission from the South, and went with his family over to a grove, called from him Walker's Grove, near where Plainfield now stands, and there established a settlement and a home. There he lived until his death. As soon as he went there, preaching was established; and a few families joining him, a class was organized in 1829—probably the first class organized in the bounds of the Rock River Conference. James Walker began with the horsemill, but soon after added a sawmill and a better gristmill. For years these were the only accommodations for miles around. In 1833 black-walnut lumber was hauled from his mill to build the first frame store in Chicago. This was erected by P. F. W. Peck, on the southeast corner of South Water and La Salle Streets. James Walker also kept the first post-office; had a store, where a few general articles could be obtained by the settlers. He also for years kept the stage stopping-place on the road from Chicago south through Ottawa. When Will County was set off, he was chosen one of the three county commissioners, and was soon sent to represent the county in the Legislature of the State. He frequently held these offices. When the Black Hawk War was on hand, in 1832, all the people from Ottawa to Chicago, in three companies, were mustered into the United States service, and James Walker was chosen captain of the company whose headquarters were at Walker's Grove. The record of these companies is now in the Government books at Washington.

All this time, while an intelligent leading citizen, James Walker was also a zealous, active member of the Methodist Church. His house, until Susannah Walker's death in 1832, was the home of Jesse Walker. An old settler, who often visited the Walker's Grove home, says the food was made more welcome by the fervent blessing that was asked at the table, and the sleep more sweet by the devout prayers that were always offered before retiring at night. After he had been elected to the Legislature, the stage came along one morning and stopped as usual for breakfast. Walker was to go in the stage to the State capital. They were all in a hurry. Stephen A. Douglas and John Wentworth were among the passengers. At the end of the meal the noble wife handed her husband the Bible, and ere he left he led the family and company in prayer. It was one of the heaviest crosses of his life; but from that time, he having thus committed himself, it was easy living a Christian life in the legislative halls.

This noble pioneer layman of the Methodist Church died in 1851, at the age of fifty-seven. He had long been a sufferer from sciatic rheumatism. During the last two years he was not off of his bed except as moved by others, and the last eighteen months he was moved on sheets; and yet, says a member of the family, "never did any one go to his bedside and meet anything else than a smile and a word of welcome." He was one of the most cheerful of men, had strong good sense, integrity of character, with enterprise and energy.

James Walker's wife, Jane Walker, was, in her womanly way, equal to her husband. Having been educated by her mother, she learned how to educate her own children and to rear them to noble life. Her husband being emphatically a business man, she was called to meet all classes of men who met at her home, but she never gave offense to any. Dignified, calm, self-possessed, clear-eyed, with keen womanly intuitions, her good judgment and deep Christian faith seemed always to guide her in the right path. "A hasty or unkind word never passed her lips," is the record of one. A gentleman once said: "Nothing evil ever seemed to approach her. She reads you as an open book, and yet when you go out from her presence you feel the better for having been there."

The Pottawatomie Indians had a curious custom. A select number of women were chosen as "council women." When the chiefs met in council, these women took their seats in a circle within the council ring. They were not allowed to speak, and were forbidden to discuss among themselves or to tell to others what occurred in the council. They were the "records." They were to preserve in memory the acts of the councils, and never to divulge them only when officially consulted. In 1832, one of these councils was to be held in Milwaukee. One of these councilwomen, on her way to the meeting, called at James Walker's and committed a small boy, Shanoneise by name, to Mrs. Walker's care, exacting the promise that Mrs. Walker should keep him if she never returned. The mother was taken with cholera on her way, and died. Shanoneise was reared in the

Walker family as one of the children. When grown, he was fitted out as a child of the family, and bid to go and prosper. But the Indian blood prevailed, and he immediately turned his horse's head towards the sunset, and went to the Missouri to rejoin his tribe. There he became an influential chief, and in that capacity made several trips to Washington on business that concerned his people. On these trips he was sure to call at the Walker home to greet his old family associates.

Mrs. Walker died in 1859. For some time before her death she was troubled by diseases incident to age. Her daughter—now Mrs. Harriet W. Searles, of Joliet—took her to Iowa to visit friends, hoping that change and travel would help her. But all in vain; she died suddenly, with only a day's confinement to her bed. Jesse Walker has grandchildren, who rise up to call him blessed.

The world that receives and rejoices over the labors of our most ardent ministers too often is ignorant of how much those labors have been made possible by the noble wives who at home have cheered and aided the men whose labors we see. Jesse Walker's wife was one of these helpers. His thirty years of life given to planting the standard of the Cross was made possible because, in the days when there was little or no support for preachers' families, she looked after the family and maintained the home. She stood by the old pioneer until 1832, when she was called to her reward. In speaking of her, her granddaughter, Mrs. Searles, says: "I do not remember ever having heard a word of censure spoken of her. My father knew and loved her nearly all her life. She never complained; never looked back. God's work was her work, and her husband's cares were her cares. Tall, slender, dark hair and eyes, with a most remarkable memory, was her description. She retained incidents that hardly any one else would have thought of."

There are some members of Jesse Walker's family scattered over the West, chiefly in Iowa. They all look back upon the old pioneer as the great gem of the family. Happy the man whose life is such that he will live in the memories of people when he is gone from earth—crowned in heaven, and remembered on earth! Such are the rewards of the great, whose greatness is highest in goodness.

And in the pioneer work of Jesse Walker in Northern Illinois must ever be associated the names of James Walker and his wife, Jane, the daughter of Jesse Walker.

But from this cheerful digression we return to Jesse Walker and his mission. There are yet before us, if possible, greater works for our hero of the Cross than any that have passed before. He planted his mission, as we have seen, on Fox River, twenty miles above Ottawa. There, in connection with his school, he improved a farm and raised produce for home consumption.

At the Conference of 1825 he was continued in the mission. He was directed to erect mission buildings, the Government having promised to pay two-thirds of the expenses. The whites that gathered as helpers at the mission were the first white settlers between Chicago and Galena.

In December, 1826, Jesse Walker reported the work he was doing. "I have now closed the business of Salem Mission," he says, "for the present year, and beg leave to report that, in accordance with the instructions of Bishop Roberts, I went as soon as possible to the Indian country, and have made an agreement with the Pottawatomies, through their chiefs, for a section of land in conformity with the articles adopted by the Illinois Conference, and have obtained the best titles which could be obtained from a rude and uncultivated nation, signed by the interpreter as a mutual friend, which instrument accompanies this report. . . . I have built a house for the accommodation of the family, which consists of eighteen persons. The house is fifty feet by twenty, two stories high, with apartments. It is built of hewed logs, and roofed with shingles. We have a smith-shop, a convenience I could not dispense with, . . . a poultry-house, spring-house, and other conveniences. I have forty acres of land in cultivation, seven acres inclosed for pasture, and one acre for garden. All has cost $2,400. Our crops are good—I suppose worth $200, when secured. . . . I have talked with eight chiefs, all of whom are highly gratified with the mission, and have pledged themselves to use their influence to support it in its religious character, but can not legislate upon the subject of religion. That, they say, is a matter between the

Great Spirit and the hearts of their people; but they will defend and protect the mission family; and if the Indians will give up their children to the care and tuition of the missionaries, they will be glad of it; but they can not use coercion. The school consists of fifteen native children—seven males, eight females—and two teachers. . . . I would here state that I have built a horse-mill, and have it in operation. A door of communication to the hearts of these poor, neglected, persecuted sons of men must be opened before we can expect among them the exercises of an evangelical faith."

In 1828 Jesse Walker writes: "The Indians seem to understand me better. This is owing to the new interpreter. The old one has been turned off. As to religion, I am sorry to say I do not see that blessed work of God rising among them that I have long prayed for. They have brought four packs of cards and burnt them in my fire; and some of them have promised to quit their drinking and to go to work this spring."

John Dew, whose business it was to collect funds for the mission this year, writes (in 1828): "Brother Walker informs me that he has united in marriage George Furkee (the present interpreter, who is a half-breed) and Kita-kokish-noquah, one of his female scholars, which is the first Christian marriage ever celebrated in the nation. They have both learned to read and write."

Brother Walker reported twenty-five members in 1827, among whom was one Indian. The remainder were members of the mission family and a few whites settled near. This was the first report of members in the bounds of the Rock River Conference. In all his reports Jesse Walker looked for better times; but the reports of what he had accomplished, given above, were the highest successes ever reached. The Indians were migratory, and about this time the Government began moving them west. By 1828 the whole work was on a decline; then Isaac Scarritt was appointed to the work, not so much to labor as to close up the affairs of the mission. After reporting to the Conference of 1829, that body passed the following resolution:

"*Resolved*, That whereas the Pottawatomie Indians have disposed of their lands where the mission was located, it is inexpedient longer to continue a mission among the Pottawatomie Indians, and the same is hereby discontinued."

A committee was appointed to audit the accounts of Brother Scarritt, and another committee to take into consideration the claims of Jesse Walker to certain property at the mission station, and thus sadly closed up five of the toilsome years of this arduous worker's life.

In 1828, Jesse Walker was sent to Peoria. His work extended as far north as there were white settlers. Probably Plainfield (Walker's Grove) was one of his appointments. He lived at Walker's Grove with his son-in-law, James Walker. From this circuit in that early day he reported, in 1829, 287 members.

This year (1829) Fox River Mission, including

the territory from Sandy Creek, in Marshall County, to *Chicaugo*, was set off from the Peoria Circuit, and allotted to Jesse Walker. All over that territory Brother Walker preached that year wherever five or six listeners could be gathered together. At the Conference of 1830, from this country he reported 75 members. The name of the work was changed to Chicago Mission, and Jesse Walker still continued missionary. This is the first time Chicago appears as a Methodist appointment in the Minutes.

A month or two after Conference, Brother Walker wrote the following letter to Bishop Roberts. It will tell us something of what our pioneer was doing in those days:

"CHICAGO, November 25, 1830.

"After my respects to you, I will give an account of my labors since Conference. I reached Chicago sufficiently soon to meet the Indians at the time of payment, but the agent was on his deathbed, and he died a few days after; so that no council could be held, or anything, in short, be done with them. At length, after five days' starving and drinking, they gave them their money, and all broke up in confusion. One of the chiefs said all must be left over till the next year. I then went to see the Kickapoos, and those of the Pottawatomies that had commenced to serve the Lord. I had to follow them down the Grand Prairie. Some I found on the Ambroise, some on the Little Wabash, and some on the Fox. This has taken four weeks, in which I have been but a few nights in a house. The rains have been frequent, but the Lord has blessed me with health. I have returned to this place well, for which I am thankful. The Indians express a strong desire to settle themselves, and to change their mode of living. There are three hundred of them who attend the worship of God morning and evening, and keep holy the Sabbath-day. I can only say that there can be no doubt but if they could get some place they would gladly settle themseves, and learn to read the Word of God and till the earth. Such a place is promised them by the Pottawatomies. It is on the Kankakee, and they are going to settle there in the spring. A blessed field is open at this time for sending the gospel to the Northwest. God is raising up preachers of the right kind from this glorious work, and nearly two hundred Pottawatomies have already joined them. These have laid aside ardent spirits altogether; also, stealing, lying, . . . and all manner of sin. They keep the Sabbath day with all possible strictness, and speak feelingly of the divine influence of the Holy Spirit, and exhort each other to give their hearts to the Savior.

"I still have some hope that Chicago will some day receive the gospel. Please send me some instructions."

What a missionary spirit glowed in the heart of the old hero! Let it be remembered that when these journeys were undertaken our traveler was sixty-four years of age.

Concerning the above letter, Isaac Scarritt wrote

in 1853 as follows: "Brother Walker's ardent zeal to be the instrument of good to the Indians led him to view their improvement and prospects in religion and civilization in a more favorable light than could be indorsed by others not actuated by the same sanguine feelings. I was at the time acquainted with the history of the Indians alluded to in this letter. A leader and reformer had arisen from among themselves, who drew converts from several tribes. Many of his maxims and institutions appeared to be in accordance with the gospel, and it was a subject of much speculation among the white settlers as to whence he had derived his system, and whether it embraced the essence of Christianity. It seems they were not very anxious to put themselves under the guidance of white men, and Jesse Walker never accomplished much among them."

S. R. Beggs, in writing to the author of this work, in 1884, says: "With Jesse Walker, I visited the Kickapoos, at the head of Big Vermillion, about September, 1833. Long before we reached the camp we heard the prophet preaching. When he finished, we were introduced to him by a Negro interpreter. After the introduction, the prophet shouted, 'Ho! Ho! Ho!' very loud, and all the people—men, women, and children—came to us in single file, and shook hands with us. They had a triangle, which they said represented the ($\triangle$) Trinity. If any broke the Sabbath, they were tied up and whipped. One man was appointed to spank all the naughty children! They regarded the Sabbath, and kept it strictly. They never ate until all their religious services ended. Who taught them is not known. When Jesse Walker first found them, they were thus religious. What came of it? The Pottawatomies, coming from the East, stopped at a village on the Kickapoo River, when the roughs among the white people appeared with their whisky, thinking to have sport at the expense of the Indians. The Indians persistently refused to drink, and could not be persuaded to touch the liquor. When asked why, they said they were baptized. When asked who baptized them, they answered, 'Father Walker.' Jesse Walker baptized many of the Pottawatomies at Salem, on Fox River. These never joined the Blackhawk War, but were always true to the whites. Their religious teachings saved much bloodshed in those cruel days. At this mission was a chief named Misshell, who had received two flags—one from the English, the other from the Americans. During the Blackhawk War, to express his idea, he raised the American flag high on a straight pole; but the English flag he raised on a pole at an angle of forty-five degrees, and thus expressed his idea of the superiority of the American stars!"

In the "History of Livingston County," in whose borders many of the Kickapoos resided, we find mention of Jesse Walker's labors. The writer speaks of his success as being considerable, resulting in many conversions. It is related of his converts that they were very scrupulous in the observance of the Sabbath, always returning from their hunting excursions on Saturday night. This writer also speaks of the prayer-books the Indians had invented. They consisted of black-walnut boards, on which they rudely carved the images and figures which represented their ideas; and these, it is said, they never failed to consult at night before going to bed.

But we leave the Indians here. Jesse Walker's chief labors from this on were among the opening settlements of the whites. From 1830 on we find him busily engaged in planting the standard of the Cross in Chicago and the surrounding country. We left him in 1830 on the Chicago Mission. We have no doubt that Jesse Walker preached the first Methodist sermon in Chicago; but we have no proof of this. The writer has for years made most diligent search for facts in the case, but finds nothing reliable. If the reader will take up "Field's Memorials of Methodism in the Rock River Conference," he will find (page 48) a full account of a sermon preached in Chicago, in the summer of 1829, by Isaac Scarritt, which is the first sermon of which we can find any account. But the following circumstantial evidences may be introduced: Jesse Walker was in the habit of preaching wherever six or seven hearers could be gathered. He went up to Chicago with John Hamlin and a crew of six in the spring of 1825. There were a few people in Chicago. It would be out of keeping with Walker's character if he did not preach there. From 1825 till 1828 he was at Salem Mission, seventy miles from Chicago. He had plenty of help during those years to attend to the school and the farm. He was traveling over the country, hunting up the settlers wherever they could be found. As early as 1825, there appears on his books credits of moneys received from persons living in Chicago then. He surely must have visited the place, and it was like him to preach if he found a chance. Again, in 1828, he was on Peoria Mission, *which extended to Chicago.* During the year he resided and preached at Walker's Grove. He must surely have visited Chicago then. Besides, it has been always understood among all his relatives—many of whom lived between Ottawa and Chicago from 1825—that Jesse Walker was early at Chicago preaching to the people. This is the best evidence we can bring. Here, for the present at least, the matter must rest.

From the first we find that Jesse Walker had much influence at Chicago in the early day. He was a clerk at an election held in August, 1830, and after Cook County was organized in March, 1831, he was appointed by the Commissioners to borrow the money and go to the land-office and enter land for city uses. We also find on the county clerk's records of 1831 the following:

"July 6. By Jesse Walker, an elder of the Methodist Episcopal Church, married, Joseph Thebalt to Charlotte Tosenben.

"July 9. By the same minister, Daniel W. Vaughn to Angeline Hebart."

William See, a local preacher, moved into Chicago in 1830; the family of Elijah Wentworth appeared in November, 1830; and Mrs. R. J. Hamilton and Mrs. Dr. Harmon came in the spring of 1831. During the fall of 1830 and winter of 1831, there was quite frequent preaching. William See preached every two weeks in his own house, and Jesse Walker preached as often as once a month as he went the rounds of his large circuit. A quarterly-meeting for the circuit was held in the winter of 1831, but no regular class was formed until the summer of that year. At the time just mentioned, Stephen R. Beggs was on the Tazewell Circuit in Tazewell County, and Isaac Scarritt was on the Fort Clark Mission. Two camp-meetings were appointed to be held one after the other, one at Cedar Point, on Isaac Scarritt's work, and the other at Plainfield, on Jesse Walker's mission. To these meetings came these three preachers, and Wm. See, the lone local preacher at Chicago. Smith L. Robinson was at Galena at this time, but was not at the meeting. These five were all the Methodist preachers in 1831 between Springfield and the north pole!

From the camp-meeting held in July at Plainfield, Jesse Walker, S. R. Beggs, and William See set out for Chicago. They arrived on Monday evening, and gathered the people into Dr. Harmon's house at the fort, to listen to the gospel as proclaimed by Brother Beggs. An appointment was given out for preaching the next forenoon. The congregation of about thirty persons gathered into the log-house where William See resided at The Point, on the West Side. Brother Beggs preached again, and they had a refreshing season. At the close of the sermon the preacher (S. R. Beggs) gave an invitation for people to join the Church. Eight persons presented themselves. These were William See, Minerva See, Mrs. Lucy W. Wentworth, Sabiah Wentworth, Susan Wentworth, Elijah Wentworth, Jr., Caroline Harmon, and Mrs. R. J. Hamilton. A few weeks after, August 4th, Mark Noble and family arrived in Chicago. Brother Noble, his wife, two daughters, and a son all joined the class. At first William See was appointed leader, but soon Mark Noble became the leader in more senses than one. This was the first Christian society ever formed in Chicago. For a few months in the spring of 1833, by removals and the appearance of the cholera, the class was left very small, but new members coming in early in the fall of that year the society recovered itself, and from that day there has never ceased to be a growing Methodism in that stupenduous city.

In the fall of 1831 Jesse Walker was appointed to the Mission District and in charge of Deplane Circuit. This circuit included all the country outside of Chicago down to the Illinois River. Very little was done, however, that year on any of the circuits on this district on account of the Black Hawk War, which, while small in itself, kept the people in a state of fright all summer long. The people gathered in barricaded log-houses at Dupage and at Plainfield for a few days, and then all fled to Fort Dearborn, at Chicago, where they lived a long time, until the cholera brought to the place by General Scott's troops drove the people back to their homes. S. R. Beggs's house at Plainfield was turned into a fort, and with the crowd that gathered there for protection was Jesse Walker and his family; and when they all fled to Fort Dearborn, Jesse Walker went with the crowd. This brought four Methodist preachers into the fort. They were Jesse Walker, S. R. Beggs (who was stationed at Chicago that year), Isaac Scarritt, and William See. Most of these took their turns in preaching to the people while shut up in the fort. The year on all the circuits was nearly a failure. Jesse Walker reported but thirty-four members from his Deplane Circuit.

The next year (1832) Brother Walker was appointed to the Chicago District, and also in charge of the Chicago Mission. The district included four charges. These were Chicago, Deplane, Peoria, and Pekin. He had for his workers S. R. Beggs, Zadoc Hall, and Jesse Haile.

Before Conference his beloved wife, Susannah, had died. The poor man was now alone, without home, only as he found it with his children. He immediately procured the old log-house at Chicago in which William See lived when the first class was formed in 1831, as a lodging-place for himself when in town, and as a place of meeting. This is the famous Father Walker's Log Church which appears in all the annals of early Chicago. It was the first church, or meeting-house of any sort, in the city. It was a double log-house, situated at The Point, on the west side of the river, about two hundred feet from the point where the two branches united. There was a door at each end, and a connecting door in the inner partition. Brother Walker fitted up one-half of this house as a meeting-place, and in the other he lodged by himself when he was in the village. Up to 1836 there was a room of some note on the North Side called Watkins's School-house, which was often used as a meeting-house. The first quarterly-meeting of John Sinclair's appointment as presiding elder was held there in 1833.

The above will be explained by the following notes. The quotation is from John Watkins, the first school-teacher in Chicago. He says:

"I commenced teaching in the fall after the Black Hawk War of 1832. My first school-house was situated on the North Side, about half way between the lake and the forks of the river, then known as Wolf's Point. The building was owned by R. J. Hamilton; was erected as a stable. It was twelve feet square . . . After the first quarter I moved my school into a double log-house on the West Side. It was owned by Rev. Jesse Walker, and was located near the bank of the river where the north and south branches meet. He resided in one end of the house, and I taught in the other. On Sundays Father Walker preached in the room where I taught."

"Jesse Walker was my successor in 1832," writes S. R. Beggs. "Myself and wife attended his first quarterly-meeting. The meeting-house, parsonage, parlor, and kitchen were all the same old log-house that we formed the first class in in 1831. Mrs. Beggs and myself were permitted to dine with the old hero. His stove was one of the box kind, with one griddle-hole. Here he boiled the tea-kettle, fried the meat, and boiled the scanty vegetables, each in its turn. He had for his table a large chest, and when dinner was served we surrounded the chest, and having good appetites, the dinner was refreshing."

The first Sunday-school in Chicago—first a union, now the First Presbyterian—was commenced in August, 1832. From April, 1833, to August, the school was held in the log church.

Rev. Jeremiah Porter arrived in Chicago May 4, 1833, and preached his first sermon in Jesse Walker's meeting-house. He organized the First Presbyterian Church on June 26, 1833. After the organization, the following service occurred: "At our first communion season," says Mr. Porter, "in that old school-house of logs, sitting on oak slabs, we had very little to suggest present luxuries, except one silver cup, brought by Major Wilcox from his own table. . . . That house, called Father Walker's, at The Point, on the West Side, witnessed the first communion season of our Church on the west shore of Lake Michigan, except at the Stockbridge Mission, at Green Bay." The first Methodist communion in Chicago had occurred in January, 1832.

James Rockwell, who had a great deal to do with Chicago Methodism from 1834 till 1838, in speaking of various matters, says: "I arrived in Chicago May 18, 1834; Jesse Walker missionary; a log church; the Bible lay on the center-beam. It was held sacred by the whites and Indians. At the Indian payment we had some disturbance in our worship. On arriving once for evening prayer-meeting, we found the Indians had stored pork, saddles, blankets, etc., in the house. Father Walker requested their removal; said they were desecrating God's house. The things were all removed at once. Being encamped near the house, they became quite noisy through strong drink. A kind word from the preacher made all quiet, which showed their respect for one they knew to be their friend."

The Methodists—as we shall see—built a neat frame-house in 1834. Until then, to accommodate the three sections of the city, the meetings were divided between the log church, Watkins's school-house, and Mark Noble's house, on the lake-shore, south of the fort. It is rather a curious fact that all sides have had the *first* Methodist Church. The first church, the humble log-house, was on the West Side; the first frame on the North, which was finally moved to the South Side, where the one lone Methodist society in the city worshiped from 1838 to 1845.

We now go back a little, to bring up the thread of our narrative. In the winter of 1832, Jesse Walker was on the Deplane charge, and was also superintendent of a district. Brother Beggs, from Chicago, went down to Walker's Grove to assist Brother Walker in holding a quarterly-meeting. At the close of this meeting, Beggs and Walker set out for Chicago on one of the coldest days of that year. It was thirty miles to the first house. A brother, T. B. Clark by name, started with them with an ox-team laden with provisions to aid in sustaining the coming quarterly-meeting, for provisions were scarce and high in Chicago. The preachers reached the first house, and put up for the night. They waited long for Clark and his ox-team, and then set out on a fruitless search for him. He did not come up till midnight. The next day they all arrived safely in Chicago, and met a warm reception from William See and wife. The meeting commenced with interest, and increased in power until its close. Sunday morning, after preaching, at 10.30 A. M., Jesse Walker invited the little band around the sacramental board. It was a season long to be remembered, that *first communion season* in Chicago. Who were the communicants has not been recorded; but we know all the members of the class that joined in 1831 were yet living in Chicago, and were still members of the Methodist Church.

Going back to our connections, we add that in the summer of 1833 many people began to come into the country. There was quite a class formed on the Des Plaines, ten miles west of Chicago. We have no record of the appointments Jesse Walker filled; but he certainly had members out of the city, for at the Conference he reported forty members; and we know there were not more than eight or ten at that time in Chicago.

Jesse Walker was returned to Chicago in 1833, and John Sinclair was appointed to take charge of Chicago District.

In July, 1833, Jesse Walker married again, and settled in his last earthly home, in a log-cabin on the Des Plaines River, ten miles west and a little north of the center of Chicago. The first quarterly-meeting for Chicago for the year was held in the fall in Watkins School-house. There were present John Sinclair, presiding elder; Jesse Walker, circuit preacher; William See and Henry Whitehead, local preachers; Minerva See, Charles Wissencraft and wife, Mrs. R. J. Hamilton, and Mrs. Caroline Harmon. These constituted the entire Methodist family at that time. The Nobles and Wentworths had moved in the spring of this year, and settled upon the north branch of the Chicago River.

In the spring of the year 1834 the rush began to come into Chicago. Adventurers of every kind began to appear; but among these there came many Methodists, who added strength to the small society. Among these were Grant Goodrich and Robinson Tripp, who remained members of the Methodist Church in Chicago to their death.

Little of interest occurred in the life of the pastor, more than the regular work of the ministry in caring for his little but increasing flock. But he performed one more eventful service that needs recording, and then the records of his service will be nearly ended. We refer to his building the first real Methodist church in Chicago.

The Catholics erected a small frame chapel, with bell, on State Street, in 1833. The Presbyterians erected a chapel and school-house on the alley between Randolph and Lake Streets in the fall of

1833. These were the first two churches of Chicago; the Methodist was the third. All these years the Methodists were hanging on to the humble log church on the West Side. We do not know why this church was placed on the North Side. It was probably because there were no members left on the West Side, and but two or three on the South Side. Just then the North Side was struggling for supremacy, and it seemed as though the main city would be there. The ground was higher and dryer, and the first good buildings were erected there. The building of the new church must have been largely managed by Jesse Walker; for he signed the contract for building, and no doubt, as was almost universally the custom of those days, furnished most of the material and raised the means for building. The building was erected, and stood on the corner of North Water and Clark Streets until its removal to the South Side in 1838. We may know something of this first Methodist Chicago building by scanning the following very particular contract. This is about the last official business of any account Jesse Walker ever performed:

"We, the undersigned, agree to build a Methodist Episcopal Church, 26 x 38 feet, agreeable to the following specifications, for the sum of $580:

"Good pine timber for sills; 12 feet posts and plates; joists $2\frac{1}{2}$ x 6 inches; studs, braces, rafters, and tie-beams, 3 x 4 inches; sheet and shingle the roof; elliptic cove roof; floor $1\frac{1}{2}$ inch, grooved and tongued; seats with board backs, and a rail of separation down the middle; 11 window-frames and sash, 24 lights each, primed and glazed complete; a neat pulpit, 6 x 3 feet 6 inches, steps up one side, panel work with molding, and pilasters, and seat inside; the pulpit to be raised four inches on a platform for table and chairs; 2 eight-panel 1½ inch front doors, with moldings, the front and one side to be planed; a neat cornice in front, and returned on one side; base around the floor,—the whole to be done in a workmanlike manner.

"HENRY WHITEHEAD,
"JOHN STEWART."

"I agree to accept of these propositions given by Henry Whitehead and John Stewart, on the part of the Methodist Episcopal Church. Signed on the 30th day of June, 1834.

"JESSE WALKER."

Some of the smaller timbers were sawed from timber up the north branch. When the house was torn down some time about 1860, Henry Whitehead secured a brace made of this timber he had made with his own hands, to keep as a relic. We believe this was destroyed by the fire of 1871. This Henry Whitehead was an efficient Methodist worker in Chicago for fifty years after this building was erected. After this building was removed, in 1848, to the corner of Clark and Washington Streets, it was twice enlarged, so that, in 1845, when it was removed to make way for the stupendous brick built by Rev. Wm. M. D. Ryan, it was a curious-looking affair, 52 x 76 feet in size, with ceiling less than twelve feet high.

At the Conference of 1834 Jesse Walker reported twenty-five members and one church at Chicago. This was the second church in the bounds of the Rock River Conference. The first was built at Galena in 1833.

Brother Walker had had his eye upon Chicago from 1825. In that time only one other man, S. R. Beggs, had shared the charge of the new field. He had hoped and longed for the day that had now come; and when Chicago Methodism was placed on a sure foundation, and John T. Mitchell had been secured as the pastor, the faithful pioneer, after thirty-two years of constant labor, at the age of sixty-eight, at the Conference of 1834, took a superannuate relation, and settled down quietly on his farm on the Des Plaines. Here he entertained the travelers that passed his way, did a little of farming, sold milk in the city, and in these quiet ways strove to earn a living for the short time yet allotted him on earth. His stepdaughter says, while here he never omitted family prayers morning and night, no matter who might be stopping with him. He was greatly loved by the Indians, and sometimes gave them the last food in the house.

He remained at this place for a year. When his Conference was in session in Springfield in 1835, he passed from earth on Sunday, October 5th. William See was at Root River (now Racine, Wis.) in 1836, and as he disappeared from our notice in 1834, he may have gone to Racine that year. Edmund Weed, one of Jesse Walker's old Plainfield members, was also at Racine with William See. It was probably these families that are referred to in the following notices. It will very likely appear, when the history is written, that Jesse Walker was the first preacher at Racine, and perhaps formed the first class there. The following incident will give us some facts in the case, as well as explain how Brother Walker came to his death: John Sinclair went on to the Chicago District in the fall of 1833, and left it in the fall of 1835; so that this incident must have occurred some time during those two years. John Sinclair came to Illinois at an early day; but he says that through all the years in the new country, he was never permitted to reach a new neighborhood ahead of any Methodist preacher. At length he received word that a few families had settled on Root River, Wisconsin, and he felt that his opportunity had come for going to one place heretofore unexplored. He lived on his farm near Ottawa, Ill. He set out on a trip to Root River to visit the new settlement. On his way, he called at Jesse Walker's house. After greetings were over, Brother Walker remarked that he was very tired, as he had just returned from Root River, where he had been to establish an appointment. John Sinclair said he then gave up the attempt of being first.

By 1835, there must have been quite a settlement around Racine; for we are led to the following sad recital: "The cause of his death was a severe cold he took on his way to camp-meeting. In crossing Root River, he found the water deeper than he had calculated on. He got very wet, took cold, and died in about six weeks.

"His last moments were such as might be expected from his long and laborious life in the way of doing good. To a ministerial brother who visited him shortly before his death, he said that God had been with him from the time of his conversion, and was still with him. His last moments were tranquil, and he died in full and confident hope of a blessed immortality."

He was buried near his home; but when the Rock River Conference was in session at Plainfield, in 1850, his remains were removed to the cemetery of that place and reinterred. The members of the Conference—the present writer in the company—gathered around the new tomb to look upon the remains, which had already been decaying for about fifteen years. A. E. Phelps, Isaac Scarritt, and John Sinclair spoke tender words of recollection, and then the body was covered once more, to rest till the last trump! A neat monument stands over his grave, to mark the last resting-place of this pioneer preacher without a peer.

WILLIAM SEE.

Jesse Walker was appointed to Chicago Mission in 1830. He resided at Walker's Grove, and traveled over the country from Ottawa to Wisconsin. In July, 1831, with S. R. Beggs as helper, Mr. Walker went up to Chicago to hold a two days' meeting. On Sunday a class was organized, which from that day has rated as the first Christian society of any kind organized in Chicago. Of this class William See became the leader.

To this Brother See must be given the honor of being, with his wife, the first resident Methodists of Chicago, the first Methodist preacher, and the first class-leader of the now extensive Methodism of the great city.

I have not been able to fix the date of William See's arrival at Chicago. His name occurs as a voter on a poll-book of a general election held in the house of James Kinzie, August 2, 1830. Mrs. J. A. Kinzie, who heard him preach in the spring of 1831, says: "He has recently come to the place." The Government made a treaty with the Pottawatomie Indians around Chicago in 1821, in which it agreed to furnish them a blacksmith and a schoolteacher for ten years. David McKee became the first blacksmith, and he was succeeded by William See, in 1830, who no doubt went to the place in that year.

Mr. See was born in Charleston, Virginia, in April, 1787. When a young, man he went to Kentucky, and from there to Palmyra, Missouri, where he owned a farm upon which he lived. There he married Minerva Moss, and remained until his three children were born—Elizabeth in 1811; then George W.; then Leah, who afterward became the wife of James Kinzie. At Palmyra, Mr. See joined the Methodist Church, and began preaching. About 1820 he moved to Morgan County, Illinois, where he remained until 1825, when he was admitted into the Illinois Conference, and appointed to Peoria

Circuit. This work included most of the country north of the Saugamon River, including what are now Peoria, Tazewell, Fulton, and Schuyler Counties. The only Methodist work north of Mr. See, to the north pole, was Jesse Walker's Indian Mission, on Fox River, established that year. The country was all new, and William See's work was to explore the new settlements. He was very active among the first settlers, forming societies wherever four or five Methodists could be found. He organized the first class in Schuyler County, at the house of Mr. Hobart, father of the twins Norris and Chauncey Hobart, who were afterward noted Methodist preachers. Let the reader remember that Mrs. Lucy Wentworth was at this time one of his members, at Lewistown, in Fulton County.

Mr. See traveled this circuit two years. At the Conference of 1827 he was elected and ordained a deacon, and then, at his own request, was discontinued. The probable reason was the want of support for his family, as many of the best men of that day who had families were obliged to locate for the reason just given. We know but little of Mr. See for the next three years. In 1828 a meeting of great interest was held at Farm Creek, on the Peoria Circuit, by S. L. Robinson, the circuit preacher, at which meeting Jesse Walker and William See were efficient helpers. He must have been appointed Government blacksmith at Chicago some time in 1830, for we find him voting, as before mentioned, at Chicago, in August of that year. When he learned the blacksmith trade we do not know. His son-in-law, in a letter to the writer, says: "He was a blacksmith and a gunsmith; in fact, could turn his hand to almost everything, from building a mill to tinkering a clock."

In 1831, Cook County was organized, including the territory now embraced in Iroquois, Kankakee, Will, Dupage, Cook, Lake, and McHenry Counties. The County Commissioners' Court held its first session March 8, 1831, at which time William See was appointed clerk. This is equivalent to being the first county clerk of Cook County, at Chicago. The records, as kept by the clerk, were preserved in the old court-house until 1871, when they were consumed by the great fire, that devouring monster that ate up so many precious things. Those old records contained many interesting items. The court met part of the time "in the brick house in Fort Dearborn, in the lower room of said house." At a session held June 6, 1831, the court adjourned to meet "until court in course, at the house of William See." The clerk was a poor speller. Most of the officials of every sort of that day were poor scholars. They had grown up in the rough times of the West, and had not formed great acquaintance with the schools in a land where there were no schools. They can in history make this boast, however: They were, any of them, as good scholars as Andrew Jackson or Abraham Lincoln. In the records at Chicago we find "Sail of lots," "Auxineer," etc. We find in the document:

"April 22, 1831, by William See, an ordained

minister of the M. E. Church, Joseph Papin to Maryan Sargarma.

"April 24, Wm. D. Schanks to Elizer Jane.

"July 24, by Rev. William See, William Anderson to Susan M. Wentworth."

Two marriages were performed by Jesse Walker; one June 6th, the other July 9th.

Mr. See held the office of clerk until April, 1832, when he resigned and was followed by Colonel Richard J. Hamilton.

During all these years, from 1830 to 1834, the testimony is that William See preached frequently, in the absence of the regular preacher.

The ten years specified in the treaty with the Indians expired in 1831, and Mr. See was thrown out of employment. In the new country, it was difficult to find the means of support for a family, and we find him moving about trying to find means of living. In the fall of 1831 he settled on a farm near Plainfield, where, for a time, he kept a house of entertainment. It was the day of immigration, and the most ready means of taking in a few dollars was by entertaining the numerous travelers. On nearly all roads, in that day, these log-house hotels were kept within four or five miles of each other. Jesse Walker kept one of them on the Des Plaines, in 1834. The family of the writer of these sketches kept one sixteen miles from Chicago, at Hegewich, in 1837; and the writer lived with David Pierce, who kept one at Hammond, in 1840.

In the spring of 1832, Mr. See was driven back to Chicago by the Black Hawk War. About 1835 he went to Wisconsin, and built a mill on Root River, about two miles above the mouth, at Racine. Henry Whitehead found him there in 1840, when he was on the Root River Circuit. About that time he left Racine, and spent some time mining near Mineral Point. He afterwards settled at Clyde, Iowa County, in Western Wisconsin. There he built another gristmill on a stream called Otter Creek, it being the first mill for grinding wheat in that country. His son-in-law, James Kinzie, who was living there, furnished the capital as an offset to Mr. See's work, and owned a half-interest in the mill. Mr. See continued to run the mill until about 1850, when he sold his interest to Mr. Kinzie, and went to Texas. He remained there a couple of years, then returned to his old home at Clyde, traveling all the way from Texas on horseback.

His first wife died at Clyde, about 1847. On his return from Texas, he remarried twice, and lived for a while in Pulaski, a town near Clyde. Here he engaged in farming, in which occupation he continued until his death. He died in August, 1859, and was buried by the side of his first wife, in the town of Clyde.

Letters from his personal friends state that during all these years he continued preaching as opportunity occurred. "He was a member of the Church and a preacher when he died," writes his son-in-law. "He was," says another, "about five feet ten inches in height, dark hair, bald on top, dark whiskers on chin, beetling eyebrows, and square chin. He was impulsive and full of energy; went for anything with his whole soul. He made a good deal of money, but lost it again in unprofitable speculations. Once, at a camp-meeting, after all the noted preachers had spoken, he was called upon to speak. He said he did not know what to say. The ground had been pretty well gone over. He was only a backwoods Southerner. One of the preachers whispered to him to give them some of his Southern fire; and he did so effectually that he soon had the audience in great excitement."

While we have the expressions of his friends, it will be of interest to note something from the other side. Before quoting, it is well to say that, in 1831, all the society in and around Chicago was made up of back-country and unlearned people, and that Mrs. Kinzie was a young married lady just from the higher circles of the East, where she had seen little but the high-style services of the Episcopal Church. We may add here that in 1836 she became the founder of the Episcopal Church in Chicago. Mrs. Kinzie says, in a letter to the writer concerning times in 1831: "There was a certain kind of holding forth by a very illiterate, untidy sort of a person named See, who called himself a Methodist." In her book, "The Early Day," in connection with her visit to Chicago in the spring of 1831, she says: "Once, upon a Sunday, we rowed up to The Point to attend a religious service conducted by Father See, as he was called. We saw a tall, slender man, dressed in a green frock coat, from the sleeves of which dangled a pair of untidy hands. He stepped briskly upon a little platform behind a table, and commenced his discourse. His subject was the fear of God. 'There was a kind of fear,' he told us, 'that was very near alienated to love—so nearly that it was not worth while splitting hairs for the difference.' He then went on to describe this kind of fear. Becoming a little bewildered, he paused and exclaimed: 'Come, let's stop a little while and clear away the brush.' At last, closing, he said: 'Which fear may we all enjoy, that together we may soar away on the rolling clouds of ether to a boundless and happy eternity, which is the wish of your humble servant.'"

It must be remembered that this visit to the meeting at the Point was before the forming of the first class. We suspect the preacher was in the "brush" and unusually embarrassed; for the Kinzies were very aristocratic people, living down near the lake on the North Side, who seldom appeared in these early meetings; and it is probable their unexpected appearance, with this new visitor from the East, threw our modest Brother See off his balance. We would pay a price for his views of his success on that eventful Sunday.

To all of which it is due to him to add yet more from his friends. S. R. Beggs says: "William See was, to say the least, an average preacher. His practical and theological attainments were above the average, and if he murdered the king's English, as Mrs. Kinzie says, the best of all, thank God, he murdered sin also. He was in good company. He was of muscular frame, nearly six feet high, dark hair, blue eyes, an intelligent face, affable and communicative, and, best of all, religious. He would have thrown some collegiates of this day in the shade."

STEPHEN R. BEGGS

Was born in Rockingham County, Virginia, March 30, 1801. His father was of Irish descent; his mother's family were from Holland, but were both born in Virginia, land of Negroes, (no more) Presidents, and Rebellion. The parents were both members of the Methodist Church before they were married, and they had been Methodists forty years when they went to the better land. If Stephen was an ultra Methodist, it was bred into his very life and being. When he was two years of age the family moved West, and after stopping two years in Kentucky, settled on the Ohio River, in Clark County, Indiana, about seventeen miles above Louisville. From a child Stephen was under religious impressions, and when quite young commenced to pray, and continued that wholesome custom until his conversion, which occurred when he was nineteen years of age. This auspicious event occurred in 1819, at a camp-meeting held at Jacobs' Camp-ground, seven miles from Louisville, where two hundred other souls were born into the kingdom of God. In six months he was appointed class-leader, and in 1821 was licensed to preach. He was received into the Missouri Conference in October, 1822, and was appointed to Mt. Sterling Circuit, Indiana. In 1823 he was sent away to the Missouri River, in the Boonlick country, and in 1824 he was continued in Missouri, being on the Fishing Creek Circuit, which extended about seventy miles along the Missouri River, embracing settlements west of the State line. He received for the year of toil and arduous labor twenty-three dollars. By the end of the year the clothing he had obtained two years before was well-nigh worn out. His close-bodied preacher-coat was something like Joseph's coat of many colors, in consequence of the blue and gray patches. But there was help at hand. The sisters united, and made him cloth of blue and white cotton, twilled, and very coarse. All hands then turned in at this *Preachers' Aid Society*, and made a coat, cut in the genuine Methodist preacher style. The pantaloons were of another and inferior kind of cloth. This was his Conference suit, in which he set out for Conference, which was held in Missouri. The weather being warm and dry, one could scarcely tell what his new coat was made of, it was so colored by sweat and dust. A sister, by washing and ironing, set him to rights, and Brother Beggs says he " was as genteel as any of the preachers." By Mr. Beggs's request, Bishop Roberts transferred him to the Illinois Conference, and he was appointed to Rushville Circuit, on Blue River. He visited his father's house after an absence of two years, and was, by a father's hand, refitted and reclothed ere he set out to the more genteel circuit in Indiana. In 1827 he was on the Wayne Circuit. During the year he fell into doubts, and for six months there hung a sad gloom over his mind. He went to visit his parents in Clark County, and one evening retired to secret prayer to the old spot where, years before, he had for hours wrestled in prayer to God. There, while in deep struggle, the day dawned, the clouds broke, and his sky was again clear. For six months afterward his peace was as a river. In 1830, Mr. Beggs was appointed to Tazewell Circuit, along the east side of the Illinois River, opposite Peoria. This was his first circuit in Illinois, and ever after his appointments were in this State. While on this circuit he married his first wife, whom he found at Holland's Grove, near Washington, Illinois. Mr. Beggs's account is this: "The first round on my circuit I fell in with the family of William Heath, a brother-in-law to Samuel Hamilton, who had lately come from Ohio. Brother Heath had a daughter that I concluded would make me a good preacher's wife. During the year I proposed marriage for the first time in my life. I was married, after traveling nine years as a single man, the 1st of September, 1831, by Jesse Hale." That fall Mr. Beggs and wife set out on horseback for Conference, which met at Indianapolis, and to pay a visit to Brother Beggs's brothers. At this Conference he was appointed to Chicago Mission, he being, as appears elsewhere, the first preacher really appointed to the place. During the winter (1832) he purchased a claim and house at Walker's Grove, near Plainfield, and his house in the spring of the year was for a time barricaded as a fort, all the people of the country gathering there for protection from the Indians. It was the time of the Sac War. The party remained in Mr. Beggs's house a few days, and then all set out for Fort Dearborn, at Chicago. While here, Brother Beggs preached and did duty as a soldier in turn. An incident, which occurred while he was on sentry duty, will illustrate one of his most prominent traits—confidence. Standing sentinel, not exactly on the "walls of Zion," but within the palisades of Fort Dearborn, he was approached by the officer of the day going his rounds. What mischief could Mr. Beggs look for in a fellow-soldier? The officer advanced without permission, and with kindness of manner accosted the unwary sentinel. "Fair piece, that," referring to Mr. Beggs's gun. "Yes, tolerable," was the reply. "Does she go easy? Let's see." The officer, to satisfy himself, took the piece without opposition, and walked off toward the guard-house. Brother Scarritt interceded for the new sentinel, and he was permitted to defend Chicago with his musket. In 1832, Brother Beggs was appointed to Deplane, which circuit embraced the regions about Plainfield and Joliet.

In 1835 he was appointed to Bureau Mission. From that time until 1850 he ranged over the country between Peoria and Joliet, doing effective labor as a camp-meeting man and a revivalist. He had a quiet home at Plainfield ever since 1831, and in quiet, peaceful old age awaited the angelic escort which came to convey him home. Few men in the Rock River Conference ever performed more ministerial labor or were the means of the conversion of more souls.

For the part he took in establishing Methodism in Chicago, see life of Jesse Walker. He died in 1896.

JOHN SINCLAIR.

John Sinclair came into the bounds of the Rock River Conference in 1833 as presiding elder of the Chicago District. He was born in Loudoun County, Virginia, April 9, 1793, and was forty years old when made presiding elder of Chicago District. When he was six years of age his father moved into East Tennessee, where the opportunities for attending school were limited. The father, however, was a good scholar, and taught John and the other children the elements of an English education. Mr. Sinclair related of himself stories of study amid difficulties. Reading by firelight, he was enabled to make some advancement in information. He once remarked that he had heard it said that "a little learning is a dangerous thing," but he had never had enough to expose him to danger. From a child he manifested a love for the Scriptures, and, by reading the Book for himself, was made to feel the great necessity of devoting his life to the service of God. When twenty years of age, with his father's family, he settled in Lexington, Kentucky, and, in February, 1819, was married to Lydia Short, who in 1865 was yet living. A year after this the conviction of his sinfulness became so powerful he began to seek religion, and united with the Methodist Episcopal Church. Soon after, in a class-meeting, he was powerfully converted; and so clear was the evidence, he never doubted his adoption into the family of God. He at once began to exhort his fellows to flee the wrath to come, and was appointed the leader of two classes. The impression was soon made upon his mind that he ought to preach the gospel; but his wife was not so easily persuaded that it was best for him to give himself and herself to the trials of the itinerancy. One night, when he supposed all were asleep, he lay struggling in prayer; and in the midst of his anxiety, he heard a noise. "It was not," he wrote, "the voice of God, it was not the voice of an angel; but it was the voice of my wife, saying, 'Go, and do all the good you can.'" This was in September, 1824; and in the same month he was admitted into the Kentucky Conference, and appointed to Winchester Circuit. In 1825 he was appointed to Mount Sterling; in 1827, to Hopkinsville; in 1828, back to Winchester. In 1830, on account of a feeling that slavery was an evil, he transferred to the Illinois Conference, and was appointed to Jacksonville. In 1831 he was appointed to Sangamon Circuit, with A. E. Phelps. In 1833 he was made presiding elder, and appointed to Chicago District, during which service he held quarterly-meetings in Chicago, dedicated the first Methodist church built in the Rock River Conference, which was at Galena, and failed to get to Root River ahead of Jesse Walker, as related elsewhere. The district embraced nearly all the territory in the Central Illinois and Rock River Conferences. He left his wife on Fox River, six miles above Ottawa, where he had made a home, and spent his days traveling over the new country. The roads were without bridges, over vast plains, without a stake or mark to direct his course, except the points of timber miles apart. In 1835 he was removed to Sangamon District. This removal he thought a mistake, but bore it patiently. At the close of two years he took a supernumerary relation, on account of the ill-health of himself and wife. In 1838 he was appointed to the Ottawa District; and from that time he remained in the bounds of the Rock River Conference until his death. In 1855 he was appointed to Evanston. He was able to preach but little; and as Evanston needed a pastor more than a preacher, he was a good man for the place. After the Conference, when asked where he was to labor that year, he remarked that he was going to Evanston as a "professor." "Professor of what?" the astonished querist inquired. "Why," replied Sinclair, modestly, "as a professor of religion." After a service of two years, he settled down in Evanston, remaining in that quiet place during his closing years. There was no man who cared for consistent piety that did not love John Sinclair. When he was tired, God took him to receive his crown. It was long his wish that he might not linger when called to pass away, and he hoped he should not in his last days become a burden to his friends. After his wanderings to and fro, he was permitted to die at home. His death, when it came, was sudden; but he was ready. A short time before his departure he said to his friends: "Do n't weep for me when I go away. Do n't," said he, "put on mourning.

It seems to me that it is very improper to mourn for a minister who has gone to so good a place as heaven." This was his dying sentiment. He died some time in the winter of 1861, aged sixty-nine years.

John Sinclair was simple and playful in manner, and childlike in innocence of heart. He was often seen weeping when there was cause; for he had a tender heart within him. There is a morose melancholy, and there is a light and trifling spirit. John Sinclair had neither of these; but he had a vein of the most quiet humor one ever sees—a humor that was not out of place in connection with the most religious scenes. Indeed, the early preachers partook of this pleasantry more than the dignified latter-day ones; and it must be confessed that many of them, as the Haneys and U. J. Giddings, carried their jokes too far. But to relieve the tedium of travel and toil, the earlier preachers indulged more in joviality than would be seemly nowadays. We give an instance, to illustrate not only Mr. Sinclair's pleasantry, but that of most of the old-style preachers. John T. Mitchell, Peter Akers, and Sinclair were returning from General Conference in June, 1844. Mr. Akers had charge of a Mrs. and Miss Seeman, who were coming West. They came to the canal somewhere between Joliet and Ottawa; and as the high waters had carried away the bridge, the stage in which they were traveling was obliged to ford the canal. Mitchell and Akers got out of the stage, and stood on the bank. The drunken driver ventured in, and midway overset the stage, drenching passengers, trunks, and mails. The driver opened the door, and pulled out the dripping passengers one by one. Taking Miss Seeman on his back in a ludicrous manner, he waded to the shore, and, with little ceremony, dumped her on the bank. At this J. T. Mitchell laughed. Sinclair came over with a stage-horse, and took up Mr. Mitchell behind him. Going over, he stopped in the middle of the canal, and told the then newly-appointed Cincinnati Book Agent that he had done wrong in laughing, and that he must apologize, or he would drop him in the deep water. John T. gave proper tokens of repentance, the young lady forgave him, and the party hastened on to Mr. Sinclair's home on Fox River. "John Sinclair," says Peter Akers, "may have had his faults, but he was seldom if ever charged with any; . . . and if his speech and his preaching were not with enticing words of man's wisdom, they were often in demonstration of the Spirit and of power."

We have not in these pages narrated many serious adventures or hairbreadth escapes. If a half of the perilous adventures of the early men were written here, we would have room for but little else. But as a specimen, we give this concerning John Sinclair: In the winter of 1837 he came near losing his life. He was crossing the prairie between Vermillion and Ottawa, when suddenly the wind changed to the north. The earth was covered with slush. Before he reached Coles Creek he got down to walk to keep himself warm.

His leggings became so heavy with ice he was obliged to slip them off and leave them. His horse's legs became so loaded with ice he could hardly go; and his own were so heavy he could not remount his horse to cross the creek. He was obliged to hold on to the stirrup, and let his faithful horse drag him through. At last, exhausted, almost frozen, he reached a house, to find relief from the impending danger.

Appointments: 1824, Kentucky Conference, Hinkstone; 1833–34, Illinois Conference, Chicago District; 1835, Sangamon District; 1836–37, Peoria District; 1838, Ottawa; 1839–42, Ottawa District; 1843, Rock River District; 1844–46, superannuate; 1847–50, Rock Island District; 1851–54, Chicago District; 1855–56, Evanston; 1857, superannuate; 1861, he died.

PETER R. BOREIN.

In 1837, Chicago was in a bad way. The work on the canal, on which the city depended for existence, was commenced July 4, 1836, and had gone on for six months. Laborers and speculators flocked to the place, and when suddenly there was a collapse of all things in the whole nation, Chicago felt the crash as no other section did; for when the work on the canal ceased, there was nothing left to live upon. There was money enough; it was as plenty as butterflies in summer, and just as valueless. And while Methodism in the city suffered with the general calamity, it had special ills of its own. The church was on the North Side. There the rising city first began its business; but by 1837 all business had gone over to Dearborn, Clark, and Lake Streets. The dwellings of citizens were growing up southward. The North Side was deserted. The grand hotel built there in 1836, from whose steps Daniel Webster spoke in 1837, became the abode of washerwomen. Besides, then the Presbyterian and Baptist Churches, who had buildings on the South Side, had all the prestige and position. No people of prominence belonged to the humble Methodist Church; they were all in the two Churches named. The failures of the day prostrated all the Methodists that had anything, and those that could, left the place. The leading member — a lawyer — failed, with $60,000 of debt upon him.

When Chicago Methodism was in such a plight as this, Peter Borein came; and it is probable that no other Methodist preacher ever went to the city who set so important influences in motion. In two years he took that little Methodist Church up from its feeble condition till it became so strong that it, in those days, overshadowed all others! If any other man can lay claim to as great a work as Peter Borein, it was Wm. M. D. Ryan, who went to Clark Street in 1844. For an account of his peculiar work, see Field's "Rock River Conference History."

Peter Ruble Borein was the son of Greenbury and Mary Borein—or Boreing, as the parents spelled their name—and was born among the mountains of East Tennessee, on Sinking Creek, in Washington

County, November 17, 1809. His father was a
poor farmer, illiterate and wicked, of English descent; his mother was of German origin. The occasion of his conversion is interesting. In 1828 an
uncle of Peter's, Harris by name, lived in the
neighborhood. The Methodists had penetrated into
the region, and had begun to fill the land with
their fame. Several camp-meetings were held, and
wild rumors were afloat that the Methodists threw
a "spell" over the worst of men, and the preachers
held them until they got religion. Out of curiosity, Mr. Harris went to witness the wonderful
works. The mighty spell of the Spirit came upon
him, and he was glad to take his place among the
seekers. He was soundly converted. The keen-eyed circuit preacher saw in the new convert material for a worker, and before the meeting was over
he was given charge of a class, which met nine
miles from his home. One Sabbath, as Mr. Harris
was riding home from his class-meeting, he saw a
group of youngsters standing by a store at the
Corners. After passing them, his soul became so
burdened for the boys he turned back to exhort
them. He agreed, if they would promise to attend
the next camp-meeting, that he would furnish a
conveyance, and see that they were provided for
during the meeting. There were thirteen of them,
and they all promised to go; and when the meeting
came, the thirteen went, and every one of them was
converted. One of these was his nephew, Peter
Borein. This occurred in August, 1828, on Brush
Creek. When the boys went home, they were sub-

jected to severe persecution. William McBride received a severe flogging; young Peter was summoned into the presence of his father and informed that he must either give up his Church or his home; "and," said the father, "I will give you till to-morrow to decide." "You need not wait until to-morrow," said Peter; "I can tell you what I will do to-night; I will leave my home." And picking up a little bundle containing all his earthly possessions, he left his father's house and went to reside with his uncle, Harris. He at once became a great worker in the mountain Church. For years after there were many who remembered Peter's first prayer. It ran about thus: "Lord, have mercy on my soul. Been to camp-meeting; got religion; been happy ever since. Lord, have mercy on Billy McBride's daddy. Amen."

Eighteen months after Peter Borein's conversion, Mr. Harris moved his family into Southern Illinois, taking Peter with him. He settled near Jacksonville, in Morgan County. Peter commenced laboring in a brickyard, which employ he continued after he entered college, to gain means to pay his way. Encouraged and assisted by friends, he entered Illinois College in 1830, where he remained two years. While there, such was his piety, and the indications of genius he exhibited, and the rapidity with which he advanced in his studies, that he won the esteem and attention of his teachers and fellow-students. He acquired a habit of study, which he never lost. The year before his death he commenced the study of

Hebrew, and in six weeks, with the aid of a lexicon, he could read the Hebrew Bible very well. On leaving school, he was immediately licensed to preach, and in 1832 was received into the Illinois Conference, and appointed to Canton Circuit, with Peter Cartwright as his presiding elder. In 1833 he went to Rushville; in 1834 to Henderson Mission; and in 1835 to Quincy, to which place he returned in 1836. In December of this year he married Miss Lucinda Burns. At Quincy he was eminently useful, and distinguished himself as an able and eloquent minister of the gospel. But becoming mingled with anti-slavery movements in his last year, he became with some very unpopular. At the Conference at Rushville, in 1836, he made a memorable missionary speech. So great was the enthusiasm created, the preachers emptied their pockets so completely for contributions that many of them had to borrow money to return home. His classmate, Zadoc Hall, says: "He always stood number one in his Conference studies." His oratory was of the word-painting style. Had he lived he would have been a Simpson. At one time he was picturing the wavering soul. Long he held the soul swaying between the Church and the world. Every inducement in heaven, on earth, and in hell was used to induce the wavering soul to cleave to Christ. The recording angel stood in heaven, with deep suspense, weeping—if e'er angels weep—over the impending calamity. At last the soul became fully immersed in the world. He was given up of heaven. The recording angel, with one sweep of the pen, blotted his name from the Book of Life. An eminent lawyer, who was a frequent hearer of Mr. Borein, undertook in company to tell something of his power, when the tide of tender memories rushed upon him in such force the tears rolled down his cheeks, and his emotions choked his voice. Three young bloods stood leaning against a tree at camp-meeting, listening to Borein's preaching. One after another began wiping his eyes, when one of them turned to the others, and said: "What the —— are you crying about?"

During the last winter of Mr. Borein's life more than three hundred were converted in Chicago; and so great was the respect for him, whenever he passed along the street, clamor would cease, even in the drinking saloons. His name was on every tongue, and when Augustus Garrett, the auctioneer, would be selling a handkerchief, he would exclaim: "You will want this if you go to hear Borein preach."

But his Master called him away ere he became an idol. He had finished his course; his crown was ready. "Who that heard his last sermon," says Grant Goodrich in a lecture, "can ever forget it, whether he shall reign with him in heaven or wail with the lost?" It was of the vision of the dying Stephen. As he spoke of the beatific sight which burst upon the raptured vision of the dying martyr, Borein seemed to catch a glimpse of the glories which Stephen saw. There seemed a supernatural radiance glowing upon his countenance, and a prophetic fire burning upon his lips. "God," he said, "had not seen fit fully to reveal to us the locality or the form of heaven; but every one, he presumed, had had some mental conception of heaven and its inhabitants. He believed in the next world, as in this, there were degrees in Christian attainment, and that in that better land some would occupy positions higher than others. Sometimes his imagination had conceived heaven as a vast amphitheater, with seats rising in one grand circle, tier above tier, up to the very throne itself, and from the lowest seats the white-robed ones strike the exultant song of redemption. It is caught up from rank to rank, growing louder and sweeter as it rises. In unison the angel choirs strike their harps, and from every golden lyre-string of saint and angel, of cherubim and seraphim, is poured the jubilant rapture of adoring song, until heaven becomes filled with an atmosphere of richest melody."

"Who shall dare to say," continues Grant Goodrich, "that God in that hour did not permit his soul to catch some of the dying strains of that heavenly music in which he was so soon to join? 'None knew him but to love him.' He was a nearer impersonation of Christ than I ever expect to see again on earth. In his words and looks there was a holy charm—a something that awed, and yet captivated you. As an effective preacher I have never heard his equal. I have heard men of more varied learning, of more brilliancy and depth of thought, and more polished diction, but none of that moving, winning power, that seized the heart, and wrought conviction, and made his hearers willing captives. There was a persuasive earnestness, a yearning tenderness, that made his hearers feel that his heart would break under the awful sense of their danger. There was a silvery music in his voice, a melting cadence in his tones, that fathomed the deepest well-springs of the heart, and turned the fountains of its affections toward a crucified Savior. He had great intellectual powers, blended with beauty of feature and of expression. His eyes were large, blue, lustrous."

In some sense the illiterate boy of East Tennessee was the founder of Garrett Biblical Institute. John Dempster, converted at a camp-meeting in 1812; Peter Borein, converted at a camp-meeting in 1828; Mrs. Garrett, converted under the preaching of Borein in 1839,—these are the influences that converged at Evanston in 1854. The conversion of a child may set influences at work that shall send ripples over the world, and swell to fuller tones the anthems of heaven!

We have given a glimpse of Peter Borein's last sermon. The meeting began that evening at six o'clock; and such was the interest, it lasted late into the night. The preacher went home too happy to sleep. He went out to make a few calls the next day, and on returning complained of being unwell. He went into his chamber, never to go out to earthly labor again. His disease was typhoid fever, and with much suffering he lay for fifteen days. During the time there was sickness in the family, and one child died while the father lay sick. When asked if he had any dread of death, he said: "O no; my preparation for that was made long ago."

He died at Chicago, August 15, 1839; and after a funeral service in which all Churches united, and a sermon by Rev. I. T. Hinton, the Baptist preacher, his remains were buried in the cemetery now covered by Lincoln Park. The body was afterward removed to Rose Hill.

When he lay dying, messages went out every hour or so over the city concerning his state, and inquiries concerning him were on every lip. On the day of his funeral the stores of the city were closed, and the whole city was in mourning. He was but twenty-nine years of age at his death.

Peter Borein went to his work in Chicago in 1837. He gathered the discouraged flock around him, and poured forth words of comfort He breathed into them something of his own mighty faith, and inspired them with his own burning zeal, and with them cried to heaven for help. During the winter of 1838 quite a number were converted. The preacher reported eighty-two members to the Conference, and returned to the charge. During the summer of 1838 the little church on the North Side was moved across the river, and set on the lot since famous as old Clark Street, and enlarged to double its size—the same old church in which the writer of these lines joined the Church in 1842. In December a revival commenced, deep, widespread, and powerful. Night after night Brother Borein preached like a messenger from heaven, and day after day he followed the people to their homes and shops, even into the haunts of dissipation, calling them to God. The church was crowded to its utmost capacity, and every night the altar was thronged with penitents. Religion was the absorbing theme in private and in public places. The concerns of the soul swallowed up every other thought. There were more than three hundred conversions, which was a tenth of all the population. The meetings continued from New-Year's till April.

Almost every revivalist has a peculiar way of dissecting souls that brings the charge upon them of exposing people purposely. Mr. Borein had this power more than most men. One case is in point. Mr. M., who afterwards became an efficient member and worthy class-leader, was often employed to fiddle at dances through the country. His wife was a member of the Church, but the husband refused to attend the meetings, and was called away to the country several times during the meetings to play at dances. At length one evening he was induced to go to church. Mr. Borein, as Mr. M. thought, exposed him before the whole congregation. He went home angry with his wife for telling the preacher about him. There was no truth in this charge, however. After a few nights, Mr. M. returned to the meeting again to be dissected, the preacher, as he supposed, telling the people all about him. He was angry, confused, puzzled, but under conviction. He still accused his wife of telling the preacher about him. The matter ended by Mr. M. being happily converted.

Too much "acting" in the pulpit is a serious fault; but now and then, when the wave of religious feeling is in tune, a little of the dramatic is in place. Peter Borein was a born dramatist; but he held his power in reasonable check. Frequently, when they had had a glorious time, he would introduce a favorite song to close with. There was a Negro, Pete by name, who, being tuned by divine love, could sing in strains that would move a congregation to emotion. Borein could sing also.

Standing in the altar, the preacher would sing, in rich melodious tones:

"What ship is this that's passing by?
O glory, hallelujah!"

when Pete would respond in a voice still more melodious:

"Why, it's the Old Ship Zion,
Hallelujah!"

Borein would take up the question:

"Is your ship well built; are her timbers all sound?
O glory, hallelujah!"

and Pete would answer:

"Why, she's built of gospel timber,
Hallelujah!"

And so on to the close of "Old Ship Zion."

Persons who have never listened to anything of the kind can not imagine how such strains would melt into the very souls of the throng. The words are trivial, but the tune is one of the most melodious. I have heard Pete sing, and know what a voice he had. After this, he wandered away to the world; but once again, in 1845, he had a religious spell upon him, and then we heard him pour out a song in old Clark Street, rich with negro melody.

As will be seen in the life of Mrs. Garrett, Mr. Garrett and wife were converted at these Borein meetings; and thus there can be no persons more interested in Peter R. Borein than the members of Garrett Biblical Institute.

HOOPER CREWS.

Chicago, in 1840, received Hooper Crews. Old Clark Street could not have received a more fitting man. He had been a year in our bounds—from 1834 to 1835—and had then returned to central Illinois, where he had been stationed at Springfield, and had filled the office of presiding elder for three or four years on the Danville District. Now he entered the Conference bounds once more, and never after filled appointments elsewhere, except the year he served as chaplain in the army. He was a genuine Kentuckian, with a large and generous heart and a Yankee polish. He was the truest specimen of a Christian gentleman we ever knew. He was reared by a mother that early taught him the path of life.

He was born near Pruett's Knob, Barren County, Ky., April 17, 1807. He was converted at the age of seventeen, while attending a camp-meeting held at Level Woods. From the first, he felt that his mission was to preach the gospel. In the fall of 1828, he was induced by the presiding elder to act as a supply on Bowling Green circuit. In 1829 he was admitted to the Kentucky Conference and sent to Salt River Circuit, where he remained two years. In 1834 he was transferred to the Illinois Conference, and put in charge of Galena District and of the Galena Station. The Kentucky Conference, of which he was a member, sat at nearly the same time as the Illinois, and Mr. Crews took this time to visit some friends in Illinois, and also transact some personal business. He came up with $500, with which he entered Government land. Being near Mt. Carmel, the seat of the Illinois Conference, he visited that body. The bishops, as was the case all through the Church's history, were ever on the lookout for energetic young men to man the frontier appointments. Galena, at this time, was a town of one thousand inhabitants, and one of the most important points in the State. There was but one larger town in the State, and that was Alton. Bishop Roberts no sooner set eyes on the tall, robust-looking young man than he decided to take him for the Illinois work. When he spoke to Mr. Crews about it, he said he had just received word from the secretary of his own Conference informing him of his appointment there, and doubted if it would be lawful for him to leave. The bishop said episcopacy was equal to episcopacy everywhere, and he would take the responsibility. On this assurance, he consented to go.

The Conference over, Mr. Crews and Peter Cartwright started on horseback to their appointments. Mt. Carmel is down on the Indiana line, in the southeastern part of Illinois. The distance to Galena was full three hundred miles. The two travelers took a bee-line across the prairie. Mr. Cartwright always carried a pocket compass to guide him over the sea-like prairies. Cartwright began bantering Crews, averring that his horse could outtravel Crews's horse. Mr. Crews rode his pet Luby, a dark chestnut, nearly sixteen hands high; and he thought Luby could outtravel any horse he ever saw. They aimed for the headwaters of the Little Wabash. The first day they traveled seventy-eight miles. As they started, the next morning, Crews said to Cartwright: "If you are willing, we will sleep in Springfield to-night." The distance was eighty miles. They entered Springfield a little after nine o'clock. Here they rested a week. From Springfield they steered for Lewiston; from Lewiston to Knoxville, which then consisted of a few shanties. Cartwright was bound for his first quarterly-meeting for the year in Burlington, and at Knoxville the two presiding elders parted. From thence Mr. Crews went on to Rock River. He arrived at the river in the midst of a drizzling rain. There was an island in the river. To this he forded. He threw his saddlebags over his shoulder, and swam the river to the north shore. Twenty miles up the Mississippi, which he was now following, he came to Cat-tail Swamp. As he went in, the horse began to flounder, and Mr. Crews went over the horse's head down into the mud and water. The horse gained the shore; but when Mr. Crews went up to catch him, he playfully darted off. Every time Mr. Crews came up to the horse, he would play this trick. The whole afternoon was spent in this game. It began to grow dark, and there was no house for twelve miles; and just as our traveler began to grow alarmed, he caught the horse. It now commenced to rain, and it became very dark. About daylight he came to Plum River. He dismounted, and sat down at the root of a tree. He wrapped his blanket around him, and sat waiting for the day. When it was light, he saw a ferryboat, and soon discovered a rope which was attached to a bell in a tree. He pulled the rope, and the ringing bell soon brought the ferryman. His first house was the home of Mr. Davison, a man who, in 1803, brought the first Methodist preacher into Illinois; who was a member of the first class in Illinois in 1803, and also of the first class at Galena in 1829. (See Davison.)

It was now the 17th of October, and Mr. Crews hastened on to Galena. He found there Mr. Kent, the Presbyterian minister, who had been there since 1829. There was a small Methodist church built in 1833, on the ground where the present (1896) church stands. Mr. Crews and Kent made arrangements by which they were not both to be absent from town on the same Sabbath. Old numbers of the Galena *Advertiser* speak thus of Galena at this time: "The houses are of wood, save two, and are built principally on two streets, called Lower and Bench Streets. There are about fifteen stores, and about the same number of groceries [these, in that day, were liquor-shops], and all appear to be doing well. Three clergymen reside here—Presbyterian,

Methodist, and Episcopal—all industrious and pious men." And again: "There are twenty places where ardent spirits are sold—retailed by the glass every day of the week, the Sabbath not excepted. One-half of our merchants transact more or less business on the Sabbath. There are more gambling-houses than places of worship, and twenty or thirty professed gamblers residing in the city."

Mr. Crews says: "I had not been long in the country before I found I should want the money invested in my horse to pay for board; so I sold him for $160. I sometimes walked to my appointments; at other times kind friends would loan me a horse; and when the river was open in summer, I went to Rock Island by boat, when I was able to pay my passage. Several times I walked twenty miles to Plattville, to Mineral Point, forty miles to Hamilton Grove, and once to Rock Island. I generally walked to Dubuque; and once, in walking to Vinegar Hill, was nearly frozen to death." It will be remembered that the places named above were circuits or missions on the Galena District. The dangers to which he was exposed fell out as follows: He started out to hold the quarterly-meeting at Vinegar Hill, ten miles from Galena. Soon after he started, it commenced snowing very hard. He concluded the safest way was to go direct to the Mississippi; and he kept his eye on a line of trees to keep himself from straying from the right direction. He became wet with perspiration, as it was not cold; but suddenly the wind came down from the northwest. He was hungry and weary.

The wind was directly in his face. He did not feel the cold much, but began to be very sleepy, so much so that he fell down several times. He began to fear the worst. He thought of his mother—that directing saint of his—and of what a sad thing it would be to perish, and his body be eaten by wolves. He would fall more often, and only the above thoughts were sufficient to arouse him. Finally, near sundown, he reached the house of Mr. Simmons. He went right in without ceremony; sat down in a chair, speechless, but not senseless. As he went in, the woman of the house, frightened, ran out. Mr. Simmons came in, and, understanding the position, at once drew the chair back from the fire. A tub of water was brought, his feet were bathed, and water poured on his head. In a short time he had the most painful sensations he ever felt. He was then wrapped in blankets, and put to bed, where he went to sleep. In the morning he felt very sore. His face, ears, and hands were blistered. He remained with Mr. Simmons four weeks, and when he left was not yet able to pull on his boots, and was obliged to wear overshoes. Mr. Simmons took him in a sleigh to Galena; and, after all this, refused to receive a cent for his trouble.

Mr. Crews had not been in Galena long after his first coming until the young men of the place organized a theater. These shows had a very bad effect. They demoralized everything. Hardly a meeting or decent gathering could be held, there was such a "craze" over the new theater. Mr. Crews felt constrained to oppose the performances. This aroused the ire of the young bloods, and there were dire threatenings. One Monday morning, Mr. Crews met Dr. Graw in the post-office. The latter immediately said: "Mr. Crews, I had made up my mind to cane you; and if I had met you yesterday, I should surely have done it." Crews replied: "I doubt it very much." The doctor looked at Crews, amazed. "You don't mean to intimate," he said, "that you would not have submitted?" "You will never cane me, unless I fail to cane you," Crews replied; whereupon Dr. Graw replied: "You have more pluck than I thought you had." Mr. Crews observed: "I have preached nothing but the truth. Convince me that I am wrong, and I will take it all back. You know that I have preached the truth." "Yes," said Graw; "'tis true. Go ahead; and I will help you all I can."

Mr. Jordan, a young clerk in a store, was steward. He had raised on subscription enough to pay Mr. Crews's board; but when the theater was attacked, many of these wished to withdraw their pledges. Brother Crews told the young steward to return the money paid, but that he was bound to remain. By this he was thrown upon his own resources. He rented a room, and moved his few things into it, and began to board himself.

To return to the danger of freezing. He was returned to his room in Galena; but he was not fully recovered. One night, about two weeks after his return, he awoke very sick, and began to vomit. He arose to procure some water. He had no sooner touched the floor than he fell headlong. He lay there all night. When morning came, he hoped no one would come in; for he did not want to see any one. He felt as though he would rather do anything than receive a favor from the people there. The day passed away, and nobody came. The next day, a young man, a Baptist, came in on an errand. Mr. Crews pleaded with the young man to tell no one of his condition. This led to some remarks; and the young man explained so clearly to Mr. Crews where he was wrong, that he began to be sorry he had acted thus. He sent for Dr. Newhall. He came and prescribed. Soon several persons came in, brought bedding, food, and everything that he could desire. They nursed him, and seemed to vie with each other in their care for the poor, lonely, sick man. He owned afterward that he felt very much ashamed of himself for having distrusted them. They were all conquered. Dr. Nelson, a famous revivalist, a converted infidel, came to the place, and, beginning a meeting, seventy souls were added to the Church.

At the Conference of 1835, Mr. Crews was stationed at Springfield. Two noted events occurred at this time. He came up, as we have seen, from the Kentucky Conference in 1834; and at the Illinois Conference of 1835, when he had been in its bounds but a year, and had been traveling but six years, he was elected one of the delegates to the General Conference. The delegation was: Peter Cartwright, Simon Peter, and Hooper Crews. This shows that at that early time in his history he was a man of mark. The other noted event was his marriage to Miss Mary F. Smith, of Russellville, Kentucky—a woman who for forty years after, as the wife of Hooper Crews, was honored wherever she went.

There are two sorts of men. The men of one sort are always the same. Wherever they go they fill the required duties, and go on. Men of the other stamp are always meeting with events, for they are men that create events. Mr. Crews was of the latter stamp. He could not be at a place without doing something. If there was nothing going on, he stirred up something. While at Springfield one of these events occurred. It was a hard place. July of the second year came, and there had been no revival. The wicked had become bold in opposition. But for some cause, the pastor began to feel that there was to be a change. When the final hour came, the day was rainy and forbidding, and the congregation was small; but finally, when the meeting closed, the sun shone out. The evenings were short, and the services began before dark. As Mr. Crews went out his door to go to the church, he saw the people coming in crowds from all directions, as if moved by some great excitement. The church could not hold the people. They sat about the altar; everywhere. The services began with the usual forms; but from the first there was a profound, hushed emotion. It was like the deathlike stillness that often precedes a storm. The preacher had gone on but a few minutes with his sermon, when the feeling in the audience became so intense that he stopped, and began to invite mourners to the altar. Then the storm burst! Such a scene as occurred is seldom seen. It seemed as though the entire audience desired to reach the altar. Penitents knelt in all parts of the house. The people began crying mightily to God. At the close of the meeting it was announced that eighteen had been converted. As Brother Crews was about to close the meeting, it occurred to him (as a temptation) that this might, after all, be but a wild freak of the people that would not last; and so, to test it, he announced a prayer-meeting for sunrise the next morning. At one o'clock the preacher lay down to rest. He did not wake till broad daylight, and rose alarmed, thinking he was too late. He opened the doors of his house, to behold a sight! The church was crowded. People were standing in masses about the door; they were crowding about the windows to get a glimpse inside. The meeting began, and all that day until night the service continued without an intermission. Prayers, sobs, cries were mingled all day long, and shouts of victory rose above the song and prayer! This wonderful revival lasted about ten days, and one hundred and twenty persons were received into the Church. Only twenty-seven of these were females—a curious proportion. Some of the converts became ministers; others made permanent members of the Church, going up at last to heavenly crowns.

At the time Brother Crews was appointed pre*si*ding elder of Galena District he was but twenty-seven years of age, making him the youngest elder that has ever served in the Conference. We heard Hooper Crews preach more or less for thirty years, and never heard him preach a sermon but what was excellent and in place but once. This exception was a dry sermon on the support of the ministers, to a promiscuous crowd, at eleven o'clock on Sunday, at a camp-meeting. There was a time when it was a common saying: "Listen to A. E. Phelps for eloquence; to Hooper Crews to be made better." For a prominent man, he was the most modest person we ever saw. None but the Great Head of the Church knows how much he suffered from underestimating himself. A fault how rare! Few men live in the affections of the people of the Northwest as Mr. Crews does. He was a delegate to the General Conference several times; but he never ranked high as a leader in his Conference, from the fact that he carried the staid manners of the pulpit into the Conference, where all who would get a hearing must be prompt, pointed, and pertinacious.

Chicago was, in 1840, when Hooper Crews went there—in church as well as in secular matters—beginning to recover from the crash of 1837; and from the date of Mr. Crews's appointment Chicago Methodism has had an upward tendency. There were at the commencement of the year 150 members; at its close 189. Mr. Crews remained there two years, and during his term prosperity, with many conversions, had attended his administration. The church built in 1834 had, in Peter Borein's time, been enlarged, and now it was double in size;

so that the original North Side church formed a quarter of the large, low church of 1845.

When Mr. Crews finished his time in the Clark Street station, he was made presiding elder of the Chicago District. From this time on he never failed to do effective work. In 1878 he took his last appointment; and while serving his third year at Oregon, Ogle County, he died, and went to his rest. He was then seventy-three years of age. His last sermon, one of rare beauty and power, was on Thanksgiving-day, in 1880. Soon after he passed from earth, and his remains were deposited in Rose Hill Cemetery, near Chicago.

His service in the ministry was fifty-three years, forty-one of which were in the bounds of the Rock River Conference. No other man, up to this time, can say as much.

Hooper Crews was a member of the General Conference in the years 1836, 1840, 1856, 1860. He never being a very active man in Conference business on the Conference floor, and men of the opposite being generally selected as delegates, Mr. Crews was for the greater part of the time passed by. Every man has his work. Being an efficient delegate was not Hooper Crews's forte.

For a man of his force and power he was one of the most diffident of men. He always mistrusted his own abilities. He was not of an emotional temperament, but yet, like men of that class, he was subject often to feelings of complete discouragement. A man who speaks without paper has a great advantage, and also a great disadvantage.

When free he can soar; and if he has "liberty," the inspiration of the hour will often take one of this sort up to what seem superhuman efforts. But if, on the other hand, there is no inspiration, no liberty, the discourse often falls flat; or, if the audience does not perceive this, the preacher feels it, and despondency follows. Often preachers in this predicament wish for a vestry door by which to escape unnoticed. Sometimes they even wish they had never been born. Mr. Crews, more than most men, was subject to these failures. On one occasion, when he had preached at a camp-meeting at eleven o'clock on Sunday, he felt so bad, some people, who for a time were led into Free Methodist measures, induced him to go to the altar for prayer. To those who knew the sublime piety and purity of Brother Crews this seems almost an insult.

He was supplied in 1828 to Bowling Green Circuit. On this, his first circuit, he had one of these sad experiences. He became so discouraged he determined to abandon his work. But he had a noble mother whom he loved; and as she had sent him forth with joy to his first work, he could not endure the thought of meeting her in the character of a deserter, and so he determined to wander away and lose himself among the Indians of Canada. He wrote to the presiding elder that the charge would be vacant. He had one more appointment out. He resolved to fill that, and then abandon the work. After the dismissal, a local preacher, Berkitt by name, said: "Brother Crews, you ought to lead class." "I do not feel like leading class," he answered; "but if you will lead, I will ask the people stay." Mr. Berkitt agreed, and at the close of the class-meeting gave out preaching for the evening. Of course, Berkitt had to preach, though young Crews was present. Berkitt knew nothing of the young preacher's purpose, but chose a text that upset all Brother Crews's resolutions. As the preacher sat down he said in an undertone: "Brother Crews exhort." But Brother Crews had resolved to exhort no more, and arose to close the meeting as shortly as possible. But rising to his feet, he began to talk, and had unusual liberty. He then took the hymn-book to close the service. But Berkitt exclaimed: "Invite sinners forward." "There is nobody here who desires religion," said Crews. "You are mistaken," persisted Berkitt. "Invite them." And so the reluctant about-to-be deserter from the army and battles of the Lord obeyed the persistent demand, and called for penitents. The first to respond was a notorious infidel, who no sooner stepped into the aisle than he fell flat to the floor. This was a signal for a general move, and every unconverted person in the congregation went forward for prayers! The journey to the wilderness was indefinitely postponed!

We can not close without one more incident. This time the poor, disconsolate man proposed to flee, not from, but to, his mother. It was in 1848. For two years the Chicago Methodists had had trouble with James Mitchell, their presiding elder. Clark Street Church was against, Indiana and Canal Street Churches were for the elder. It was a quarrel about trifles that might have been settled had there been some strong, quiet hand to hush the passions of men. At the Conference Mr. Mitchell had been unanimously but gently condemned. The two last-named Churches at once resolved to receive no man from the Conference as elder or pastor who had voted against Mr. Mitchell. R. A. Blanchard was absent from Conference, and did not vote, and was for that reason sent to Canal Street. Hooper Crews was an old Chicago pet. It was thought surely they would not treat him unkindly. But the leaders had made opposition a principle, and while they strove to treat Brother Crews kindly as a friend, they were reluctant to receive him as an elder. On a certain Saturday Mr. Crews met the Canal Street Quarterly Conference. Much disputing arose. The Conference adjourned to Monday evening. During the time that lapsed, Mr. Crews learned all that was going on, and became disheartened. In the forenoon he went over to R. A. Blanchard's. His face was as grave as death. He was the very picture of sorrow. The following conversation ensued:

"Brother Blanchard, I came over to tell you that I can not be at your Quarterly Conference to-night."

"Why, Brother Crews, what is the matter?"

"Well, I have concluded to leave the district. We are going to pack our goods, and I am going home to my mother, and that is the last of Hooper Crews."

"That will never do," said Blanchard. "At

any rate you must be over at the Conference. I can not be left alone. You know the difficulty I am in."

He consented to be present. At the meeting the discussions were long. Some one proposed to adjourn the meeting till another night.

"Can you be with us, Brother Crews?" Mr. Blanchard asked. Before knowing or without thinking, Mr. Crews consented to attend. He was present. The storm blew over, and Brother Crews remained in the Conference just thirty-two years after that, to do efficient work.

ASAHEL ELIHU PHELPS

Was, no doubt, all things considered, the finest pulpit orator that appeared in the Rock River Conference in the first fifteen years of its history, and in prominence on the Conference floor he stood with John T. Mitchell, Luke Hitchcock, and Philo Judson. The writer, on going to Mt. Morris, in 1847, secured a boarding-place near which stood a modest frame house. When told that Brother Phelps lived there, he asked if Brother Phelps was a preacher. The answer was emphatic: "I guess he is a preacher!"

Mr. Phelps was born in Sussex County, Delaware, March 21, 1806. His father, Asahel Phelps, was a soldier all through the War for Independence. He (the father) was a native of Connecticut; had a good common-school education; was an adept in vocal and instrumental music, and taught singing-school for years in the neighborhoods around him.

Mr. Phelps's mother, Agnes Houston, was a native of Delaware. There were nine children in the family, of which A. E. was the seventh. His parents were, from an early day, devoted members of the Methodist Church, who strove to rear their family on strictly religious principles. His father died about 1837, having been a Methodist for fifty years. Asahel, from a child, was taught to pray morning and night, and his mother, early in his childhood, in prayer devoted him to the ministry. At five years of age he became deeply convicted of sin, and so fervent were his religious anxieties, he fled to his mother for aid and relief. She read to him appropriate Scriptures, and knelt with him in prayer. But when he was ten years of age, that mother died, leaving him to be tossed almost helpless, religiously, on the waves of life. But this loss only deepened his desires to be a Christian. In his sorrows, the only person at hand whom he dared trust was an old colored man, familiarly called "Old Tom." But though "Old Tom" was a Christian, he had—like some wiser ones of even this day—some erroneous notions. When Asahel went to the old colored man for aid, he was told that the proper time to become a Christian was at twelve years of age. He had such confidence in the old man's opinions, he gave up sadly to wait. But the two years that were to pass seemed long, and all through them the ardent boy longed for their ending. At length his birthday arrived, and as he laid him down on his bed to rest the night before, it was with a joyful, anxious heart; for the dawning of the next day was to be the hour of his Christian freedom. On that morning he was to become a child of the King! In the morning he arose very early, and falling upon his knees, gave himself to the service of God. He at once performed every duty that presented itself, and in a few months was happily converted. From that hour his life was joyful. He never after went to the world for enjoyment, but found a heart full of pleasure in the religion of the Lord Jesus Christ.

When eighteen years of age, his father sent him to his uncle, Littleton Houston, in Charleston, Ind., to learn the cabinetmaker's trade. This incident gave him to the Church in the West. On going to his new home, he was very lonely. He found no Eden like his Christian birthplace! There were few young people who were Christians. There was opposition to religion that Asahel had never found before. He kept his Church letter in his trunk, and wavered. He still observed the forms of religion, but his soul was in darkness. For months he lingered in this eclipsed condition; but at last, driven by a feeling of despair, he went to the altar, and there again rose upon his soul the dawning of the morning.

He was soon appointed class-leader, then exhorter, and finally he received license to preach. At the Quarterly Conference where he was licensed he found much opposition. An old local preacher said "he had too much topsail for the hull, and would surely capsize." There must have been some truth in this, for until Mr. Phelps's death there were indications of this being the fact. Taking on ballast alone kept him in trim.

In 1828, when twenty-two years of age, Mr. Phelps was admitted into the Illinois Conference, and was appointed junior preacher on the Kaskaskia Circuit, with Peter Cartwright as presiding elder. At that time the Illinois Conference, which took in all the country northwest from Ohio, had but fifty-nine preachers.

His first work was a six weeks' circuit, on which the preachers traveled five hundred miles in making a round, preaching every day. The next year he was on Lebanon Circuit with John Dew. Mr. Dew was a scholar and a great student, and by his aid Mr. Phelps made great advance in his studies. In 1830 he was appointed to Salt Creek Circuit. Here he first met Charlotte Catterline, a miss of sixteen, who rode to the preaching on horseback behind her father, then a live exhorter. A. E. Phelps was married to Charlotte Catterline by John Sinclair, at Athens, in the fall of 1832. His "Lottie" made him a worthy companion the remainder of his days, and still (1895) lives to cherish his memory.

In 1838, Mr. Phelps was appointed presiding elder of Mt. Vernon District. From this time till his death he filled the office of elder, excepting the four years (1846–49) he was agent of Mt. Morris Seminary, and the two years he was stationed at Galena (1849–51).

When the Illinois Conference was divided, and the Rock River Conference was organized, in 1840,

Mr. Phelps remained on the Illinois side. The south line of the Rock River Conference was then nearly as it is to-day, being bounded by the Illinois River; but the General Conference of 1844 added to the Conference the territory now embraced in the Central Illinois Conference. The preachers in the newly-added territory came with the appointments. By this means Rock River gained such men as A. E. Phelps, Richard Haney, Henry Summers, and Zadoc Hall. From that time Mr. Phelps was a power in the Conference.

Brother Phelps could never let error pass without hitting it. There were many peculiar forms of error and manners of combating them in Central Illinois that are out of date now; and amid these scenes Mr. Phelps found a sphere of activity for which he was peculiarly adapted. The Churches of those days (1836–1850) were divided against each other, and, under the guise of opposing error, the ministers in the pulpits delighted in overthrowing imaginary champions. Besides, error was rife in the West. Speculation and affairs incident to a new country kept religion at a low point; and wherever this is the case, the people will run greedily after every new light. While this was the case in general, and while most Methodist preachers were schooled to overthrow "strange doctrines," Mr. Phelps was especially pugnacious. He could never come in contact with wrong in any form without "pitching into" it. I have among my papers a seminary manuscript paper (the *Amphyction*) in which there is a labored article by Mr. Phelps, wherein he scores a student who had taught infidel ideas. In narrating some of Mr. Phelps's debates, it should be added that they were popular only because Mr. Phelps made them so. Anything glittered in his hands. Others tried to follow his example; but the encounters generally lacked interest. In Central Illinois, John Luccock, H. Richie, Francis Smith, and others tried their hand at the work, but never made the thing popular. John Luccock was really an abler man in this line than Mr. Phelps; but he was so unmercifully savage he carried the sympathies of the people over to the opponent. Once at a Rock River Conference session, when Mr. Luccock was scoring a Baptist, half the members of the Conference who were present became indignant at the speaker.

A. E. Phelps's first attempt in this line was on this wise: Being stationed in Peoria in 1837, he found there a very popular Universalist preacher, Huntoon by name, who was drawing crowds after him. He had the field to himself, while the other Churches and preachers lived by sufferance. Mr. Phelps was not the man to endure this state of things, and resolved to make an attempt to change this tide, and so began in his own pulpit to answer the sermons preached by Mr. Huntoon. The latter took up the themes, and answered back. This warfare from behind their own citadels was kept up until Mr. Huntoon was so completely vanquished he left the field. Mr. Phelps's success turned the attention of the Church to him; and, for this reason, until his death he was pressed more and more into the field of debate. The first debate where Mr. Phelps met his opponent face to face was also at Peoria. In 1842 he was presiding elder on the Peoria District. During the year a Universalist preacher, Chase by name, appeared at Peoria. Mr. Phelps attended one of his meetings, and was called upon to pray at the close of the service. In the prayer, he prayed with ardor for the conversion of the speaker. Mr. Chase was so provoked he arose and challenged Mr. Phelps to a public discussion. The challenge was accepted, and a noted public debate followed. Mr. Phelps was not only posted and eloquent, but shrewd. He put the Universalist on the defensive. It is much easier to pick flaws in diamonds than to prove one's own paste-gems to be pure. The arguments of Mr. Chase were utterly overthrown, and even—that worst of calamities to a debater—the laugh, turned upon him. He was so completely disheartened he soon left the country.

In 1847, Mr. Phelps held a debate with a Universalist at Farmington. At the close Mr. Phelps, having time left after the close of his argument, proceeded to arraign the false and the wandering before the judgment. The descriptions of the great day were terrible, awful. All souls were awestruck by the vivid pictures of the last great day. The audience became wild, and hung with painful suspense upon the speaker's lips. Mr. Gardner, the Universalist debater, himself seemed utterly overcome. His face became as pale as death. Such a trembling seized him he was compelled to take hold of the table by which he stood, to prevent falling to the floor. When Mr. Phelps sat down, the outburst of emotion was irrepressible. Sobs as of whipped children were heard on every hand. There was scarcely a dry eye in the whole throng. Mr. Gardner died soon after; and it was said by his intimate friends that he never recovered from the gloom that took possession of him under that supreme closing speech. The debate broke the power of Universalism in that region so fully it never recovered from the stroke.

We have no space in which to follow up these debates. He met Mormons, Unitarians, Campbellites, and all sorts of people; and on every occasion the universal opinion was that the opponent was completely vanquished. On one occasion a Campbellite abandoned the debate, saying in public: "Our doctrines are correct; they can be sustained; but Mr. Phelps is too strong a man for me to meet;" and yet this man had challenged the whole Methodist Church to meet him. On another occasion the Campbellite failed to come to time, and abandoned the debate. It is not saying too much to assert that, in this line, no man has arisen in the Methodist Church equal to A. E. Phelps. His manner, his eloquence, his argument were peerless.

As a presiding elder, Mr. Phelps took great pains to aid and improve the young men who held appointments on his districts. He had been a helpless young man himself once, and knew what the young men most needed. Many a young man was set forward to a nobler life by the encouragements of his presiding elder. Occasionally, however, like others, he made mistakes in these attempts at direction. Somewhere near 1845, F. A. Read was a young man on a circuit among the new settlers south of the Illinois River. There was on the circuit a local preacher who expected the preachers to make his house their home. By vermin, grease, hog, and hominy, Frank Read had been obliged to abandon this place and seek better entertainment elsewhere. At the Quarterly Conference, one Saturday forenoon, when the question, "Are there any complaints?" was asked, the good local preacher arose, and in a long speech informed Elder Phelps that his house had long been the preachers' home, but that Brother Read refused to stay there. Brother Phelps strove to do his duty, and kindly admonished the young preacher. On adjournment, to make amends, Mr. Read led the way to the local preacher's house for dinner. The main dish, besides the corn-bread, was a pile of rancid fat bacon, floating in a sea of grease. Mr. Read was very polite on the occasion, and was careful to help the elder to a good supply of the delectable bacon. Phelps tried to eat. Read urged the meat upon him. "Take a little more meat, Brother Phelps; you must be hungry after your long ride." Mr. Phelps soon arose from the table and went outside the house, sick under the effect of the emetic. There was meeting in the afternoon. At its close, Frank Read led the way back to the house of the local preacher. Mr. Phelps, remembering his lecture, dare not refuse to go. Mr. Read conducted him to the house, and went to the stable to look after the horses. Mr. Phelps saw the same old ocean of fat going on to the table, and taking his hat went out to seek Read. He exclaimed: "For God's sake, Read, is there no other place?" "Yes," said Read; "there is a nice place up yonder at that white house." "Take me there, do; I shall die here!" was the answer. And by the way, the old preachers have no fear to mention storms, floods, persecutions; but for the sake of many dear, well-meaning people, they generally keep silent on the subject of vermin, filth, hog, and hominy—often greater ills to bear than storms or winters.

Mr. Phelps acted as agent of Mount Morris Seminary from 1846 until 1849. In this last year he was stationed at Galena, where he remained, having grand success, until 1851, when he was appointed to his last charge—the Rock Island District.

We now draw near the close of his life. In 1852 he held a debate with Mr. Summerbell, a "Christian" preacher, at Henry, Illinois. Mr. Phelps resided twenty miles away, at Princeton. One of his children was very ill at the time, and at the close of each day's debate he would drive home, sit up with his sick child much of the night, and then return to Henry in the morning. This, with other overwork, had much to do with the ending of his life. The old story of overwork had come to be his experience. In March, 1853, tired, worn, sick, he came home from a quarterly-meeting and took to his bed, telling his family that he had come home to die.

He rapidly failed. Most of the time he was delirious, being engaged often in holding his quarterly-meetings; but in his conscious moments he spoke cheerfully of the great future. He was calm and happy. At last he became wholly unconscious, and sank away quietly into the arms of death. This closing day of his life was March 20th. The funeral sermon was preached by Martin P. Sweet, father of T. E. Sweet; the text, 2 Tim. iv, 6. His body was laid away to rest in the Princeton Cemetery, where, under a graceful monument, adorned with an acorn dropping from its shell, the weary body lies asleep.

It is an ungracious task to portray the faults of these old arduous and worthy laborers. It would be difficult to find any man without faults; now and then we mention them to point a moral. A. E. Phelps and Dr. Eddy, more than any other Rock River men we have known, seemed to be ambitious of preferment. But Mr. Phelps's chief fault, too glaring to be unseen, was an oversensitiveness on the subject of his reputation. The true way is to do the right and pass on. Mr. Phelps failed here. He seemed ever to be fearing that some person or word would tarnish his reputation. He, who had the least cause to be troubled about this matter, seemed to be most concerned about it. An instance will illustrate. In Conference one day the seminary was under discussion. Richard Haney had the floor, standing just back of where Mr. Phelps sat. Mr. Haney made some remark concerning "our efficient agent." Mr. Phelps sprang excitedly to his feet, exclaiming, "Deficient in what?" "I said *ef*-ficient," Mr. Haney blandly responded. Mr. Phelps looked foolish.

A chapter might be written concerning the innocent tricks of presiding elders to accomplish their purposes. The life of Peter Cartwright, fully written, would be full of these incidents. We give one of Mr. Phelps's maneuvers. F. A. Read was admitted to the Conference in 1844, and appointed to work in the bounds of Elder Phelps's Washington District. During the year Mr. Phelps took a great fancy to Mr. Read, and greatly desired to hold him for work in the district. But at the Conference of 1846 a great call came from the newer regions of Northern Wisconsin for preachers. It was a hard thing to send men with families to the missions, where the support was meager and the labors the hardest. Accordingly, the bishop was selecting every young unmarried man to send to the missions of Wisconsin. To save Frank Read, Mr. Phelps had him discontinued from the Conference, and sent him to work in his district as a "supply." The next year Mr. Read was admitted on trial again. This accounts for the crooked record that numbers *F. A. Read* among those admitted on trial in 1844 and in 1847.

When U. J. Giddings and the writer of these pages were on the Middleport Circuit in 1849, we fell in with an intelligent man lately from Boston. As we entered into conversation, the stranger asked if we knew "the great Mr. Phelps, of the West," and went on to say that Mr. Phelps was in Boston on an agency, and preached in Bromfield Street Methodist

Church one Sabbath morning. The news flew over the city, and at night the place of preaching was so crowded hundreds went away without hearing him. "And," continued Boston, "Mr. Phelps is spoken of to this day in Boston as the greatest pulpit orator that has appeared there for years."

Mr. Phelps was the leading delegate of his Conference to the General Conference of 1852, and was the real leader in the Annual Conference business at the time of his death, giving place to Luke Hitchcock.

A. E. Phelps's appointments were as follows: 1828, Illinois Conference, Kaskaskia; 1829, Lebanon; 1830, Salt Creek; 1831, Sangamon; 1832, Alton; 1833, Carrollton; 1834, Carlisle; 1835–36, Pekin; 1837, Peoria; 1838–42, Mt. Vernon District; 1842–44, Peoria District; 1844–46, Rock River Conference, Washington District; 1846–49, Agent Rock River Seminary; 1849–51, Galena; 1851–53, Rock Island District. March 20, 1853, he died.

JOHN CLARK

Was one of the noblest of the pioneers of the West. He was born in Hartford, Washington County, New York, July 30, 1797. His parents were members of the Baptist Church, and quite poor. John was obliged to work at light wages wherever he could get employment, and when eighteen went as an apprentice to learn the tanner's trade, at which business he was employed two years. At the age of twenty he began to seek religion, and was converted in his father's barn when engaged in secret prayer. In

June, 1820, when but twenty three years old, he was admitted into the New York Conference, and appointed junior preacher on Leyden Circuit at a time when Joshua Soule, afterwards a bishop in the Church South, was yet a circuit preacher in the Conference, as was also Alexander McCaine, one of the chief lights of the Protestant Methodist Church. John Clark came down to us from companionship with Peter P. Sanford, Freeborn Garrettson, Billy Hibbard, Tobias Spicer, Noah Levings, Nathan Bangs, and others of note in the Church. He was presiding elder on Plattsburg District from 1828 to 1831, and was in this last year stationed in New York City. In 1832 he set out for the lonely regions of Lake Superior, to take charge of missions among the Indians there. At Sault Ste. Marie and at Green Bay he labored until 1836, when he transferred to the Illinois Conference, and was appointed presiding elder on Chicago District, when that district extended from Green Bay to a point one hundred miles south of Chicago. In 1840 he was sent to Mt. Morris District. At this time he was the chief agent in organizing the Rock River Seminary, and was the leading man of the Conference. In 1841 he went to Texas to assist in planting Methodism in that country while it was yet a separate republic. He was there appointed presiding elder on a district, and was elected as a delegate to represent the Texas Conference in the General Conference of 1844. The stormy times drew on which severed the Church South from the Methodist Episcopal Church, and John Clark, siding with the Northern portion, did not care, even had it been safe in that preacher-hanging country, to return to Texas. By invitation he joined again his old Conference, by division now Troy Conference, and was appointed to Poultney District. With the exception of two years, he served as presiding elder until 1852, when he again returned to the Rock River Conference, where he had endured so many hardships, to find a land of churches and railways. He was absent eleven years, but in that time nearly all the improvements of the country had been made. He returned to find but few of his old comrades in the Conference, and was appointed to Clark Street Church. During his two years there he was instrumental, as Mrs. Garrett's pastor, in securing the endowment of the Biblical Institute. In the summer of 1854, while stationed at Clark Street, he resided at Aurora, where he died suddenly of cholera, July 11, 1854, after being in uninterrupted service for thirty-four years, and that in six different States of the Union. He was in all respects a noble man; but he lacked that winning warmth of nature that makes a person live in the affection of friends rather than in their respect. He was born to command, rather than to win, and yet won by the bold utterances of a grand mind. No presiding elder of the early times has left so many to remember him, and everywhere the old settlers speak of the camp and quarterly meetings John Clark attended. "John Clark was a great, noble man," says William Kimble, one of his preachers of 1840, "well-formed, large-sized, quite handsome, high forehead, large gray eyes, clear heavy voice, a good singer of Methodist hymns, powerful in prayer-meetings, and an excellent manager of camp-meetings; quite ambitious, with a good stock of self-respect." T. C. Gardiner, visiting Chicago in 1853, says in a letter to the *Herald*: "Brother Clark has been thirty-three years in the ministry without having looked back all that time, as alas! too many do in these office-seeking, gain-getting times. He is still young in spirit, and fresh in thought, and vigorous in action, though ripe in years, having kept up with the age instead of falling behind it. . . . He is in full sympathy with the spirit and improvements of the present day, not having had such educational advantages in his youth as are afforded to this generation; yet so disciplining his mind by thinking—the only scientific method—and so developing his mental energies in ministerial studies and labors, that now, in knowledge, in attainments, and in pulpit ability and efficiency, he is among the first; and in manners and address he is a model for all."

BARTON H. CARTWRIGHT

Was born in the State of New York, March 9, 1810, and was one of a family of eleven children. His father, a Baptist preacher, traded his home in New York for military land in Illinois in 1822, and started at once to prepare a home in the West for his family. While on this trip he sickened and died; so from that time, young Barton, having no home, was tossed about in the world. "When fourteen" (this is Barton's account of the matter), "I renounced the world, and went over to God's side. O how he blessed me! I had to tell it, and have been telling it ever since; and every year there is more to tell, and the old, old story is richer, more precious every day."

In 1833, when twenty-three years old, he left for Illinois, to look after his father's property. All the travel from the East in that day was down the Ohio and up the Mississippi. Young Cartwright shook hands with Black Hawk at Cincinnati, he being on his way to Washington, a prisoner. He met him again at Flint Hills, and Rock Island afterwards. Cartwright landed in Iowa at Burlington, and four miles back found two cabins, in one of which resided, alone, his brother Daniel, whom he had not seen for nine years, and who afterward became a traveling preacher in Iowa. He soon crossed into Illinois, into Henderson County, and stopped at the house of Solomon Perkins.

Barton Randall was, in 1833, the preacher on Henderson Mission. He was preaching to log-cabin congregations, to seven or a dozen persons, among the grove settlements. Mr. Cartwright, the first Sabbath after his arrival (the first in May), heard of one of these appointments a few miles from the place where he was stopping, and went to the place. A small company had gathered, but the preacher lay up-stairs sick. Mr. Cartwright clambered up the wall by the aid of the pins driven into the logs, and presented his Church letter to Mr. Randall. Without further words the preacher told Barton he must hold meeting below. He had never done such a thing; but he must either comply, or there would be no meeting. At last he consented, and made his first attempt at exhortation. After meeting, Mr. Randall crawled down-stairs, and told Mr. Cartwright that he must fill his afternoon appointment at Mr. Reece Perkins's, on Swan Creek.

"But," said Brother Cartwright, "I do not know the way."

"I will send a boy," was the answer.

"I have no horse, and can not go on foot," Cartwright rejoined.

"You can take my horse," said Randall.

"I may not return it," said Cartwright.

"I will risk it," said Randall.

Such was the brief settlement of the matter, and our inimitable Barton set out to fill his second appointment. The next week he received license to exhort. At a quarterly-meeting, at which Peter Cartwright presided, in March, 1834, Barton Cartwright received license to preach, and was at once commissioned by the presiding elder as a missionary to Iowa.

Brother Cartwright was already prepared to go over into the Territory with an ox-team to break prairie. He strove to get rid of the appointment; but Peter had set his grasp upon him, and there was no escape. Accordingly, one of the first ministers Iowa ever received set out with his large Hoosier wagon and four yoke of oxen, with breaking-team whip twenty feet in length, and uncouth appearance, to form a Methodist circuit in the new land. He preached his first sermon in April, 1834, in the cabin of Dr. Ross, which was on the bluff back of the Mississippi River, at a place called Flint Hills. There were two stores and several shanties in the place, which has since been transfigured into the proud little city of Burlington. There was one other appointment, which was on Skunk River, six miles west of Flint Hills. The sermon preached in April was the first of any kind preached in that part of Iowa; but Barton Randall had been before him in the Territory, he having preached near Dubuque. In April, Mr. Cartwright formed a class of six members at Flint Hills. Dr. Ross and wife were of the number. This was the beginning of Methodism in Burlington, and the first class in Iowa. In 1840, Mr. Cartwright was on the circuit, in the bounds of which Iowa City was laid out in this year; and he was permitted to preach the first sermon in that town. The next year he preached the first sermons ever preached in Lyons and Comanche. While on the Comanche Circuit, in 1841, he heard of a new settlement some miles in the country, and went out to explore. He put up over night at the house of the chief man of the neighborhood. Several politicians—office-seekers, we presume—were there for the night also. When it became known that they had a preacher in their midst, the host walked the floor very gravely for a time, and then very gruffly remarked:

"Gentlemen, I once had an uncle worth ten thousand dollars eaten out of house and home by Methodist preachers."

"They must have had sharp teeth," Cartwright dryly made answer.

In the morning the man charged the preacher a dollar—and it took the last dollar he had—for his very poor fare. Not long after the man was running for office, and the dollar worked against him. People could not endure such a breach of the laws of Western hospitality. To save his fame the official—or would-be official—sent the dollar in a letter to Cartwright. Brother Cartwright returned it, wishing him to apply it on the ten thousand dollars the preachers had eaten. That "dollar" defeated his election.

In the fall of 1834, Mr. Cartwright was received into the Illinois Conference, and in Illinois and Iowa since then performed valuable labor. He had little polish, but a vast fund of good sense and a talent for work. He had for many years taken an active part in Conference business, making at times dry speeches that brought the crowd out in laughter; and the laughter was always in the right direction, and his speeches to the point. Barton H. Cartwright—witty Barton, youthful-hearted Barton, genial-souled Barton—remained a member of the Rock River Conference; and if he has less fame than Peter Cartwright (to whom, by the way, he was not at all related), it is not because he was less worthy. He did good service as chaplain of the Ninety-second Illinois Volunteers. He died in 1895.

It is probable that to Barton H. Cartwright belongs the credit of forming the first class in Iowa.

Barton Randall preached at Dubuque what, it is likely, was the first Methodist sermon in Iowa, in the fall of 1833. In the following spring, May 24, 1834, he formed a class at Dubuque, which is sometimes claimed as the first in Iowa. But let us see. Brother Cartwright does not remember the date of the organization of the class at Burlington; but the following facts will give some clue to the truth: When he was sent to Iowa, Peter Cartwright had been asked for a preacher by Dr. Ross and other members, who were already on the ground. The people were ready, and waiting for the preacher. The preacher went about the 1st of April. He at once settled his appointments, and, as soon as possible, united the few members in a class, with Dr. Ross as leader. The date is forgotten; but Mr. Cartwright persists in the opinion that it could not have been later than the last Sunday in April, and then, probably, a week or two before the class at Dubuque was formed. At some one of the early appointments of Brother Cartwright in the cabin of Dr. Ross, a visitor appeared in the person of J. M. Jameson, a preacher from Missouri. He gives us this account of B. H. Cartwright: "He was a young man, in vigorous health, and of good proportions, dressed in plain linen pants, home-made cotton vest, common shoes, without socks, no coat, and a common chip hat. But the dress was no disparagement of the man. His text was Col. i, 18. I have never forgotten his sermon, which would do him no discredit now in his maturer years."

HENRY WHITEHEAD

Was born in Chatham, England, June 17, 1810, and came to the United States about 1831. John Clark, then missionary to the Indians on Lake Superior, writing at Sault Ste. Marie, August, 1833, says: "My recent visit to Green Bay has prevented my building; but I hope to commence preparing timber to-morrow. In this work I am almost wholly alone. My only sure dependence is upon Henry Whitehead, from Troy, New York, who has nobly volunteered his service without charge, except for board, while he is in my employ. He is late from England, and by trade a joiner." Brother Whitehead could not have rendered John Clark much service; for we find him landing in Chicago, September 17, 1833. When Mr. Whitehead arrived at Chicago, Jesse Walker was absent at Conference. After Mr. Walker returned, they had regular preaching every Sabbath, followed by class-meeting. William See and Henry Whitehead preached in Mr. Walker's absence. On the first Sabbath evening of Mr. Whitehead's arrival, he preached in the evening from John iii, 16, in the log church at The Point. He also began to assist the Presbyterian minister, Rev. Jeremiah Porter, in holding meetings at the Fort.

At the first quarterly-meeting of the year, held in October, 1833, by John Sinclair, presiding elder, and Jesse Walker, Mr. Whitehead was licensed to preach. He had before served on a preaching "plan" in England. He was the first local preacher licensed in Chicago.

June 30, 1834, Henry Whitehead and John Stewart entered into a contract with Jesse Walker to build a frame church, 26 by 38 feet, for the Methodist society. This church was completed during the summer, and was the first Methodist church-building of any kind in the city, if we except Father Walker's log church at The Point. It stood on the North Side.

July 31, 1834, Mr. Whitehead was married to Elizabeth Jenkins. July 31, 1884, the fiftieth anniversary of this wedding was observed by a social gathering at his house. There were present two sons and one daughter—wife of Dr. Arthur Edwards—and nine grandchildren.

He moved to Joliet about 1835; and from then to 1840 he was a local preacher on Joliet Circuit.

At the first session of the Rock River Conference in 1840, Mr. Whitehead was admitted on trial, and sent to Root River Circuit, where he remained two years. From 1842 till 1844 he labored on the Troy Circuit. In 1844 he went to the Sylvania work, and in 1845 to Elk Grove. In 1846 he took a superannuated relation, and settled once more in Chicago, where he resided till his death.

When the General Conference established a Book Depository at Chicago, Henry Whitehead was already on the ground with a small stock of books, which he was selling on his own account. This store was made the nucleus of the new depository, in which for several years he had charge of the book department. In 1853 he was superintendent of the Clark Street Sunday-school.

A few years ago he took charge of Biglow & Mains's Western Depository of Sunday-school Music-books—a position he held till death, which occurred April 10, 1885. The day before his death he was in his office down in town. In the night he was taken severely ill, and by six o'clock in the morning he was gone. A few minutes before death, unable to speak, his eye sought rapidly in turn the faces of those he loved; and then a smile of unutterable joy told that the weary pilgrim had caught sight of the spires of the Celestial City.

Through all these years of Henry Whitehead's Chicago life he was a modest, cheerful Christian, rallying to the help of the Church and pastor whenever help could be rendered. He was all people's man, the friend of every Christian.

For nearly fifty years he was identified with the Methodist work in Chicago. At Clark Street, Wabash Avenue, and Trinity Churches his character and life particularly shined forth as a glowing light. His name is precious to every one with whom he was associated in Church relations. The people regarded him with the highest admiration and affection for his peculiar Christian graces. The pastors who were so fortunate as to be associated with him found in him a true friend, a cordial supporter, and efficient assistant in all the interests of the Church. He was a model class-leader, whose fertile mind, pure heart, and positive experience and triumphant testimony and uncommon power in prayer, made him a power in the class-room. He was the inspiration of every society and encourager of every pastor with whom he came in contact. His almost prophet-like eloquence, his musical voice, his knowledge of the Scriptures, his fervent piety, made him unusually a force in the class-room, love-feast, prayer-meeting, and revival service. Mr. Whitehead was widely known in Chicago by Christians of all Churches. His business integrity, religious zeal, and charity commanded the respect and won the love of all who knew him; and his death was mentioned with profound regret by many of the foremost citizens of Chicago, and his praises were in all the Churches. For forty years he walked among the Churches in a frail body, which was subject at times to most severe attacks of pain; but amid all, he never lost his patience or his exultant experience. So powerfully would he at times be baptized with the Holy Spirit, his body seemed too weak to stand the glory and shouts of triumphant spiritual joy that often attended his groans of physical pain. His final illness, as we have said, was brief. It lasted from midnight until morning; and when the morning came to him it was morning forever! He left behind his wife, who had journeyed with him for fifty-one years, and four children, one of whom was the wife of Dr. Arthur Edwards.

SOLOMON F. DENNING

Was born in West Chester, Pennsylvania, November 20, 1813. His parents were both members of the Methodist Church. His father died when he was ten years of age, and his mother when he was fifteen, leaving him, their only child, to depend upon himself. His father was from the north of Ireland; his mother came from Scotland. We copy entire the account of his life given in a sermon preached before the Rock River Conference in 1893:

"'The home of my parents, as far back as I can remember, was the house of prayer and religious worship. When I was but nine years old, father was taken in glorious triumph to the Church above. Two years later, mother followed him, and I was left to continue the struggle of life alone. At the age of seventeen, under the labors of J. B. Ayers, in Harrisburg, Pa., I was converted, and joined the Methodist Episcopal Church. In 1833 I turned my face towards the West, working at my trade, that of a tailor. I reached Peoria, Illinois, in the spring of 1835. There being no Methodist preaching there, I soon went to Springfield; gave my certificate of membership to the pastor, Hooper Crews. I remained there till January, 1836, when I settled in Princeton, Illinois. I was in a short time appointed classleader by S. R. Beggs. The class-meetings and preaching were held two miles northwest of Princeton, at the residence of Abraham Jones. November 30, 1837, I was married to Miss Mary Zearing, of Dover. Soon after, our house was opened for religious worship, which continued till the first Methodist Church was built. In 1841 I was licensed to exhort. In 1842, was licensed as a local preacher, and recommended to the Rock River Conference, notwithstanding my opposition to it. So little confidence did I have in my ability or fitness for the work, I refused to attend the Conference, which that year was held in Chicago. The appointment was as junior preacher on Princeton Circuit, with Harvey Hadley as preacher in charge. I thought this appointment at home would surely kill me. I had been elected clerk of Bureau County for four years. Three years had passed. I was acquainted with nearly every one in the county. But thanks be to God, I survived. The court did not want a resignation, but granted me a deputy for the balance of the term, and what I feared would break me down proved to be for the best. I was among my friends. If I made a blunder, they kindly overlooked it. The circuit included Princeton, Center Grove, West Bureau, Tiskilwa, French Grove, Knox Grove, Troy Grove, Green River, and several other places. It was a year of long rides, some prosperity, but very little pay. I remember, one quarterly-meeting, the presiding elder, John Sinclair, came forty miles. When the dividend was made *pro rata*, the elder received twenty-five cents, preacher in charge $2.50, and junior preacher $1.25. The balance of the year was better pay.

"The Conference of 1843 was held in Dubuque. A long ride in a buggy. Here the first ordeal of Conference examination was passed; and we raised no question as to where our next appointment would be. It was read out for Milford Circuit by Bishop Andrew. We soon found out that the parsonage was at Plainfield, in the eastern corner of the circuit, about sixty miles from Princeton. As soon as possible we loaded our goods in a two-horse wagon, and, with wife and children in a buggy, we started on our first itinerant move. We were taught to believe that the voice of the Church was the voice of God, and we submitted all into God's hands. Toward evening on the second day we reached Plainfield. In a day or two we were settled in the parsonage or skeleton of a preacher's house that had never been finished, and located on a lot without any inclosure. A Bible agent rode up to the house and said: 'Well, Brother Denning, are you living out of doors here!' But it was a home for the year, and the Church received us with open arms and warm hearts. The circuit included the territory from five miles east of Ottawa to Plainfield, lying between the Kankakee and Fox Rivers. We preached at Plainfield, Plattville, Morris, Milford, Newark, Oswego, and at many places in the intervening territory. A young man was sent from the Illinois Conference as assistant preacher, but on his way his horse died. I borrowed one for his use during the winter. In the meantime an effort was made to buy him a horse, but all I could get was $30. The Quarterly Conference decided that he should return home till he could procure another horse. I gave him the money collected, and have never heard of him since. Two Church trials, one at Morris, where two women were expelled, and one at Milford, where two men were expelled, occurred. One was a quarrel between women, and the other a quarrel between two families on farm matters. But I had a safe counselor in Rev. Brother Bibbins, father of R. K. Bibbins, of this Conference. We afterwards had glorious revivals at Newark and at

Oswego. At the latter place I had but little help, and labored until I was so hoarse I could not speak. I gave up and went home, to find that it was more than hoarseness. My lungs were affected, and for six weeks I despaired of ever having my natural voice again. But God in his infinite mercy brought me out of it.

"The Conference of 1844 was held in Milwaukee. Here I passed my second examination, was admitted into full connection, ordained deacon, and appointed to Sycamore. Without murmuring or complaining, we loaded our goods in a two-horse wagon, and started, crossing Fox River at Oswego. The water ran over the front part of the buggy, with wife and children in it, but we got safely over. We found the parsonage on Brother White's farm, four miles north of Sycamore; but we were met with a hearty reception, and were soon at home among kind-hearted Methodist neighbors. This was another large and laborious charge. Wesley Lattin, a local preacher, was employed as assistant. Our preaching places were at Sycamore, White's School-house, Brush Point, Union Grove, Ohio Grove, Genoa, Elias Crary's, Chicken Grove, Currier's, and at Kendall's.

"This year the land was coming into market, and many farmers had to save every dollar to pay for their land or lose it, so that my receipts were only $50 quarterage, and $48 table expenses, including horse-feed and firewood. It was a hard year of work and of family affliction, as well as in money matters; but fortunately for us, one of our nearest neighbors was Dr. Harrington, father of W. S. Harrington, formerly of this Conference.

"It is rather a strange incident that so many of us who are now living have seen the land from Fox to Rock Rivers sell at $1.25 per acre. In 1846 a whole school section in Plato, Kane County, sold at $2.50 per acre.

"During this year we had a wonderful revival in the village of Sycamore, services being held in the old court-house. The whole community seemed stirred by the spirit of God. We needed help, and sent for Elder St. Clair, who came. The sheriff, Walrod, was converted. He turned the bar out of his hotel, and his dancing-hall into a prayer-meeting room. At this meeting a young man, just beginning the practice of law, Andrew J. Brown, now of Evanston, and a large number of influential persons, were added to the Church. We also had a fine revival at Brush Point, and some conversions at Genoa.

"The Conference of 1845 was held at Peoria. On the way to Conference, we spent the Sabbath at a camp-meeting eight miles from Peoria. Sunday night I was called upon to exhort and to invite mourners to the altar. The crowd being great, the weather being warm, the effort was too much for me. I took cold, and by the time I passed my Conference examination I was sick and had to take my bed. I was in the home of an old friend from Pennsylvania. Dr. U. P. Golliday, a local preacher, attended me. I had all the care I needed, but did not get to the Conference-room till the day of adjournment, and was confidently expecting that I would be returned to Sycamore, as I was assured by vote of Quarterly Conference and by the presiding elder; but when the appointments were announced it was 'Chicago City Mission.' As soon as Conference adjourned I started towards home; went ten miles that evening, taking quinine pills every hour; stopped over night with a free-hearted Methodist family; early next morning I continued my journey, taking my pills every hour, reaching the home of my wife's father, at Dover, having traveled fifty miles. Resting here a day or two, I continued my journey, reaching home the second day.

"The following week we went to the mission, to find it all in the country, a large territory lying between Chicago and Wheeling. My home was to be at Union Ridge, twelve miles north of Chicago. There was no parsonage, and no house that could be rented. Brother Morton had a house on the ridge, with a lean-to. This unplastered room he gave to us. The next week he moved our household goods. A German vacated his old log cabin, which I rented. I filled up the chinking, and whitewashed and cleaned up the cabin, and moved into it, paying one dollar a month rent. We were glad to get settled in our own home.

"The charge included all the territory from Chicago to within four miles of Wheeling, and from Whisky Point, eight miles southwest of Chicago, to Grosse Point, where Evanston now stands. As soon as we were settled, the work of building a parsonage was begun. The members were all poor. I drew up a subscription and secured $120. I went to Chicago and contracted for lumber. Brethren hauled it. I hired a carpenter in Chicago; boarded him myself, and in about six weeks had a house up, 12 by 24. We were putting the roof on the shed part, when it began snowing. Nothing more could be done until after January. A carpenter from the circuit made the doors and sash in Brother Wheedon's woodshed. By assisting the carpenter, we succeeded in getting the building all inclosed, and by the middle of February we moved into it, in the midst of a snowstorm; and living in a kitchen we found much better than in the old log-cabin, which would leak when the snow melted, and let the black water run down on our beds. When spring came, after doing the lathing myself, I hauled the sand and lime, mixed the mortar, and tended the mason, and finished the parsonage, leaving me out of pocket, after all my work, ten dollars. This was Chicago City Mission! One hundred dollars mission money, of which the elder, James Mitchell, received twenty-five dollars. My portion, with all other receipts, amounted to two hundred and thirty-eight dollars."

We have given in full some of these details to illustrate the way we all did in those days. There was hardly a Rock River Conference preacher at that time but went through the same experiences. We built parsonages and churches with our own hands in all parts of the Conference. The first Methodist Church built in Chicago, on the West Side, in 1843, was built mostly by volunteer work, the present writer lending a hand.

"The Conference of 1846 was held in Galena, and we were returned to the mission for the second year. Our house was opened for preaching until a school-house was built. A number were converted at several appointments. The year closed pleasantly. Salary about the same as the preceding year.

"The Conference of 1847 was held in Chicago. At this session I was appointed recording secretary, which position, by the blessing of God and the kindness of the Conference, I was permitted to retain until at the last session (1892) of the Conference, when failing health compelled a resignation. We were sent this year to Little Fort, now Waukegan. This was another large, laborious work. I had Daniel Beckwith as assistant the first year, and John Hodges the second. The circuit embraced about all the territory in Lake County. It extended from the lake to Fox River. We had a great revival at Sand Lake; a large number of converts and additions to the Church. I baptized fifteen by immersion in Sand Lake at one time. These immersions were caused by the Campbellites, who had built Antioch and spread their notion of baptism all over the country. We had a large number of accessions at other points on the charge.

"Our next move was to Joliet Circuit, in 1849. By the advice of the presiding elder, Hooper Crews, we moved to Lockport. The appointments were at Joliet, Chelsea, Francis, Lockport, Yankee Settlement, and Dryers School-house. A small church was built this year in Lockport, but not finished inside. Temporary pulpit and seats were provided.

Revival services were held in connection with our quarterly-meeting, Elder Crews being with us. Colonel Manning, who was the mainstay of the Church, was happy when he saw his daughter Mary converted. The church at Chelsea was inclosed, but not finished. Temporary seats and a pulpit were prepared, and a number were converted and added to the Church. The city of Joliet had in former years been a station, and there seemed to be no prospect of building up a Church without a resident pastor and preaching every Sunday. I proposed at the last Quarterly Conference that it be made a station, which proposal was adopted; and at the Conference of 1850 a preacher was stationed there. Lockport Circuit was the same work as the previous year, with Joliet left out. We remained at Lockport; had a pleasant, prosperous year. The church was finished and furnished, and was dedicated by Dr. Crews. Everybody thought it was a beautiful little house of worship.

"From Lockport we moved to Morris, with William R. Irvine as assistant the first year, and —––— Hewitt, an eccentric English local preacher, the second year. The charge was still called Newark Circuit; but it had been divided by taking off all the eastern part. Brother Irvine resided at Newark in the parsonage, and I rented a house in Morris. Our new church in Morris was completed and dedicated by John Clark and O. A. Walker, the presiding elder. There was a large increase in membership, and we had another pleasant and rosperous year.

"At the Conference of 1853 I received my appointment at Ottawa. A new parsonage had just been completed, into which we moved as soon as it could be cleaned out. Here we had a comfortable home and many warm friends for two years. The church-edifice had been woefully neglected; and our first business was to collect money for calcimining, papering, and painting, which we did, with a wonderfully improved condition of the church, at a cost of $200. Our salary, first year, $464; second year, $496.

"The Conference of 1855 was held in Rock Island. It was the time when the Conference was divided, Central Illinois Conference being formed. Near the close of the session I ascertained that I was likely to be appointed in the southern section. I then made the only request I ever made of the bishop with regard to my appointment, and that was, if I was likely to fall into the southern portion, my preference was to remain in the Rock River Conference. I was sent to Sterling. I was busy writing up the record, so that the bishop could sign it before leaving the Conference room. Some of the brethren near me said I spoke up, and said: 'Sterling? Where is Sterling?' I had never heard of it before. One brother near me said: 'Denning, you know where the Rock River Rapids are, don't you?' I responded, 'Yes.' 'Well, that is Sterling,' was the answer. So I went to Sterling, having G. W. T. Wright as my colleague. This being the first appointment of a resident pastor to that place, there was no house to move into. My family went to wife's father's until I could find a resting-place. There was not a house in the village that could be rented. I had sold my office in Princeton to procure money to send my oldest son to school at Mount Morris, and succeeded in getting two members of the Church to join with me in buying a house, partly finished, each one paying $200. After putting in $100 more and doing a good deal of hard work myself, we had a comfortable home for two years. Brother Wright, having no family but his wife, procured rooms over Brother Brink's store. For preaching-places we alternated between the court-house and an old stone school-house, a half a mile further up town. We preached at Sterling, Gap Grove, Genesee Grove, Frasier's near Coleta, and Rock Creek, where we formed a new class.

"The second year, Sterling having been made a station, I was continued as pastor. A brick church, costing $9,000—the contract for which had been let about the time we came to Sterling—was completed in February, 1857. The dedication occurred at the time of a great freshet and freeze-up. Dr. Hitchcock, the presiding elder, conducted the services; but surroundings were such that but a comparatively small subscription could be procured, and the Church was left with an embarrassing debt. It was the time of the terrible 1857 failures. There was no general revival, but the year closed with double the number of members.

"At the Conference of 1857 I was assigned to Polo. Family sick, and no house in Polo for us to move into. I went to my appointment, sixteen miles off, preached three times on Sunday, and back to Sterling after preaching Sunday night, for about a month, and then came down with bilious fever. Soon after I recovered, a house was purchased in Polo for a parsonage, and we moved into it. We had no meeting-house in Polo at that time. I preached in the old church at Buffalo Grove, two miles from Polo, and in the Presbyterian Church in Polo. I soon organized a class at Polo, meeting in the parsonage for that purpose. I remained at Polo the second year, and had the largest revival of any during my ministry. About one hundred were converted, and seventy-five were added to the Church.

"Our next move was to Belvidere, in 1859, where we remained two years. We had a goodly number of conversions, and a pleasant time. From here we went to Roscoe in 1861, where we spent two years, and had a glorious revival. At the Conference of 1863 we were sent to Harvard. Here we received our oldest son home from the army with a dangerous gunshot wound just above his right knee. But we were glad that he could come directly home, so that we could take care of him. Here it was that we received the sad news of the death of President Lincoln. I never was more stirred in my life than when preaching his funeral sermon, with our church draped all around the house, altar, and pulpit, and so crowded with people that all could not get inside. We had some conversions, but no sweeping revival.

"In 1865 we went to De Kalb, where we had two successful years. Repaired another dilapidated church; had a peaceful time, with some conversions.

"In 1867, through the good providence of God, it was our lot to be returned to Sterling, First Church. J. H. Alling was appointed to the Second Church. Those who still remained with the old Church, which had been divided the previous year, were united heart and hand for the work of the Lord. Our house of worship, which had been sold for part of the debt, and bought back, was still in financial trouble. There was a judgment against part of the trustees for $1,000. Mr. Forbes agreed to cancel this for $500. I went to work, but could only get $350 subscribed. I wrote to him. He replied: 'You are the only preacher who has tried to do anything. I will see you when I come out.' He came. I had raised something over $400. His agent said if it was put into notes at six per cent interest it would be accepted. It was done, and the judgment was canceled; and we all united in singing the doxology. But what was best of all, God gave us nearly one hundred conversions. We had one very peculiar case. A family lived across the street from the parsonage. The man had attended the meetings night after night, but stubbornly refused to bow at the foot of the cross. One night, after the services were closed and I was about to retire to rest, his wife came, and said her husband was in great trouble. I went over, and found him on his knees, crying aloud to God for mercy. I talked and prayed, but he found no relief. I went for Brother Hess, who could sing. We kept on until near midnight, when he came out, shouting happy. Then his wife began to pray for mercy, and she, too, was converted.

"I was returned to Sterling for the third year. Ascertaining I could not rent the house I was occupying for another year, I contracted for the building I now live in. This I built from money I saved from my home in Princeton, which I had before entering the ministry. Having a family of five children, four of them to educate, I never saved anything from my salary; and have spent at least $1,000 over and above what I have received in preaching the gospel to the poor.

"At the close of my third year in Sterling I took, in 1870, a nominal appointment five miles east of Sterling, and went with my wife to visit our relatives in Harrisburg, Pa., the home of our childhood. On our return, I was appointed by our presiding elder to supply Coleta for the balance of the year, but I remained in my home at Sterling. My presiding elder said there was no necessity for a man of my age to move, and at the Conference of 1871 I was appointed to Sugar Grove. The Conference year closed with but little success. The next Conference was held at Rockford, in 1872, and I was appointed to Sterling Circuit.

"The Conference of 1873, which was held at Mendota, was the only session from which I have been absent since my admission to Conference. Just before Conference I was taken with a violent attack of bilious fever, and was lying very sick during Conference. I was appointed to Sterling Circuit another year.

"The Conference was held in Sterling, in 1874. My health being so much impaired, and being sixty-one years of age, I was placed in a superannuated relation. In fact, for years I had been so afflicted with rheumatism that I was ill fitted for effective work in the winter season. It was a sore trial to me to give up the regular itinerant work. But while I was not in the work I had no thought of backsliding, and have always found something to do. . .' For the past seven years I have been the leader of the class which meets on Sunday morning at the close of public service."

I have given this account of work in detail from the pen of Brother Denning to say, first, that it is a fair showing of the kind of work and the sort of fare most of us did and had from 1840 to 1870; and, second, to say that, though all this work may not seem brilliant or grand, it was the work that had to be done to give the splendid fruitage of to-day, and it seems to me that no one should deny the claim to the sums the stewards allow these men, now superannuate, from year to year. The brilliant young men of to-day will have to do some such plodding work when age comes upon them. For purity of character, for lasting friendship of all, S. F. Denning for fifty years has been a model.

RICHARD A. BLANCHARD

Was, in 1842, in the strength of his buoyant soul, and preached in a way to be remembered. To show his appreciation of the people of Belvidere, he took Miss Mary Brooks to wife, the couple being married in public at a camp-meeting held on Beaver Creek, in 1843. This was one of the happiest of marriages, and few preachers are blest with so fitting a wife as Mary Blanchard proved to be. Her home until the death of her husband was always a charming one. R. A. Blanchard was born in Madison County, New York, December 27, 1816, and moved to Wayne County with his parents when eight years of age. Long before he was converted he felt that if ever he became a Christian he must preach the gospel. He was converted when seventeen, at a camp-meeting near Sodus, in September, 1832. His conversion was at first like the glimmering of daylight, and then the sun of righteousness appeared in full beam. He at once began to preach in his sleep, so as to wake his parents in the night-time. This was made known to his pastor, who sought an interview with the young Christian. Finding that he had impressions of his duty to preach, the pastor brought his case before the society, and, on recommendation, he was licensed to exhort in October, 1836. His license to exhort was regularly renewed until August, 1840. At this date, while attending the seminary at Lima, where he had been about two years, he was licensed to preach, and at the same time recommended to Conference. Before the meeting of the Conference he fell in with John Clark, who was then in the East looking for young men for the work in the West. He started for Illinois in a one-horse gig, accompanied by Rev. Sias Bolles, who had also been induced to come West. They both arrived in time to be received into the Rock River Conference, at its first session in 1840, at Mt. Morris. S. Bolles had been admitted to the Genesee Conference in 1836. Mr. Blanchard was appointed to Buffalo Grove Circuit. Luke Hitchcock was then on the Dixon Circuit as a supply. Mr. Hitchcock was soon selected by the trustees to act as agent of the new Rock River Seminary, and Mr. Blanchard went to the Dixon work, to supply Mr. Hitchcock's place. When he went to Dixon he found that everybody was talking of Luke Hitchcock in a manner that made it disagreeable for a successor. One day Mr. Blanchard preached a funeral sermon, and after preaching was sitting in a back room at Mr. Hitchcock's house. In another room, separated by a thin partition, a company was gathered who began comparing the two preachers. One of those grandiloquent persons that use great words without knowing their meaning, put in this grave opinion: "Mr. Blanchard is quite an exceptionable preacher, but I must say that the Rev. Mr. Hitchcock is the most diabolical preacher I ever heard." Whatever that word may mean, the gentleman intended to pay Mr. Hitchcock the highest kind of a compliment.

From Dixon Mr. Blanchard went, in 1841, to the Freeport Circuit. It is not needful here to insert the list of his appointments. He was one of those even, good, hard-working, tried men, who rise slowly but surely, and who are often called to fill difficult places where prudence and perseverance are needed. He was in Galena and Chicago, at Belvidere and Mount Morris, and charges of that sort, until 1860, when he was made presiding elder on the Rockford District. He continued in the eldership until 1869, when he was stationed at Roscoe. He was never brilliant as a preacher or as an elder; but by attending carefully to every part of his work, he made one of the best presiding elders the writer ever had. In 1872 he was appointed to St. Charles, one of his old favorite places. He continued to fill his place there until August, 1873. At this time he took a trip to Belvidere. While there, he rode with the pastor into the country, where he had property, to attend to some business. On his way he complained of pains; but taking simple remedies, he felt better. He attended to his business, took dinner, and then returned to the parsonage occupied by Joseph Odgers at Belvidere. Going into the parlor, he sat down on the sofa. Mrs. Odgers, being in the next room, hearing a noise, stepped into the room, and saw Mr. Blanchard sliding helpless from the sofa. He was lifted up; physicians were sent for; but it was too late. He was gone. The toil of the workman of thirty-three years was over. This occurred August 19, 1873. In social life he was one of the most genial of men; but in all his geniality, nothing gross or impure ever passed from his lips. His piety was deep and abiding. As a member of Conference, from the first he was one of those who took his part in the proceedings, and generally had some word of wisdom to offer. There are on the Conference floor two classes of men who are at fault. The first class of men are always striving to get in a word, whether wise or unwise—oftenest unwise—on every matter that comes up; the other class never are known in the Conference business. R. A. Blanchard was a member of neither class. He took the medium ground, and generally spoke only when there was reason for speaking. The only exception to this was that, in his early days, he was such an admirer of Hooper Crews he seemed to think he was the special guardian of Mr. Crews's character, and strove often to defend it when it did not need any defense.

Mr. Blanchard was a member of the General Conference in 1868.

MILTON BOURNE,

For many years a laborious member of the Rock River Conference, was born in Attleboro, Massachusetts, in 1810. When he was but four years of age, his father moved to Wallingford, Vermont, and a year after settled in Pawlet. Here young Milton grew up, and, when about twenty years of age, was converted. He was religiously inclined from a child, and never saw the time he did not observe habits of prayer. He was led to give himself to Christ because of the wonderful restoration of a sister from sickness. About the time of his conversion, two local preachers, Elias Crawford and Joseph Ayers, went into the town where he lived, and began a meeting, which seemed to arouse the country. It was the first young Bourne had seen of the Methodists. A society was formed at Pawlet, and grew in power and strength.

In 1826, Pawlet was taken in as an appointment on Cambridge Circuit, and Daniel Brayton and Joseph Eames appeared as circuit preachers. Brother Bourne continued a member for eight years, and was then made leader of the Pawlet class. In 1834 he volunteered to go as a missionary teacher among the Indians at Lake Superior, where John Clark had been a year or two superintendent. He traveled in company with D. M. Chandler by stage and canal to Buffalo, on the old steamboat *Michigan* to Detroit, by steamboat to Mackinaw, and by a small sail-boat to Sault Ste. Marie, where he and his companion were kindly received, August 24th, by John Clark and family. The superintendent at once removed to Green Bay, and left Brother Bourne in charge of the mission at Sault Ste. Marie. This charge he undertook September 1, 1834. There was a Methodist society of thirty-eight members among the Indians, and the *charge d'affaires* at once became preacher, school-teacher, and superintendent of the mission-farm. He was obliged to do his own cooking, and for two years was the only white person within a hundred miles. The Indians adopted him into their tribe, and gave him a name well fitting his character. They called him Omemee, or Dove.

At the end of two years, Brother Bourne returned to Vermont, and spent a year at school. In 1837 he went up to the Troy Conference with a recommendation for admission. At the seat of Conference he found John Clark, then presiding elder of the Chicago District, hunting for preachers for the West. Brother Bourne was admitted to Conference, and was at once, with others, transferred to the Illinois Conference, when he was appointed to Thornton Mission, which embraced all the territory from Joliet to Blue Island. The next year he went to Forked Creek Mission. In 1839 he married Miss R. Miller, of Dayton, on Fox River. At the Conference of 1839 he was appointed to Roscoe Circuit, where he remained two years. His appointments after this were: 1841, Joliet; 1842, Sylvania, in Wisconsin; 1843, Racine; and in 1844-45, at Mount Morris. In 1846 he was appointed presiding elder of Ottawa District. This district, on which he continued four years with acceptance, included all the country between Fox and Rock Rivers, from Peru to Belvidere. In 1850 he was transferred to Knoxville District, where he remained four years. After this he was appointed to circuits as follows: 1854, Macomb; 1855, Peru; 1856, Buffalo Grove; 1857, Milledgeville; 1858-59, Roscoe; 1860, Winnebago; 1861, Harmony; 1862, Chemung. When at Winnebago, he was taken with sickness, which came near removing him from labor. He recovered; but the disease induced a sort of physical lethargy, which thereafter greatly impaired his acceptability. He passed into a superannuated condition without knowing it. Accordingly, in 1863, by advice of friends, he reluctantly took a superannuated relation. This, to an old itinerant soldier, is one of the severest strokes in life. To be called to retire from laboring with a noble band of ministers, with whom one has associated for years, is a disappointment too bitter for tears. No wonder one prayed that he might cease at once to work and live!

Brother Bourne at once removed his family to a small farm near Macomb, Illinois, where he undertook to prepare a home for his wife and children. Being compelled to labor harder than he was able, he soon sank under disease, and in the spring of 1865 he departed this life, in the joy and faith of the gospel. He labored without intermission on circuits and districts in Illinois twenty-six years, nineteen of these years in the bounds of the Rock River Conference. He married a second wife in 1850, his first having died a year or two before. Milton Bourne was never brilliant, but quiet, sound, deep, safe, true, argumentative, and reliable. He delighted to dissect the metaphysical dogmas of fate, foreknowledge, and the quibbles of Universalism, laying bare all the illogical conclusions of the old-time errorists. Like *too many* others, he graduated in ministerial study early in his ministerial life, and began to fag mentally before his time. Always unassuming and retiring in manner, he was never a leader, but a safe adviser and aid. His is the memory of the just.

SIAS BOLLES,

The preacher at Elgin, in 1840, was born in Williamstown, Vermont, September 5, 1810. His father was a farmer, and young Sias worked on the farm summers, and attended the district school winters until eighteen years of age, when he learned the trade of tanner and shoemaker. He was converted September 20, 1832, at the age of twenty-two, and soon joined the Methodist Episcopal Church. In two or three years he left his business, received license to exhort, and went to the Wesleyan Seminary at Lima, New York. Here he remained until April, 1836, when he was employed by the elder on a circuit. In September of that year he was admitted to the Genesee Conference, and sent as junior to Sodus Circuit. He came to Rock River Conference in 1840, and, being appointed to Elgin, began his first year's work in the West in a small wood-colored frame church in a village that had a little cluster of buildings. He continued to fill appointments in our bounds until 1856, when he was transferred to Minnesota, where he was present at the organization of the first Conference in that State. There he has done efficient work as presiding elder, and as preacher in some of the best appointments.

Bishop Janes told us at his first visit to the Rock River Conference in 1848, that we "must neither wear out nor rust out, but burn out!" This, Sias Bolles seemed to verify more than any man we have known. Abel Stevens was pleased in an *Advocate and Journal* editorial to class him with Spurgeon. He used to be the man-of-all-work in the Conference, ever ready, ever interesting. His chief forte was speaking at anniversary meetings, and on those occasions we never knew him to fall behind any "illustrious stranger" that stood upon the same platform. At the Rockford Conference of 1849, A. E. Phelps and Mr. Bolles were the speakers at the Sunday-school anniversary. Mr. Phelps was the eloquent man of the Conference. This evening he went beyond himself, and carried the audience up among the stars. We thought that for once Mr. Bolles would fail; but he arose, and in his natural conversational, homelike way commenced with a simple illustration concerning his daughter's first examples in arithmetic; from this he went on, up, up, up, until Mr. Phelps was forgotten. At Rock Island in 1855, M. L. Scudder, Bible agent from New York, was present to speak upon the Bible cause. He was put number three on the list. Amasa Lord led the way with his telling statistics; Mr. Bolles followed with the most glittering Bible speech we ever heard, and the grandest effort we ever knew him to make. Dr. Scudder arose to make the closing speech, but he remarked, "Brother Bolles has taken the wind out of my sails;" and he strove with poor success to interest the audience. The silvery words of the weeping preacher will never cease to echo in our hearts. Brother Bolles became one of our first Church dedicators, raising such sums at dedications as had never before been heard of in the West. He had a wonderful faculty of working himself down to the feelings of the people, and there was so much of the spirit and sympathy of religion about him he won all hearts. During his first year at Elgin he undertook to paint the church. The chief tavern-keeper of the place—Tibballs by name—had made his threats that he would turn the first preacher out of doors that came into his house as a minister. Mrs. Bolles had commenced a school, and among her scholars were the tavern-keeper's children. These, taking a fancy to their teacher, frequently invited her to tea. At one time they persuaded their mother to invite Brother Bolles also. He went. Mr. Tibballs was affable and social. After tea, Mr. Bolles remarked that he wanted to paint up the church to help the looks of the town, and consulted Tibballs concerning the cost, etc. Mr. Tibballs was communicative, and closed by handing over five dollars—a very large sum for that day—as his portion towards the painting. When asked afterwards why he did not carry his threat into execution, "O," he rejoined, "I did not know of Bolles then; he's an exception."

Six years after this, in a company, the remark was made that it was hard to listen to Mr. Bolles and not shed tears. A very wise young lawyer thought it a weakness to cry at the stories of a haranguing preacher, and said he would give any minister five dollars that could make him weep. Not long after this conversation, Mr. Bolles went to Elgin to preach a funeral sermon. The young lawyer went to hear him. Remembering his sneer, he nerved himself against the preacher's influence; but in twenty minutes Ed. Harvey sat with the tears trickling down his cheeks. After service, he stepped up to the preacher, and said: "Mr. Bolles, I wish to present you with five dollars." Brother Bolles thanked him kindly, and took the gift as a special providence, for he had not sufficient money to pay his way back by stage to the city.

The year at Elgin closed in 1841, with 174 members; and William Vallette, a man rather after the Bolles sort, was sent to the work. Ever since then Elgin has pursued the even tenor of its way. Brother Bolles returned to the charge in 1850, and put on a wing to the old narrow church, and still strengthened the old society.

JOHN W. AGARD

Was the only son of Horace Agard, a popular presiding elder in the State of New York for many years. He was born in the town of Odessa, Schuyler County, New York, May 6, 1811. He spent most of his time from three to sixteen years in school. From 1827 to 1830 he worked on his father's farm. At that time he entered the Oneida Conference Seminary at Cazenovia. In 1831 there was a great revival there, under the labors of Zachariah Paddock. On Saturday, March 19th (these exact dates are given as indications of Mr. Agard's exactness in all details), at the first meeting he attended, he was convicted of sin; on Sunday evening, the 20th, he went to the altar for prayer; on Monday, twenty minutes before twelve (noon), March 21st, he found peace in believing. According to his nature, he at once set about active Christian work. He was soon made a class-leader, and soon a steward in the Church. In March, 1834, he married Marcia Thomas, and went to live in Nichols, Tioga County. September 1, 1836, he settled in Wyoming, Stark County, Illinois.

Soon after his conversion he began to feel that it was his duty to preach the gospel; but to avoid this, he gave up his studies, and gave his time to secular life. But as his convictions deepened, he resolved to secure a home for his family, and then enter the work. In 1841 he made a profession of Christian perfection. Now his call to preach became more imperative. In 1845 he was licensed to preach, and recommended to the Rock River Conference. He joined the Conference that fall, and was sent to Peru. In the work he was the same painstaking, methodical man that marked all the doings of his life. He passed gradually upward, till he filled such appointments as Indiana Street, Chicago, Aurora, and Dixon. In 1855 he became presiding elder of Chicago District. He continued in the relation of presiding elder until 1864, when he took a superannuated relation, and returned to business at Wyoming, where he continued to reside until himself and daughter, by death, were left alone. Then, in 1880, they secured themselves a pleasant home in Chicago.

As a man he was intensely devoted to the right as he saw the right. No one expected intolerance on the one hand, or compromise on the other. His honest soul said: Give me the facts and the law, and the verdict will be welcome, whatever becomes of me. He became one of the best business men of the Conference, always being in the right on a question of law. Quiet, a little too sedate, he lacked the moving power of a Crews or a Hitchcock to stand high as a presiding elder. But, like all men of his quiet, thoughtful turn, he failed to be fully appreciated according to his merits. His success was greater on stations than on districts.

In justice to the truth, we can not afford to hide one fact here. When the War of the Rebellion broke out, there were but three men in the Conference but what had gone over to Republicanism and Lincoln. Previous to this time politics was of so little interest to preachers, the writer does not know which way the old-time men voted. We have no idea what was the politics of any of the older men. We only know, whenever a clear case of God and humanity is made out, you may expect to find Methodist preachers flocking to that side. So when the Democratic side went for slavery and oppression, and the new party under Lincoln was going for free soil, free speech, and free men, it did not need a prophet's vision to see where the Methodist preachers would be found. For reasons we can not determine, John W. Agard was one of the three—Nathan Jewett, D. C. Howard, J. W. Agard—who, through a too great leaning to "law and order," were on the opposition side. When the war broke out, Mr. Agard was on the Aurora District. He was so bound to law that he at once pronounced the new greenback—the money issued by the Government as an extra war measure—to be unconstitutional; and, it is said, refused to receive it as quarterage. This thing pressed him from the district, made him unacceptable in the station, and was the leading cause of his retirement. But it was not his nature to be a bitter partisan.

Well, at last, in his quiet Chicago home, this tender, brave, wise, loyal heart ceased to beat! He had become a sweet, ripe, saintly believer. Through much suffering he came to the ending, October 10, 1881. His last words were: "Jesus," "enough."

JAMES R. GOODRICH was born at Swanton Falls, Vermont, in 1805. He was converted when eighteen, and entered the New York Conference in 1828, being appointed to Pittsford Circuit, with Salmon Stebbins as preacher in charge, at a time when John Clark was presiding elder in the same Conference. In 1829, Brother Goodrich went to Chazy with Daniel Brayton, who afterward kept tavern in Mount Morris, Illinois, and under John Clark as presiding elder. In 1837 he was transferred, with Salmon Stebbins, Milton Bourne, Jesse Halsted, and William Gaddis, to the Illinois Conference, and appointed to the Milwaukee Mission. In 1841 he was appointed presiding elder of Green Bay District, in which relation he continued until 1844, when he became presiding elder of the Chicago District. At the close of the year he superannuated and went into merchandising at Dubuque. He was feeble in health, but desiring to labor, he took work in 1859, and was stationed at Marengo. Soon after, he retired again to his Dubuque home, where, after years of physical suffering, on March 15, 1886, he peacefully passed to his home in heaven. He was refined in his tastes and manners, a scholarly, pure, accomplished man, whom everybody loved.

GEORGE DAVISON.—In the life of Mr. George Davison we are permitted to present some rather unique history. If all accounts can be trusted, he was a member of the first class formed in Illinois and the founder of Methodism in the State. His own account is thus given. Previous to 1803 he came up from Tennessee and settled in Jackson County, Illinois. One night he fell under conviction, and saw the necessity of being converted. He waked up his wife, and asked her what he must do. She said he must pray. But he answered: "I don't know how; do you?" "Yes," said she. "I have been praying for three weeks! Praying will make you feel better." She prayed for him, and he was converted; and then he prayed for her, and she was converted also. Next morning they held a council about sending for a minister. It was finally decided that he should go to Cincinnati in search of a preacher. He undertook the journey of five hundred miles on horseback, and secured the promise of a preacher. Accordingly, Benjamin Young was appointed to "Illinois" in 1803. A class was soon formed, of which Davison and wife were members. But this man Young soon turned semi-infidel, and began to preach against religion. But

Davison stood firm, and went again to Cincinnati for another preacher. In his account of this, Mr. Davison says he secured another preacher, named Samuel Hamilton, who began demolishing the teachings of Mr. Young, and proved a man of the true stamp. We know what is said of Mr. Young is true; but as no man appears in the Minutes of this time named Samuel Hamilton, if the account is correct it is likely that Mr. Hamilton supplied the work for a part of the year, as the Minutes give us Joseph Oglesby as the preacher to Illinois in 1804.

In 1827, Mr. Davison removed with his family to Galena, and became a member of the first class in that place in 1829. Dr. Newhall, who in those days edited the Galena *Advertiser*, and who has preserved much of Galena's history, speaks, in 1860, of Mr. Davison's piety and consistency in the warmest terms. In 1834, Hooper Crews found this man living near Savannah, and it is probable he was a member of the first class formed in that place. He died at Savannah in 1850.

JAMES F. CHAFFEE was born November 5, 1827, in Wyoming County, New York; was converted at the age of thirteen in the town of China, and joined the Free Will Baptist Church. He came West to McHenry County, Illinois, and made his home near Hebron about 1845. Here he found no Free Will Baptists, and joined the Methodist Church merely to find a religious home for the time, having no idea of ever becoming permanently a Methodist. But he soon found that he was at home in the Methodist Church, and resolved to enter her ministry. At the age of nineteen he received license to exhort. In 1848 he was recommended to Conference from the McHenry Circuit, and was the same year admitted to the Conference, with W. P. Jones and A. D. Field, and appointed junior preacher on the Carthage Circuit. This occurred four months before he was twenty-one years of age. He was afterward appointed to Oquawka, Monmouth, Knoxville, and Lewiston charges. In 1855 he was appointed to Jefferson Street, Chicago, where he remained two years. In 1857 he was transferred to Minnesota, where, as presiding elder, and college agent, and pastor in the larger cities, he has continued to do work that will live after his earthly work is done. Tall, with imposing presence and elaborate delivery, he stands among the able men of his Conference.

MRS. EUNICE BUSH has a record here, because, according to our plan, we have desired to enter the names of such as did any special work in the bounds of the Conference. Mrs. Bush must take place among the worthy pioneers. She was born in Oneida County, New York, in 1800, and was, accordingly, eighty-five years old at her death.

In early life she became a Christian, and at her death had been a member of the Methodist Church sixty-five years. In 1836 the family came to Illinois, and in 1838 settled at Sterling. In this last year, Barton H. Cartwright, who was at the time on the Buffalo Grove Circuit, formed the first class at Sterling. Mrs. Bush, with her husband and four others, composed this first class. Mrs. Bush remained a firm and faithful member of this society until her death—forty-seven years! Mr. and Mrs. Bush not only were a part of the first class, but when the time arrived for erecting a church they gave the grounds on which the church and parsonage now stands. Their house was always the home of the preachers, and their means were freely given to sustain the Church.

Not quite two weeks before her death she was at Church, and, remaining for class-meeting, spoke of the comfort religion gave her, and of the blessed hope of heaven which then inspired her. A day or two before the end she manifested a greatly-increased interest in the prosperity of Broadway Church and its new pastor. It would have been a comfort to friends had she died conscious; but by a sudden stroke of paralysis she died December 16, 1885.

MR. LUTHER BEAL, of Sandwich, Illinois, in many of the tests which we have chosen to apply to laymen whose record finds admittance here, excelled any man we have known. His pure devotion to the Church wherever he resided, his pure gentle spirit, his cheerful-hearted companionship, ever made him the peculiar friend of the right-spirited pastor. The preachers loved to be in his home, and loved to have him in their homes.

Mr. Beal was born in Maine in 1823. About the year 1858 he removed to Illinois, and entered mercantile life at Lacon. Here he showed the peculiar spirit of the man. His means were limited, and it was peculiarly necessary that he should prosper. His partner was a devout Presbyterian. Both had faith in the providential power of God. And so each morning they would go down to the store, go to the back part of the room, and kneel down and pray that God's blessing might be on them through the day, and that all things might prosper in their hands. Such men deserved to prosper, and they did prosper.

About the year 1865, Mr. Beal removed to Earl, where he still continued storekeeping. This removal was made partly so that the family could be nearer the seminary at Aurora, where their only child—Ellery H. Beal, of Rock River Conference—was being educated. Mr. and Mrs. Beal were now becoming advanced in life, and their greatest joy being the hope that God would take their son for the ministry, they made the business of their lives bend to this end. Earl at this time had a small, discouraged Church; but the coming of such a man as Luther Beal, with the influence of such men as James Walcott, David Moar, and others who joined at Earl about this time, set the Church on its feet, and a more prosperous Church than that at Earl in those days (1865–68), I never knew.

In the spring of 1867 a fire at Earl swept out all the business houses. Mr. Beal's store went with the rest. There were no buildings to occupy, and the trade of the town for a time became demoralized, so that Mr. Beal was almost obliged to go elsewhere. He selected Sandwich as a new home. Here he opened up a store once again. He had not been in Sandwich three months until he was made superintendent of the Sunday-school, and at once he was advanced to every position in the Church he could be induced to fill.

He was converted at fourteen years of age, and his life in the Church was nearly fifty years, but all this time his spirit was young and boysome. For forty years he filled some prominent lay office in the Church. For twenty-five years before his death he was an invalid; but his last illness was short and severe. Through all these years, and finally when near his end, he was cheerful and resigned. He did not expect or desire longer life, but longed for his home "over there." His expressions were wonderful gems of religious experience. He died October 8, 1885.

When MR. BENJAMIN BOWMAN died, the Methodist Church lost a noble and heroic member. He died at Blaine (old Round Prairie), November 18, 1884. He was born in Luzerne County, Pa., February 27, 1810, and was, as we see, seventy-four years of age when he died. In 1831 he married Miss Frances Parks, sister of that well-known, well-loved local preacher, Samuel Parks, once of Round Prairie. In 1841, Mr. Bowman removed to Boone County, Illinois, where ever after he resided. When nineteen years of age he gave his heart to the Savior, and found a reception so clear he never after doubted that he was a child of a

King. He joined the Methodist Church; and, from that on, it was his greatest luxury to do for and to give to the Church. He was a man of strong character and strong convictions. He believed in religion. Often his prayers were marvels of power. He read the literature of the Church, and was unusually intelligent. He belonged to a large family of staunch Methodists. Bishop Bowman was his cousin and schoolmate. His brother, Samuel, was a member of the first class at Dixon, and was the superintendent of the first Sunday-school there. His brother Elijah, the father of Ada, the wife of Rev. G. L. S. Stuff—with himself—was one of the most ardent supporters of the old Round Prairie Church. When the writer of these lines built the first church in all that region, the two Bowmans—Benjamin and Elijah—were on hand with financial and other aid.

We shall never forget their labors of love in those days. Being an anti-slavery man and a man of strong opinions, there could be no doubt of the side Brother Bowman was on when the Union war was upon us. He gave five sons and one son-in-law to that cause. Three of these soldier-boys lie in the Blaine Cemetery. When the war commenced, there were but three sons old enough to go. These went, and as soon as two others became old enough they went also. Mr. Bowman, in 1861, was a man of some means; but I heard him say the country could have it all if necessary to put down that most uncalled-for, unreasonable rebellion! This is what he said to his sons, most of whom were married men: "Boys," said he, "I do not tell you to go. I wish you to be free in this matter; but if you do go, remember that you can leave your families in my hands and they will be cared for. None of your interests shall suffer while you are gone, and you shall not be the poorer for going; and if you are wounded or dying, I will go to your aid."

When Elijah, the first of these to die, a brave, noble, Christian boy, lay dying at Donelson, the father flew to his relief, but arrived only in time to bear the body of the dear boy back to a Round Prairie grave. Such fathers and sons in the North to back our Illinois Grant is what made the Union arms triumphant!

But after years of valiant Church service, this warrior fainted by the way—this pillar began to crumble. For two years before his death he was almost blind. An operation gave him sight, but other ailments set in, and he began a decline. But to death—the grand departure—he looked with joy. He knew in whom he had believed. He was no disciple of a doubting Thomas in that last hour! He was saved strongly and gloriously. "Blessed be God," says one concerning him, "who gave Methodism such heroic souls!" Wasted and infirm by the toil of seventy-four years, the body at length went down to the earth to be buried in the cemetery his own hands had prepared. But such men never die! His influence will linger about the precincts of Blaine till years and years are past!

Mr. ELIAS CRARY was born in Wallingford, Vermont, in 1794. He was the son of Captain Elias Crary, a Revolutionary soldier. He was converted in 1817 under the ministry of John Dempster, and in 1836 went to Illinois and settled at the south end of Chicken Grove, in Kane County. In old age he removed to Geneva. For nearly half a century he was a class-leader, and often held other official positions. His Christian life was one of unusual zeal and faithfulness, and when old he was always still in his place at Church. He departed from this life September 16, 1876, and was laid away in his last resting-place by Hooper Crews, Robert Beatty, and others.

On settling at Chicken Grove, his house at once became a preaching-place. The class was formed there in 1837, and for years the meetings were held in his house. Whenever there were quarterly or other meetings at Mr. Crary's, the upper floor was removed in the center, and thus a gallery was formed, where many of the congregation found seats. The present writer attended one of those meetings in 1840, sitting up in the gallery while he listened to a sermon by Josiah Whipple. Staying over night with others, we found a bed on the softest side of the front-room floor. When such men as Elias Crary went into the new West, they filled a place in the mission of the Church which preachers could not fill. Quartermasters are often as serviceable as generals.

Mrs. LUCY WALKER WENTWORTH was born in Maine, October 20, 1785, and was converted and joined the Methodist Church at Bangor under the first Methodist preaching in that place. She was engaged in teaching school until her marriage with Elijah Wentworth. Soon after this marriage the couple started West by way of the Ohio River; stopped awhile in Kentucky; then went on to Lewistown, Fulton County, Illinois, where Mrs. Wentworth was a member of the Church, when William See was on the Peoria Circuit, from 1825 to 1827. About 1828 the family went to Dodgeville, Wisconsin, and November 1, 1830, arrived in Chicago, where Mr. Wentworth at once commenced keeping tavern at The Point, in an old log-house. William See and family were already there. Jesse Walker had just been appointed to Chicago Mission; but as there were few people there, and little to be done, Mr. Walker occupied most of his time in other portions of his work. Mrs. Wentworth urged William See to make appointments for preaching on the Sabbath. He argued that no one would come out to hear him. She made an appointment for him at his own house—afterward the famed log meeting-house—and went around and personally invited the people to come out to meeting. All the white people of Chicago but three families attended. Mr. See kept up regular appointments after that. Until 1832 the meetings were often held at the Wentworth tavern. In the spring of 1833 the Wentworth family moved on to a farm eight miles up the north branch of the river, but retained their membership at Chicago. In after years—1844 to 1849—the old people lived most of the time in the city with their daughter, Mrs. Susan Sweet. Here Mrs. Wentworth died, July 28, 1849, aged sixty-four years. Her remains rest at Rose Hill. She was a small woman, full of energy. She did what she could for temperance, Sunday-schools, and other enterprises. In 1840-42, when some Chicago Abolition Methodists persisted in sending Abolition petitions to the Rock River Conference, Lucy Wentworth's name was among the signers.

By reference to the lives of Jesse Walker and William See, it will be seen that Mrs. Wentworth and three of her children were among those that composed the first class in Chicago, formed in 1831. I suppose really Mrs. Wentworth had more to do with the forming of that class than any other.

ZEBIAH WENTWORTH ESTES. — The first Methodist class in Chicago, which was the first Christian society of any kind there, was organized in July, 1831, by Jesse Walker and S. R. Beggs. It consisted of seven members. Rev. William See — the first Chicago Methodist, the first Chicago Methodist preacher, the first class-leader — was made leader of the class. The most prominent member next to the leader was Mrs. Lucy Wentworth, who had been a second Barbara Heck in urging Mr. See on to duty, and in providing in after years a home and preaching-places for the preachers. With Mrs. Wentworth, three of her children joined this first class. Among them was her daughter Zebiah. She was born on April 19, 1810; and after her people settled in Fulton County, Illinois, where her mother was a member of the Church at Lewistown from 1825 till 1828, Zebiah was converted at a camp-meeting held near Lewistown in 1827. She at once joined the Methodist Church. She came with the family to Chicago in November, 1830, where she aided in forming the first class.

On September 4, 1837, she was married to Elijah Estes, and soon afterward went with her husband to Bay View, Wis., finding a home in a log-cabin, on the bank of the lake, three miles from what is now the center of Milwaukee. In those days she was accustomed to walk the long distance to Spring Street Church. She became owner of considerable property, and for many years managed her business with excellent ability. She gave generously from time to to time to various institutions. Among the objects of her beneficence were the Woman's Foreign Missionary Society of the Methodist Episcopal Church, the University at Appleton, the Methodist Episcopal Church enterprise in Madison, and the Welsh Congregational Church near her home; also the Bay View Methodist Church at the time of its rededication. For a number of years she felt a deep interest in foreign missions, giving at one time $400 to woman's work among the heathen. She followed with prayerful sympathy the movements of Bishop Taylor in Africa, and contributed of her means to his support. For some days preceding her decease she was restless, and longed to be free. Her mental faculties showed no sign of failing, and were perfectly clear up to the last. During the final week she read everything in the columns of the *Northwestern* of June 30th, and spent much time perusing hymns, committing to memory that one which so well expresses the feeling of a devout soul on the eve of departure from this life: "Fade, fade each earthly joy, Jesus is mine." Though long expected, death came suddenly, July 2, 1887. In fifteen minutes from the first sign of his approach, all was over. Taken by surprise, yet was she ready. The mortal struggle came to its end almost as soon as it began, and uttering a quick and earnest "Good-bye, good-bye!" to those around her, she quietly fell on sleep. She leaves an aged companion, who is highly respected in the community, with four sons and a daughter—Mrs. Rev. I. Linebarger, of the Rock River Conference.

MR. THOMAS FREEK was not a man very much known. He kept himself within his little sphere, trying to uphold the honor of his God, and doing what he could to improve the small society at Erie, Illinois, where he was so long a member. He was born at Hambleton, England, October 12, 1805. At twenty-two he was converted, and was soon licensed as a local preacher. His parents were Methodists of the strictest type, and the spirit must have been ingrained into Thomas, for I never saw a man so difficult to swerve from what he considered the right. Mr. Freek came to America in 1841, and settled on a farm near Erie. There he at once became a member of the Methodist Church, and continued to hold the relation of local preacher till his death. In 1857 we found him a crusty old bachelor, but had the privilege, in the parsonage at Albany, of marrying him to Miss Julia McKinstry, whose superbly genial nature softened the asperities of her new husband. She died in 1880.

When at last Thomas Freek's end drew near, he knew that he must go, and was fully ready. A few weeks before his death he went to Albany for better care. Almost his last words were just before he died, July 4, 1885: "Victory through the blood of the Lamb!"

As he had no children, his property was bequeathed to missions, the Freedmen, and the superannuates of the Rock River Conference.

J. W. FLOWERS came to the Rock River Conference from the Pittsburg Conference in 1850. There he was noted as an eloquent young man, and nothing more. But change of position often brings a person into better circumstances for making himself known; and from his first sermon before the Conference in 1850 until his withdrawal in 1863, Mr. Flowers was one of the most eloquent men we have had among us. There was little originality of thought or matter. He used the sermon-books too freely, and was only pre-eminent for humility and eloquence. His voice rich and musical, his manner never awkward, he would make you weep in the reading of a hymn. He dug himself out of the hills of Virginia, and though lacking education, was a polished speaker. He always took the people by storm, carrying them away with wild emotion. At a camp-meeting held at Plainfield in 1856, where Mr. Flowers had charge, things had been moving finely until one morning a brother gave us a dry, logical sermon on the evidences. The young preacher was preparing for examination the next week at Conference, and he gave us a rehash of Watson's First Part. The sermon was as dry as Sahara, and as long as a Puritan's face. The people became tired, and went to their tents, or for wood and water. The meeting, to all appearances, was gone for that day. Elder Flowers arose to exhort. Commencing calmly, he awoke the people by degrees, and in five minutes there was a stirring among the crowd like the movings of a tempest. People flocked from their tents, and came in from their walks. The preachers resting in the preachers' tent clambered to the cracks, and every soul was intent on the moving of the pool! The preacher closed by striking up one of his Pennsylvania songs, which he could sing as eloquently as he could repeat it, and rallied the people for prayer. The day was won, and the people going to work, the battle waxed glorious.

Mr. Flowers, in the Rock River and the Central Illinois Conferences, occupied some of the best positions, and was presiding elder on the Joliet District three or four years. He withdrew from the Conference under a cloud in 1863, and after that resided for some time on a farm in Iroquois County. He afterwards moved to Missouri, and entered the regular work again, being admitted on trial in the Missouri Conference, and passed on until admitted into full connection in 1869. A few years after, he died, while in the regular work.

NATHANIEL P. CUNNINGHAM was transferred in 1842 from the Illinois Conference to serve Clark Street Church. This brother was born in Pendleton County, Virginia, August, 1807. His parents being members of the Church, he was reared under the influence of Methodism. His father's house was a preachers' home, and once that meant something. Nathaniel was converted at a camp-meeting in 1825, when eighteen, and in 1827 licensed to exhort. In 1829 he was received into the Baltimore Conference. After laboring faithfully in the bounds of that Conference seven years, he was, in 1836, transferred to the Illinois Conference, and stationed at Vandalia. After this, he was appointed to Alton in 1837; to Belleville in 1839; to Peoria in 1840; to Chicago in 1842; and to Rushville in 1843. In 1845 he located for a year, and in 1846 was appointed to Paris, where he died, July 20, 1848. His year at Clark Street was his only year in our bounds. He was taken with flux, July 7th, and lingered until the 20th. When asked concerning his readiness to pass the flood, he exclaimed: "All is peace; O how good the Lord is!" A few hours before his death he asked the friends to kneel down, and then calling the name of each person, he presented them before the Lord with angelic sweetness. Calling his wife and daughter Virginia to his bedside, he gave them parting instructions, and pronounced such a benediction upon them as is seldom the privilege of any to witness. "God Almighty," said he, "bless my wife, bless my child Virginia; take care of them and keep them unto thy heavenly kingdom." Then turning to a minister present, he said: "I have not much to say to them now; but tell the congregation that the Bible is true; God is true, and faithful to his promise. I find him so, here on my deathbed; he is with me now. I find the experience of Holy Ghost religion, which I have professed and enjoyed, . . . is a glorious reality in sickness and death. . . . Tell them the doctrines, the experience, the holy living of Methodism is God's eternal truth, more enduring than the everlasting hills!" Then he gave a charge to the Conference: "Tell my brethren of the Annual Conference," said he, "I died at my post. I loved them much. I would willingly have toiled and have suffered longer, but God has given me a full discharge. I am going to a Methodist preachers' heaven!" After a few hours he fell sweetly asleep, and a heavenly smile slumbered on his features.

DAVID CASSEDAY, one of our most cheerful-spirited men, was born in Vermillion County, Illinois, on the 6th of June, 1826. His parents were George W. and Delia Casseday, who were for years prominent citizens of Danville, and who, after moving to Joliet in 1850, were influential members of the Methodist Church in that place. Being reared in a Methodist family, David, at the age of fourteen, professed religion, and united with the Methodist

Episcopal Church in Danville, Illinois. Soon he began to feel that he must preach the gospel. The world held out unusual inducements all along through his life, and the struggle between worldly offers and duty was often severe. In 1846, when but twenty years of age, he was licensed to preach, admitted to the Illinois Conference, and appointed junior preacher on Mechanicsville Circuit. During the year he was united in marriage to Miss S. R. Welch, of Perryville, Indiana. In 1847 he was appointed to Carlinville, in 1849 to Petersburg, and in 1850 to Beardstown. Here God owned his labors in a remarkable manner. At the close of the year, feeling the effects of constant labors, and seeing the necessity of a settled home for his wife, whose health was declining, and wishing to provide the means of educating his children, he located and entered into business at Joliet. But in a short time he found that his situation and occupation were not in harmony with his convictions of duty, and within a year he closed his business and was readmitted into the Rock River Conference, and appointed to Plainfield. During the first year he was called to part with his wife, who departed as the Christian departs to the better land. In November, 1853, he was married to Miss Ellen M. Hoag, of Plainfield. This union proved to be a most happy one, until death dissolved the ties that bound them, and Brother Casseday left her, who was a happy wife, a lonely widow. Being appointed presiding elder of the Galena District in 1859, he commenced a course of arduous labors which wore on his strength.

During the winter of 1861 his health began to give way, and he went to Joliet to recruit. About the close of April of 1862, after using all the means available, he gave up to die. It was found that he was afflicted with heart disease, and was past cure. But he was not unready. He sent a message to the members of the Conference. "Tell them," he said, "I wish I could have left a better record. I have done a little; done what I could; but I wish I could have left a better record. Tell them to pray for my family. Now my work is sealed up. Let me be quiet. My work is done." He remained a few hours, after he uttered this message, in great peace of mind, and then fell calmly asleep in Jesus. His connection with the Conference was not long, but he proved himself one of its most worthy members. Stout in body, hale and fresh as a mountaineer, he was as cheerful and kind-hearted as a dearest friend. There was a mellow eloquence in his voice, and his preaching was with a spirit of sincerity that won all hearts. By all who knew him he was loved as a friend, and respected as a faithful minister of the Cross. He died May 5, 1862.

> "So, whene'er the signal's given,
>   Us from earth to call away,
> Borne on angel's wings to heaven,
>   Glad the summons to obey,
> May we ever reign with Christ in endless day!"

JOHN DEW—who stands as the first preacher in the Rock River Conference who preached to the whites, and the third traveling preacher who labored in the Conference bounds—was born in Virginia in 1789, and became, while young, a member of the Methodist connection. He joined the Ohio Conference in 1813, when twenty-four years of age, and continued in active service until his death in 1840. During the time he was four years presiding elder, and two years president of McKendree College. His first circuit was Salt River—we suppose in Kentucky—and he afterwards traveled in Ohio, Indiana, Missouri, and Illinois, and was presiding elder on Lebanon District when he died. He was the fast friend of every benevolent enterprise of the Church, and " well-fitted," as one of his friends rather captiously remarks, "to pioneer for ministers of more delicate constitutions and of less vigorous faith." "No man had a fairer reputation," says H. Crews of him, "and I regarded him as one of the best and purest men I ever knew. He had few equals in his day, and in many of the best elements of a man and Christian minister he had no superior." In the early day he was often under the necessity of earning provisions for his family by his own labor. The Church too often failed to support the preachers who gave themselves to its advancement. Like most of the pioneers, his habits of life led him to take interest in all the minutiæ of life, from the points of a fine horse to the flight of a swarm of bees. A young minister, at one time, heard Mr. Dew for some days and nights at a quarterly-meeting, and thought it a great treat to be permitted to accompany the elder home. Mr. Dew was indulging in mental relaxation, feeling somewhat the depressions of "blue Monday," and as he rode along was anything but talkative. "I expected," said the young preacher afterwards, "Brother Dew would, during that day's travel, explain to me all the hard texts in the Bible; but he scarcely said a word until our horses were drinking in the last creek we had to cross; then what do you think my astonishment was to see him look up among the overhanging trees, and pointing with his whip, remark: 'Brother, do n't you think that crooked limb would make a good neck-yoke?'"

"Dew," says one of his friends, "lives in Southern Illinois, in the affection of thousands."

After an illness of two weeks he died in peace, confidently relying upon the mercy of God, September, 5, 1840, about a month after the first session of the Rock River Conference. He left a wife and seven children, besides a bereaved Church, to mourn his loss. The workmen are buried, but the work goes on!

John Dew labored in the bounds of the Rock River Conference only the one year he was at Galena. Being sent to that place, he was the first regular minister to preach in the mining regions. Rev. A. Kent went to Galena in 1829, and living there for forty years, he became an authority in religious matters. For these forty years he was wont to tell how he arrived in Galena, April 1, 1829, and that John Dew came a week after him; so that for once the Presbyterian was ahead of the Methodist preacher. This testimony was received for forty years, until corrected by the writer of these pages. In looking up the early history, in 1868, I learned these facts: John Dew was appointed to Galena at the session of the Illinois Conference in 1828. He immediately went up to his field of labor, leaving his family behind him. He visited all the mining settlements, and preached and baptized children, and laid out his work. When winter set in, he returned to his family in Southern Illinois. His appearance in April, 1829, was a return to the work he had occupied the fall before.

We do not know just when Mr. Dew organized the class at Galena; but on his return to Conference, in 1829, he left there a class of six members. In 1829, on the breaking up of Salem Mission on Fox River, the whites in the country settled mostly at Walker's Grove (Plainfield), and a class was formed there in 1829. This and the class at Galena are the oldest in the Conference.

MICHAEL DECKER, who was reared in Kentucky, and educated at the old Augusta College, went into the bounds of the Crystal Lake Circuit some time in 1841. He came up to a Quarterly Conference held in February, 1842, as an exhorter from Virginia Settlement. From the same place he came to another quarterly-meeting in June, 1842, with a recommendation for license to preach. The license was granted, as well as a recommendation to the Annual Conference. He was admitted to the Conference at its session in August, and appointed junior preacher on Burlington Circuit, Wisconsin. He was born in Staunton, Virginia, April 18, 1814. He studied for the medical profession, and practiced medicine several years. During all this time he felt himself called to the ministry. But a desire to provide for his parents kept him for a long time from the work. After joining Conference, he continued in the regular work until 1857, when he located and went into business at Franklin Grove. While there he was chosen chaplain of the Thirty-fourth Illinois, and served at the front three years during the Rebel War. At the close of the war he again entered the Conference, and was appoined to the Kingston Circuit. In 1873 he was appointed to Crete. On the fourth Sunday after entering upon his work at Crete he was smitten with paralysis while preaching in the pulpit. From thence he was taken to his dying bed. There he lingered a few days—speechless, but conscious and calm—then quietly passed away, from labor to reward. Michael Decker belonged to the great majority of Methodist preachers who make no great name, who never flame out to draw the people or establish great fame, but who do the work assigned, take care of the Church of God committed to their care, and labor on patiently from year to year, the same steady, tried men. There are the famous men who flame out and shine as stars; all have their work, and none but the Great Master knows who shall receive the greater reward.

MR. CHESTER HOISINGTON was the pioneer of Methodism in the neighborhood of Winnebago.

Chester Hoisington.

The Hoisington appointment was one of the old landmarks. Mr. Hoisington was born in Ellisburg, New York, April 13, 1808. In five years he was left an orphan, and at fifteen went to live with a sister at Royalton. Here he was converted, in his eighteenth year, while attending a camp-meeting. He sought employment soon after in a woolen factory in Vermont; and while so employed he established neighborhood prayer-meetings, resulting invariably in the conversion of souls, and, in some instances, in building up permanent societies. February 24, 1830, he married Lucy Wheeler, with whom he lived fifty-four years. In 1844 he settled in Winnebago County, Illinois. The Church early recognized him as an efficient laborer, and in 1843 gave him license to preach; and until his death he continued a local preacher in the Church. He was ordained a local deacon at the Rock River Conference at Dixon in 1867. The church building that stands at Hoisington Corners was built mostly as a result of his efforts. For months before his death he prayed ardently that he might see one more revival at Winnebago before his death. His prayer was answered. At length—May 17, 1884—this old soldier of fifty-four years in the Church and seventy-six on earth died in great peace at his residence in Winnebago.

J. A. Hoisington, a leading Chicago Methodist of 1845, was a brother of the subject of these lines.

SAMUEL APPLETON WOODBURY JEWETT was the son of Samuel Jewett, who was for many years an untiring Methodist preacher—first in Maine, and then in Illinois. Samuel was born in Newburyport, Mass., April 28, 1826. At the age of ten he was converted. Two years after this event his parents removed to Indiana, and soon after to Illinois, settling three miles east of Wilmington. Samuel was educated at the old Rock River Seminary. At the age of twenty-one he began preaching on the Wheeling Circuit. In 1850 he was admitted into the Rock River Conference, and in 1851 was married to Mary Ellen Bridgeman, who proved a most excellent and helpful wife. She gave peculiar emphasis to the oft-expressed thought that so many preachers are helped, made, or hindered and ruined, by their wives. From the first, Mr. Jewett began to take position; so that in 1859 he was made presiding elder of Mt. Morris District. From this time on, till his death in 1881, he was most of the time on districts. He was financial agent of the Northwestern University at the time of the building of University Hall; was stationed at Clark Street, at Galena, and at Aurora. He was a delegate to the General Conference in 1864, 1872, 1876, 1880. He received the diploma of D. D. from McKendree College in 1873.

Dr. Jewett was no ordinary man. The most fitting word, perhaps, would be a strong man. Large in stature, he moved slowly in all his ways, making his addresses at times a little heavy. He required time in the pulpit to elaborate thought, and the persons who listened patiently were well repaid for their pains. He wrote with great ability. On the Conference floor his presence was often seen, and his voice heard, striving to give direction to business.

In 1879 he was appointed to the Joliet District. In this capacity he preached his last sermon at the New Lenox camp-meeting. It was an able discourse, that gave tone to the whole meeting. The day after, he was taken ill, and grew worse until he died. During his sickness he was blessed with consciousness, and was trusting in the great Savior whom he had preached. "He is all sufficient;" "I will fear no evil, for thou art with me;" "This is heaven! it is brighter now!" These were some of his last utterances. "He does bless me." These were his last words. On September 25, 1881, that powerful life was breathed away, and Joliet was in mourning over one of its oldest and worthiest ministers.

ALVA GAFFIN is another pioneer of the Rock River Conference—one of those who broke the ground and blazed the paths of the new country in the days when the howl of the wolf and the visit of the transient Indian made the settler a part of the primitive West. He was born in Canada, February 24, 1805, and in 1837 settled upon a farm in North Grove, six miles north of Mt. Morris. In very early life he became a Christian. I would not cast a stone in the way of the old returner to Christ; but this record, as well as every Christian record, attests the fact that the men and women who live in the memory of the Church for noblest deeds are those whose characters were molded by an early consecration to God. When the plaster was soft, the heavenly hand made its impress. When Mr. Gaffin and his wife came to North Grove, they came as Christians. In the spring of 1838, Barton Cartwright records that he found Mr. Gaffin's log-cabin opened as a preaching-place. At that time there was no preaching nearer than ten miles, and but three neighbors within five miles. This was at once made a regular preaching-place, and a class was soon organized, of which Alva Gaffin was made leader. To that class, in a log school-house at North Grove, the writer preached his first sermon, in July, 1846.

When Mr. Gaffin died, a love-feast ticket, dated 1835, was found among his papers. Mr. Gaffin's house was famed for hospitality. In those days, when circuits were large, a "preacher's home" meant something. The tired traveling preacher loved to seek in times of rest those quiet, hospiable houses that were called, with a meaning to the name, "preachers' homes." The professors of the seminary loved to go to Mr. Gaffin's home. Henry Summers, John Clark, R. Haney, Hooper Crews, blessed the house with their benign presence.

For twelve years before his death he was helpless from effects of palsy. All these years he endured patiently. At last, without a struggle, he fell asleep in Jesus. This last event of his life occurred May 12, in 1875.

MR. JOSEPH G. GIBSON, of Ashton, Illinois, was a layman of more than usual strength of mind. He was a Scotchman, with Scotch proclivities, born at Leith, Scotland, October 8, 1806. He emigrated with his parents to Canada in 1815, and was converted at a camp-meeting in July, 1826. He then joined the Methodist Church at old Augusta Chapel, where lie the bones of Barbara Heck. Mr. Gibson removed to Illinois with his family in 1852, and became at Mt. Pleasant and Ashton a leader in all Church-work. For fifty-seven years he lived a consistent Christian life, nearly fifty of which he was a class-leader. He died in the triumphs of faith at Ashton, Illinois, November 13, 1883. He aimed to glorify God, build up his Church and kingdom, and to secure a home for himself and family in heaven.

WILLIAM GADDIS.—In 1837, Rev. John Clark brought out several preachers from the East, and introduced them to Western work. Among these was William Gaddis, junior preacher on Sycamore Circuit this year. He was a native of Ireland, and when fifteen years of age joined the Wesleyans, and at twenty was licensed to preach. He came to the United States in 1821, and continued till 1837 to labor as a local preacher, making in all thirty-two years of local preacher life. He was admitted to the Troy Conference in 1837, and the same year was transferred to Illinois, and received his first appointment, which was to Sycamore. In 1838–39 he was on Dupage Circuit; in 1840 he was appointed to Wheeling; in 1842, to Crystal Lake; in

1843, to Sycamore; in 1844, to St. Charles; in 1845, to Wilmington; in 1846, to Peoria Circuit; in 1848, to Farmington; in 1849, to Washington; and in 1850, to Lafayette Circuit. He was never in charge of a circuit but once, and then he read a whole class at Channahon out of Church without any kind of trial—a matter the elder righted up. He was one of those eloquent, good-hearted men who lacked the capacity to rule. He was a keen-witted, quick-spirited son of the Green Isle, who had at times almost the eloquence of a Bascom. He was a pious, useful man, and will live in the memories of hundreds. During the year he was on Sycamore Circuit, when undertaking to swim Deer Creek, near Genoa, he lost his saddle-bags, and barely escaped being drowned. He served the Church as a preacher for nearly fifty years, and was ever active in his labors to extend the gospel kingdom. In December, 1850, his wife died—a wife who had been a great support for nearly forty years. The loss bore so heavily upon him his health began to decline. All his earthly comforts were gone, and he longed to rejoin the companion of his toils in the better land. On the 27th of April, 1851, he preached twice with unusual energy. The next day he returned home, lying down in his buggy, unable to drive. He went to his death-couch, and continued to fail until May 8th, when, without a struggle or a sigh, he breathed his last. When asked if he had any doubts of his acceptance with Christ, he exclaimed: "Not a doubt; not a doubt!" These were his last words.

WILLIAM ROYAL.—There was no more arduous laborer in Northern Illinois in the early day than William Royal. What he lacked in talent he made up in untiring effort to reach the new settlers, and establish the means of grace among them. He was born in Monongahela County, West Virginia, February 24, 1796, joined the Methodist Church in 1817, at the age of twenty-one, and was married in 1818 to Barbara Ebey. He came West and was admitted to the Illinois Conference in 1831, and sent to Fort Clark (now Peoria) Mission, which then embraced nearly all the territory north of that point. In 1832 he was on Bloomington Circuit, and in 1833 went on to the Ottawa Mission. In 1835 he was appointed to the Fox River Mission. This embraced all the country from Ottawa northwest to Rockford. In the summer he explored the country up Fox River, and along west to Rockford, hunting up the people, establishing appointments, and forming classes. The last work of the Conference year was to organize the class at Rockford. James McKean did more work of exploration west of Rock River than any other man, and William Royal did the same work east of Rock River. Mr. Royal's appointments for 1836 were: Millbrook, Wells's (south of Yorkville), Daniel Pierce's (Oswego), McCarty's (Aurora), Hammer's (east of St. Charles), Charles Gary's, Salt Creek, Elk Grove, Plum Grove, Mark Noble's (on north branch Chicago River,) Wisencraft's (on Des Plaines,) Libertyville, Ladd's (near State line), Marsh's Grove, Deer Grove, Dundee, Crystal Lake, Virginia Settlement,

Pleasant Grove (Marengo), Mason's (two miles below Belvidere), A. F. Enoch's (seven miles northwest of Rockford), Mouth of the Kishwaukie, Lee's (near Sycamore), Seeley's (at Squaw Grove), and Hough's (on Somonauc Creek). He formed the first class at Somonauc and other places.

In 1836-37, Mr. Royal was appointed to the Des Plaines work, whose center was Plainfield and Joliet. He was still, however, on new ground. After this his appointments were in the central part of Illinois. In 1846 he was back again in the bounds of our Conference, being appointed to Little Rock Circuit, and in 1853, after being on the superannuated list for some years, he went with his son, Fletcher Royal, and other friends, to Oregon. Here he engaged in the good work of distributing tracts, and acting as agent of the Conference Tract Society. In 1860 he was appointed to the Portland Mission. From 1862 to 1867 he was tract agent again. From 1867 till his death in 1870 he was superannuated. His whole life was one of simple devotion to the work of saving souls. His closing hours were full of expressions of profound faith in the religion he had preached. At his death in 1870, he was seventy-four years of age, and had been a member of the Methodist Church for fifty-three years.

MILES L. REED.—A perfect driver, a storming preacher, was reported among the honored dead in 1857. He was born in Mt. Morris, New York, December 18, 1821, and was thirty-seven years of age at his death. The father being blind, the family was poor, and Miles did the best he could to acquire an education. In youth he was excessively fond of theatrical amusements, and was preserved from following them up by the sudden death of a young friend. By this event he was awakened and converted, in the bounds of the Genesee Conference in 1838, being at the time seventeen years of age. In 1839 he came to Illinois as a member of Horace Miller's family, with whom he resided a short time, six miles south of Rockford. Mr. Miller aided him to an education, and at Mt. Morris, as one of the earliest students of Rock River Seminary, he pursued his studies for some time. During this time he received license to preach, and in 1843 was employed by H. Crews, presiding elder of Chicago District, on Geneva Circuit, in Wisconsin. In 1844 he was employed in the bounds of the Milwaukee District, and in 1845 received into the Rock River Conference, and appointed to Plattville, Wisconsin. In 1846 he was appointed to Troy Circuit, and in 1847, on account of ill-health, he was discontinued. He literally worked himself to death. He engaged in a Bible agency for a time, and in 1851 was again admitted to Conference, and appointed to Mt. Carroll. In 1852–53 he was at Joliet, where he built a church; in 1854–55 at Lockport, where he built another church; and in 1856 was appointed to Freeport. Early in the winter there were many indications of disease, and he was soon compelled to resign his charge, when he was immediately confined to his room, where he lived, suffering, praying, and praising, until July 4, 1857, when he departed to the land where faithful laborers are at rest. On his dying couch he observed: "I have sometimes thought I might not be prepared to meet death without fear, but now I have no fear! I find a fullness in the promises of God never realized before! I have a free access into his favor through Jesus Christ, my Lord, that so fills me with his perfect love that I leave my family and all without regret, to be forever with the Lord!" Miles Reed preached in a storm, and worked in every sermon as though the fate of the people hung upon his word. He was eccentric, enthusiastic, and a great revivalist. At Mt. Carroll he had a revival which resulted in the conversion of one hundred and fifty persons, during which time he gained the epithet of "Hell Fire" preacher. He was a Benjamin Abbott polished up; a Peter Cartwright, with a deeper devotion to God and to soul-saving; a church-builder, a revivalist, a son of thunder, a man of God. Wherever he went he left a name behind him not soon to be forgotten. The first Sabbath after his death the Church at Lockport held services commemorating his life and death, and the church was draped in black. It were well if the Rock River Conference had more men equal to Miles L. Reed in zeal.

Mr. ANDREW NEWCOMER was one of the leaders in all Methodist affairs at Mt. Morris from 1846 until his death in 1885. It is a grand thing to look

Andrew Newcomer.

upon laymen who have been members of one Church for forty or more years. In the great day it will be of more account than to have been a Vanderbilt or a Wellington. Mr. Newcomer was born in Washington County, Maryland, November 25, 1810. He was a descendant of Wolfgang Newcomer, who came from Germany over a hundred years ago. His father was a miller, and accordingly Andrew's boyhood was spent in work about the mill; but he afterwards learned the carpenter's trade, but, on coming to Mt. Morris, he set up a furniture store, and afterwards became a merchant.

In 1832, being located in Boonsboro, Md., he was converted at the age of twenty-two. He joined the Methodist Church, and from that on was a reliable member. In 1834 he married Miss Eliza Hamilton, sister of William Hamilton, D. D., for years a prominent member of the Baltimore Conference. He tried his hand at editing a paper at one time, the paper being the Boonsboro *Odd Fellow*. This was in 1833.

In 1846, Mr. Newcomer came to Mt. Morris, Illinois. During the years that followed he served the Church as trustee, steward, treasurer, class-leader, and Sunday-school superintendent, and was town supervisor and justice of the peace for many years. He was also trustee of the seminary. In all these things he had the confidence of the people. He was a man of deep and earnest piety, enjoying the fullness of the gospel. His life was a blessing; his memory is fragrant in all parts of Ogle County. He died at Mt. Morris, May 20, 1885.

ANDREW S. W. McCAUSLAND was born in Virginia, June 6, 1825, and died at Ashton, Illinois, April 15, 1867. He was converted at the age of seventeen, licensed to exhort in 1846, and coming to Illinois, was admitted to Rock River Conference in 1851, when he was appointed with L. S. Walker, to McHenry Circuit. In 1852 he went to Paw Paw with S. R. Beggs. In 1853 he was in charge of Paw Paw Circuit. His appointments afterward were, Little Rock, 1854–55; Wyanett, 1856–57; and Lamoille in 1858. From 1859 to 1862 he was on the superannuated list. In the last-named year he returned to the work, and was appointed to North Prairie, where he remained two years. In 1864–65 he was appointed to Milledgeville, and in 1866 to Ashton, where he died in the spring of 1867. Funeral services were held at Ashton, conducted by his presiding elder, W. T. Harlow; the body was then sent to Sandwich for burial. The Mendota District Conference being in session at Newark, adjourned, and seventeen preachers assisted at the closing burial services.

Brother McCausland was a faithful, reliable worker. He built the churches at Plano, Sandwich, and Asbury, and the parsonage in Sandwich, all in two years. He was deeply pious, kindly in disposition, of a florid complexion and sandy hair. He was one of those quiet men whose power consists in influence and perseverance.

JAMES McKEAN, a man whom hundreds remember with the fondest recollections, was born November 24, 1795, and converted in 1824. Such was his apprehension of deserved punishment, and his sorrow for having grieved his God, he could find no rest for many days after his awakening. Great, therefore, was his joy when he obtained an evidence of sins forgiven. So manifest was the change wrought, and so powerful the witness given, he never doubted the reality of the blessing. In a short time after his conversion he began to feel it his duty to preach the gospel, but his sense of the want of gifts for the work of a minister, united with his natural timidity, were so great he paused for a time before he would enter so momentous a work. At last he yielded to duty, and received license to preach from Charles Holiday. In 1828, when thirty-three years of age, he was received into the Illinois Conference, and appointed to Paoli, in Indiana. His charges from that time were Sangamon, Vermillion, Mt. Carmel, Wabash, Paris, and Embarras. In 1835 he came into our limits, and labored on the new Buffalo Grove Mission. In 1848 he went to Prophetstown, which was his last circuit. He then took a superannuated relation, in which he continued until his death. He resided for many years at Buffalo Grove, where he died of erysipelas, May 28, 1856. During these years of superannuation, he came up to Conference almost every year asking for work; but on account of an attack of "milk-sickness" many years before, his nervous system had been unstrung, and he was afflicted with lethargy, which caused him to drop asleep frequently while sitting in the pulpit, or while on his knees at secret prayer. He was never regarded as a preacher of great talent, but his zeal and goodness made him useful above most, wherever he went. His work was accomplished by visiting from house to house, holding class and prayer meetings and protracted meetings. He was emphatically given to hospitality, the preachers always finding a home at his house. While superannuated, he still preached in the neighborhoods around. He had an appointment on the very last Sabbath of his life, but being on his death-bed he could not go. His last sickness was painful; but amid his pains he expressed a firm trust in the great Redeemer. A little time before his departure he took his wife by the hand, and in a most touching manner alluded to the trials and travels in the vineyard of the Lord along the frontiers of the West. Finishing up the task of bidding his family adieu, he fell asleep in Jesus. To Brother McKean may be given the credit of commencing more new appointments west of Rock River than any other man. In many of the prominent places of that portion of the Conference James McKean preached the first sermon, and organized the first class.

JOHN THOMAS MITCHELL was by all voices declared to be pre-eminently the leading man of the Rock River Conference from 1840 until 1844. This is a world of change, and perhaps there is nothing in it that so often changes its phases as a Methodist Conference. Ministers do not average a continuance in the work of more than ten years, and the years are ever bringing a new class of men. Between the years 1835 and 1845 there was no more influential set of men in the Rock River Conference bounds than the Mitchells. Of these there were three brothers—John T., James, and Francis T.—and their cousin, W. W. Mitchell, three of whom were the preachers at Galena within the space of ten years. The family was originally from Virginia. The father of John T., Samuel Mitchell, was a prominent local preacher for more than half a century. He moved to Illinois with his family in 1817, and settled at Belleville, St. Clair County, setting free his negroes in Virginia before he came. He settled at Platteville, Wisconsin, some time previous to 1840. At the Conference at Platteville in 1841, and again at Chicago in 1842, Father Mitchell, by special vote, was given a seat on the platform.

J. T. Mitchell was born August 20, 1810, in Salem, Botetourt County, Virginia, and was just twenty-four years of age when sent to Chicago in 1834. He enjoyed all the privileges of education at hand in his day. Removing with his father's family to Southern Illinois in 1817, he was reared amid the scenes of a new country. In 1829, John attended a camp-meeting, and becoming awakened, he set out to become a Christian, and united with the Church. He did not, however, receive an evidence of his acceptance until some months after. When attending another camp-meeting, he wrestled hard all through until the last morning, when he was permitted to feel the love of God shed abroad in his heart. In 1830 he commenced teaching school, a business through which most of our great men have graduated to honorable positions. What great man in our land is there who never taught school? At the same time young Mitchell became assistant superintendent of a Sabbath-school. He soon felt that duty called to the ministry, and preached his first sermon April 13, 1831, in Hillsboro. In the fall of this year he set out for Conference. The Illinois Conference met at Indianapolis. It was a long and tedious journey, performed on horseback. At the close of the Conference he received his first appointment, which was at Jacksonville. He came into the Conference with William M. Daily, William Royal, Barton Randall, and others, and had Peter Cartwright for his first presiding elder.

John T. at once commenced a course of study, and was from that time what every Methodist preacher must be who succeeds—a close and severe student. He studied philosophy, mathematics, general literature, and Latin and Greek. This was the course pursued by many of the preachers of the early day. All the wisdom of Methodism is not displayed in 1896! We hail with joy the *Biblical Institute* and its graduates, but there were students among Methodist preachers before 1853.

In 1832, Mr. Mitchell went to Galena, remaining two years; in 1834, to Chicago. In 1836 he was returned to Jacksonville, where he remained two years. In 1838-39 he was at Springfield. In 1840 he fell into the bounds of the Rock River

Conference, and was appointed to Chicago District, at which time he was but thirty years old. In 1843 he was stationed at Mt. Morris, and made agent of Rock River Seminary. At the Conference of 1843 he was elected one of the four delegates of the Rock River Conference to the General Conference, and at the General Conference of 1844 was elected Assistant Book Agent at Cincinnati. For four years he performed the duties of this post with ability; and at the close of his term of service in 1848—on account of the difficulties of his brother James in the Rock River Conference, and from the fact that his connections with Ohio had become so fraternal—he transferred to the Ohio Conference, and was stationed in Cincinnati. He remained in Ohio until the time of his death, filling the best stations, acting as presiding elder on prominent districts, serving as secretary in the Cincinnati Conference from 1851 to 1863, and being several times elected delegate to the General Conference. Most of these years he was also chairman of the Book Committee, which had supervision of the Western Book Concern. In every Conference where he belonged he was an ardent friend of education, leading off in educational measures. As a minister, and especially as a presiding elder, he had few equals. At camp-meetings his commanding presence swayed the throng, and some of the most sweeping meetings of that kind ever held in the bounds of the Rock River Conference were conducted by J. T. Mitchell. As a preacher, he was of the Southern type—warm-hearted, eloquent, and sometimes, at camp-meetings, overwhelming. He seemed to combine in himself the qualities of Luke Hitchcock and Hooper Crews. A business man, and thoughtful, yet emotional and kind-hearted. Tall and commanding in person, he stood, we judge, most prominent of all the men of the Conference of 1840. The question sometimes arises as to who among the preachers of the first decade of the Rock River Conference stood the noblest. Our own judgment would at once lead us to select John T. Mitchell, Hooper Crews, A. E. Phelps, John Clark, Luke Hitchcock, and Richard Haney; and some think that first of these, all things considered, was John T. Mitchell.

As early as 1836 he professed the blessing of perfect love, and this fullness was the swaying power of his life.

Saturday, March 21, 1863, he was seized with bleeding at the lungs. From this time he began to fail, and felt that his end was approaching. To a member of the Church in Cincinnati he said: "I am going home to rest; the port is in sight. You and I have often sung together here on earth; we will sing no more here, but we'll sing up yonder. My peace flows as a river. I have a desire to depart and to be with Christ."

To another he said: "I am waiting in weakness and pain, but not impatient, for God to call me home. I am ready to go at any moment." To another he remarked: "My only desire to live is to live for God, the Church, and my boys." To his Conference he sent word: "I am too young to leave words of counsel, but I hope the Cincinnati Conference will always be a burning and a shining light. This message I send to my German as well as my English brethren, for I feel a deep interest in our German work."

When his host, Brother Riddle, asked him one morning how he felt, he answered: "Struggling into life! struggling into life!"

May 26th he set out to visit his sister at Red Wing, Minnesota, in charge of his son. In the evening he was placed in a sleeping-car, in which he rode pleasantly to Chicago. On Thursday evening he left the city for Dunleith, whence he took steamboat and started up the river. At half-past seven o'clock in the morning of Saturday, May 30, 1863, while gliding along up the Mississippi River, he quietly fell asleep! Thus passed away, at the age of fifty-three, one of the noblest of the Methodist pioneers of Northern Illinois!

He was secretary of the Rock River Conference in the years 1841–42 and 1843. He was the first really settled pastor of the Methodist Church in Chicago. Jesse Walker and S. R. Beggs had preceded him, but were mere missionaries to a forming society. In 1834 the new frame church was built. Grant Goodrich, Robinson, Tripp, and many others whose names live in our memories, had come to the rising young city, and when J. T. Mitchell went there in that year all things were ready for laying the foundations of the society on solid ground. He had just (in 1833) built at Galena, the first church in the Conference, and from that he went to establish the society in the second church of the Conference. His wise plans planted the new field so skillfully it never after failed to produce fruit to the glory of God. It was a blessing indeed to Chicago Methodism to have in its first decade Mitchell, Borein, and Hooper Crews.

WILLIAM W. MITCHELL labored in the bounds of the Conference but one and a half years, and this at Galena, beginning in 1837. He was a cousin of John T. Mitchell, and may take rank as probably the first college graduate that ever labored in Northern Illinois. It is probable we did not have another until 1854, when Josiah Gibson, who was a graduate of the Edinburgh University, Scotland, came into our bounds.

William Mitchell was born in Virginia, February 16, 1815, being but twenty-two years of age when sent to Galena. He was the son of James Mitchell, of Belleville, Illinois. His grandfather, Edward Mitchell, a local preacher of some note, came from Virginia to Illinois in an early day. The father of W. W. designed him for the bar, and educated him for that purpose, but while studying in Yale College he was happily converted. This momentous event changed the whole course of his life. Whatever the father wished, God designed him for the pulpit. When he returned home and informed his father of his change of purpose, it was with great reluctance he consented to the new views; but said if he had known William was to be a preacher, he would not have given him a classical education. He was admitted on trial into the Illinois Conference in 1834, and appointed to Lebanon Circuit. He remained at Lebanon six months, and was then removed to Vandalia to take the place of the preacher there whose health had failed. While at Vandalia, in his pastoral visits he met with several persons who professed to enjoy the blessing of perfect love. He became deeply interested in the matter, and never rested until in his own heart he enjoyed the divine fullness. This gave stability to his character, and zeal and power to his life.

In 1837 he was sent away to the North to look after the new societies in and about Galena. This was a new, strange thing to have a late Yale student in the work; but his knowledge, directed by grace, was power. During his first winter at Galena a great revival took place in the Church, commencing at the close of 1837, and continued with interest till some time in January, 1838, when it was abruptly interfered with by a most calamitous occurrence. At twelve o'clock one bitter, cold night the cry of fire arose, and the little band of Methodists hurried out to see their little church, built in 1833, reduced to ashes! For five years they had worshiped in it. It had been a great struggle to erect it. Within its walls they had joined in many a triumphant song. There souls had been converted, there they had kneeled at the communion altar, there they had oft told of the triumphs of redeeming grace; but now they were without a place of worship.

On the following Sabbath Mr. Mitchell preached to his little flock in the Chamber of Commerce, an upper room on Main Street. Could he be at a loss for a text? He chose Isaiah lxiv, 11: "Our holy and our beautiful house, where our fathers praised thee is burned up with fire; and all our pleasant things are laid waste!"

A person who was present says Mr. Mitchell had scarcely read his text before he burst into tears, and could scarcely go on with his sermon.

Somewhat strengthened by the addition of twenty or thirty converts, the brave society at once resolved to rebuild. The Sunday-school was temporarily suspended. Preaching was usually held at the Chamber of Commerce rooms; sometimes in private houses. One quarterly-meeting was held in the basement of the new court-house. The new church was of brick. The citizens were liberal with contributions and service. The stones were quarried out of the hill back of the church, and many of the brick were hauled from Plattville, twenty miles away. The basement was soon ready for use. Mr. Mitchell was returned to Galena in 1838, but the church debt was so burdensome and the society so weak he became discouraged after a few months, and returned to the southern part of the State. He was never after appointed to work in the bounds of Rock River. He continued in the Illinois Conference until the Southern Illinois Conference was set off. After that, until his death, he was a member of the last-named Conference. Here he filled various appointments, being presiding elder for some time, until his death, March 9, 1869. His last appointment was to Edwardsville Station. His last year there his health failed. Removing to Richview, after severe suffering for a year he passed away in holy joy.

MR. ELISHA B. LANE, a veteran in the Church, passed away from his earthly toils February 6, 1884. He was born at Hampton Falls, N. H., May 6, 1815. When he was six years of age his father died. He came to Chicago, October 21, 1836, and there made his home during life, being in the employ of the Rock Island Railroad for several years, and for eighteen years in some of the county offices. He was converted in Peter Borein's great revival in 1838, and joined the old Clark Street Church. In 1846 he went to Canal Street Church, where he made his Christian home until his death in 1884. His was an active Christian life, he having discharged duties as a leader, steward, and trustee for years. He was a Bible-loving, patient, faithful, conscientious, energetic, every-day, consistent Christian. He died of heart disease suddenly, without a struggle.

SAMUEL GURDON LATHROP was born in Sharon, Schoharie County, N. Y., March 24, 1820. He attended school until fourteen, when he entered the cotton mills at Whitesboro, where his character was so sure and his ways so intelligent he was soon made confidential assistant. His parents were Methodists, and at sixteen Samuel was converted. He at once felt that he must enter the ministry, and he availed himself of the opportunity of fitting for college in a private class, which contained several young men from the mills. One of these was Bishop E. G. Andrews. The class met at five o'clock in the morning!

At nineteen he spoke to the proprietor of the mills concerning his duty to enter the ministry. This man pointed out the fact that his present position would soon make him participate in the mills' prosperity. But duty before prosperity is the impulse of every true man called of God for His work.

Young Lathrop spent a few months in Cazenovia Seminary, and then, in 1842, entered the Oneida Conference, and was appointed to Warren. July, 1843, he was married to Miss Cynthia Clery. While a member of the Oneida Conference he filled pulpits at Clinton, Andover, Vernon, Madison, Deansville, Earlville, Manlius, and Ithaca. In 1857 he was transferred to Rock River Conference, and appointed to Indiana Street, Chicago. From this charge he went to Dixon in 1859. Here he labored three years, and saved the Church property, which was nearly overwhelmed with debt. While at Dixon the war came; and in and out of the pulpit he was at all times for the Union. Indeed, it may as well be said that it would not take the fingers of one hand to number the Rock River Conference preachers who were not enthusiastically for the Union. Mr. Lathrop was chosen chaplain of two regiments, but in each case his Church decided that his duty lay in the pastorate.

He was afterwards at Joliet. He saw that the duties of the chaplain were performed in a perfunctory way, and determined to bring about a reform that should give the prisoners the benefit of sincere Christian teaching. Through his efforts the Prisoners' Aid Society was formed, whose purpose was to look after the religious and enlightening needs of the prisoners. The reform was beneficial and lasting. When his time expired at Joliet, he went to work as agent of the Aid Society. He filled this thankless position for three years. Scores of ex-convicts after this led happy, honest lives, as results of Mr. Lathrop's efforts while in this work.

In 1867 the Sunday-school Union of the Methodist Church in Chicago determined upon a more active missionary policy. Mr. Lathrop was called to superintend the work. During his labors, Dixon Street, Halsted Street, Langley Avenue, Michigan Avenue, Western Avenue, Simpson, and several other missions, were founded. Churches were built for four or five of the missions. During these years he had three or four services a day. The history of Chicago Methodism written in the future must, if accurate, contain frequent references to S. G. Lathrop's labors in forming these city missions, which are already prosperous Churches.

In 1869 the secretary of the Missionary Society, late Bishop W. L. Harris, appointed Mr. Lathrop superintendent of missions in Montana. With Governor Ashley, he made a tour of the Territory, holding meetings and establishing societies. Here he proved a power for good. One who knew him wrote: "No man was ever loved in Montana as

Brother Lathrop; no man had more warm friends, and the good he did there no man can know."

After two years he returned to Evanston. He took the agency of the Bible Society for Cook County, in which service he was engaged until disease prevented further work.

As he neared his end, good words came. A Nebraska editor said: "How I would love to see that dear man! I was one of seven boys whom he baptized and took into the Church thirty years ago; and what I have I owe to him." One of the Indiana Street boys said: "All I have I owe to Brother Lathrop."

While at Dixon he published "Gathered Gems," and after, "Crime and Its Punishment," and "Fifty Years and Beyond." He died November 21, 1884.

GEORGE LOVESEE was born in the State of New York in 1826, and came with his parents to Illinois, and settled in Roscoe, in 1836. His parents were originally from England, and before leaving their native land were members of the Wesleyan Church. On their arrival in the United States they joined the Methodist Episcopal Church. In this Church, George Lovesee was trained, and early became a subject of converting grace and united with the Church. So rapidly did he develop in grace and knowledge that he was recommended to the Rock River Conference in 1846, when he was but twenty years of age. He was admitted to the Conference in 1846, and sent as junior preacher to the Geneva Circuit, Wisconsin.

He was, more than most, a natural student; but for some reason was not admitted into full connection with the Conference until 1849. From the time of his admission till his death, with the exception of a year, he continued in the effective relation, and regularly received work. His last charge was Dover, where he was appointed in 1873. As soon as he commenced his work on this charge the people were greatly impressed with the ability and spirit of his preaching. His congregations increased, his Church revived, and in all his ministry before the prospect for good had not been so favorable. The Church had been a long time depressed by a combination of influences, and was now cheered by the hope of better days. The prospect was also cheering to a preacher whose labors, though always acknowledged as good and sound, were not as aggressive as could be desired. On the 5th of February he was riding in a buggy with a lady. When crossing a railway, a dashing train struck the vehicle, tossing it into the air, and killing both minister and lady. Thus passed out of the scenes of new hope and cheer so suddenly this tried man, who had worked against rather strong currents for twenty-eight years. Mr. Lovesee was one of those quiet men who are little known in Conference. He never took part in public business. He was a student, a clear-headed man; a preacher whose sermons, if popularized by some of the dash of others, would have made a fame. He lacked the peculiar "snap" that is requisite to make one of the most efficient Methodist preachers; but he was elaborate, thoughtful, solid. He excelled as a writer, and many of the contributions from his pen to our Church periodicals were works of more than common merit. His poems especially were fine. One on the Madiai, a persecuted Catholic family, in the *National Magazine* for April, 1854, is really excellent. We add one verse to verify our assertion:

> "Welcome, felon chain and fetter;
>   Tyrant power is strong;
> Right may suffer for a season
>   By the hand of wrong,
> But the pulse that razeth cities,
>   Chain it if you can!
> Thus shall muzzled thought in triumph
>   Overthrow the Vatican.
> When the moral earthquake heaveth,
>   Truth shall perch on freedom's dome,
> Vipers creep, with vultures brooding
>   O'er the fallen towers of Rome!"

MARTIN KRINBILL.—From 1840 on, for several years, the old Clark Street Sunday-school had no more faithful laborer than Mr. Martin Krinbill. He was born near Colmar, France, in 1820, and came to this country with his parents when quite small. He was converted when quite young, and his father was converted while his son was praying for him. In 1842–45 he was a clerk in a Chicago store. About 1845 he went into storekeeping, with two others as partners. But after years he went to Freeport, where he married Cynthia Atkins. He died very suddenly of heart disease, February 2, 1884. The Friday before was one of the happiest days in all his history. The great tears of joy rolled down his face as he said: "I am so happy in God." In a moment more he added: "I am so glad that I gave God my heart when a boy. He has kept me safely, and blessed me constantly; and this is the brightest day of all!" Sometimes— it may be—the Great Father is preparing his saints, unknown to themselves, for their great journey.

LEANDER S. WALKER, at his death, was the oldest member of the Conference who had done work in its bounds, excepting S. R. Beggs. His first appointment in our bounds was to Sycamore Circuit in 1837. He was born in Claremont, New Hampshire, April 24, 1809. He was converted in Michigan in 1828, at the age of nineteen, at which time he joined the Methodist Church. He was at the time an inmate of his father's family, which had removed to Michigan some time before. In 1830 young Walker went to Indiana, where, in September, 1833, he received license to preach. A few weeks after receiving this Church commission he united with the Illinois Conference, which at that time embraced the State of Indiana. His first appointment was to Jonesboro; his second, in 1834, was to Peoria; his third, in 1835, to Iroquois Mission; his fifth, in 1837, to Sycamore. From that time every charge he filled was in the bounds of the Rock River Conference.

While on the Iroquois Mission, in 1836, he married Miss Miriam Palmer, who labored with him as an efficient helper for forty-eight years,

The Illinois Conference of 1838 appointed a committee to locate the Rock River Seminary. That committee, which consisted of John Clark, L. S. Walker, Peter R. Borein, W. S. Crissey, and T. S. Hitt, met in John Clark's log-cabin, on Fox River, near Aurora, in March, 1839, when the following places were proposed: Joliet, Mt. Morris, St. Charles, Geneva, Elgin, Rockford, Roscoe, and Kishwaukie. These places were invited to enter competition. In the end, only three places made offer of assistance. Roscoe offered a subscription of $2,000, and lands which they valued at $5,000; Kishwaukie made about the same offer, and the Maryland Colony offered a subscription of $8,000, indorsed by three of the principal men, and 320 acres of land. In May the committee decided in favor of the latter proposition; and when, not long after, the trustees met to lay off the land, John Clark proposed that the town be called Mt. Morris, after Bishop T. A. Morris. L. S. Walker from that early day was an earnest friend of the seminary. Some of his last years of labor (1866–68) were passed as agent of the seminary. There surely was blame somewhere that that old first school should have been left to die! For ten years there has been no Methodist school between the Fox and Mississippi Rivers.

Mr. Walker's last appointment was at Prophetstown. While here his health completely failed, and taking a superannuated relation, he retired permanently from the work. In 1871 he removed to Clarendon Hills, and in 1878 to Rock Island, where he died at the residence of his daughter Melsena (Mrs. J. W. Stark), December 13, 1884.

It was thirty-eight years from his first labors till his last, and from his first appointment till his death fifty-one years. Fifty-six years a Christian; fifty-one a minister! In the pastorate he was much beloved, and uniformly successful. His love for the institutions and doctrines of the Church were deep and abiding. No sacrifice the Church demanded was too great. He cheerfully endured privation in the days when the heroic band who constituted the Rock River Conference at its beginning planned so wisely and well, and planted deep and broadly the foundations of religious and civil prosperity. He was, as well as an ardent Christian, a dignified Christian gentleman with spotless character. His last years were spent in great feebleness, and all the time under increasing bodily infirmities. But all this time he never doubted, never murmured. He had learned to labor, to suffer, and to wait. He was helpless, but conscious to the last, and rejoiced greatly in his preparation for death. When he could no longer speak, he wrote in his diary the following lines:

"The sacred leaves of autumn life are falling slowly,
But each leaf is gilded with the hope of glory."

He had a large family. One of them, Harriet, became the wife of J. A. Northrup, once a missionary to Bombay, India.

L. S. Walker's appointments were as follows: 1833 (Illinois Conference), Jonesboro; 1834, Peoria;

1835, Iroquois; 1836, Vermillion; 1837, Sycamore; 1838, Rockford; 1839, Crystal Lake; 1840 (Rock River Conference), Sycamore; 1841, Buffalo Grove; 1842, Mt. Morris; 1843–44, Daysville (Lighthouse); 1845–46, Princeton; 1847–48, Roscoe; 1849–50, Chemung; 1851–52, McHenry; 1853, Roscoe; 1854–58, superannuate; 1858–59, Winnebago; 1860–61, Marengo; 1862–63, Durand; 1864–65, Rochelle; 1866, Byron; 1867–68, agent for Rock River Seminary; 1868–69, Bethel; 1870, Prophetstown. In 1884 he died.

WARREN TAPLIN.—Among the young men of the Conference who have died, few have left such impressions of their worth as Warren Taplin. He was born in East Corinth, Vermont, June 16, 1834, and was converted in 1852. Being called of God to the work of the ministry, he improved every means that would fit him to be a workman that needed not to be ashamed. He graduated at the Biblical Institute in November, 1860, and at the Northwestern University in June, 1861, in which last year he was received into the Conference. But instead of taking regular work he taught at the university two years, when, in 1863, he was appointed to Yorkville, in Kendall County. Here he labored till his health failed under overwork. This failure was really due to the exertion of walking to appointments, and then in a tired condition preaching. His last sermon was preached in the Yorkville Church August 13, 1864. From this time he lingered in declining consumption till October 19,

1865, when he departed to the land of rest. His death occurred in Wisconsin, from whence his body was brought to Yorkville for burial; and after a kindly sermon by his old friend C. H. Fowler, we deposited his body in the burial-ground near Bristol Station, where he lies beside a child that died a year before, and his intelligent wife who departed a year after. While the grave remains, his name will be spoken with reverence in and about Yorkville.

WILLIAM DRAKE SKELTON was born in England in 1835, and in 1855, at the age of nineteen, came with his father's family and settled in Chicago. Not more than a week passed after his arrival before he was appointed in charge of Marengo by the presiding elder. He was converted in early childhood, and had been licensed to preach before coming from England. Not long before his death he remarked to a friend that one of the earliest things he could remember was the enjoyment of the love of God in his heart. This early piety gave strength to his character, and induced him to urge upon the young the blessedness of loving the Lord in early years. His father intended him for the profession of law; but after three years of work in a law office, he came home one day and said, "Mother, I can't be a lawyer;" and that ended his labors in that line. He was admitted to Rock River Conference in 1856, and appointed junior preacher on the Chemung Circuit. His appointments thereafter were Harrison, Flora, Rockton, Elizabeth, West Indiana Street, Chicago, Rockford, Sycamore, and Princeton. In 1858 he was united in marriage with Eleanor L. Lawsha, with whom he had become acquainted when on the Chemung charge. He died at Princeton, January 9, 1874. During his last sickness his thoughts were as full of his work as ever. To one friend he said: "Brother W., you ought to be doing more good than you are; you might be very useful." To a brother in the ministry he said: "This gospel I have preached sustains and cheers me; it is all I expected to find it." When asked by one how he felt, he said: "Peace, peace; no ecstasy. I am trusting; I know Him." Two weeks before his death he was asked if he had any message for his brethren of the Conference. He replied: "Yes, tell them not to overwork as I have done, and fall in the midst of their years." He saw so much work to be done for the Master it filled all his dying thoughts. He was buried beside his father in Graceland Cemetery, Chicago. The writer of these pages was for many years statistical secretary of the Conference, and from time to time, as old ones were taken from him, he sought out new men as assistants. W. D. Skelton served as assistant for some time, but was drawn away into higher secretarial duties, and was fast rising in the business work of the Conference sessions, as well as in importance as a preacher in the pulpit. He was one of those growing men whose possibilities are only known as the years go on. At the early age of thirty-nine he was loved, trusted, and looked upon as one just beginning to rise. He was neat, precise, pure, a model of a Christian minister.

Marshall Sherman.—Few persons are remembered in the country, from Dundee to Elgin and the regions round about, with greater affection than Marshall Sherman, almost a life-long local preacher. He was born in Connecticut, April 15, 1799. When a child his parents moved to Franklin County, Vermont, where he lived until 1837, when he moved to Illinois and settled between Dundee and Elgin. He had married, in 1822, Miss Sarah Wanzer, who shared his toils for forty-three years. Mr. Sherman, from early youth, was an active, a real live member of the Methodist Church. He was licensed to exhort in Vermont in 1830 by Joel Squire, and not long after was licensed to preach. This license was renewed every year until he was ordained local deacon in 1840.

His daughter married Joseph Lewis, who was on the Elgin Circuit in 1842. When her first husband died she married a Brother Adams, a local preacher at Beloit, and became a noted religious worker through all the regions round about.

Brother Sherman, after being confined to his bed in a partially paralyzed condition for ten weeks, died November 21, 1879, in New Hampton, Iowa.

Marshall Sherman was one of those men that made himself felt and known wherever he went. His preaching glowed with a holy ardor, and went forth with power.

Elihu Springer, who appeared in our bounds in 1835, was born in Bond County, Illinois, July 21, 1811; and was the first native of Illinois who labored in the bounds of this Conference. Mr. Springer was reared by pious parents, who, amid the noise of battle and din of savage life, were true to their Christian integrity. "The first thing of which I have any recollection," says Brother Springer, "was my father collecting the family around the family altar." McKendree, Jesse Walker, Joseph Oglesby, and others, were visitors in his father's house when he was a boy, "and the impressions made by their faithful instructions," says he, "are engraved as with the point of a diamond on the pages of my recollection." In September, 1824, at a camp-meeting held on the old Shiloh campground, St. Clair County, he was happily converted, and immediately became connected with the Methodist Episcopal Church. In the fall of 1827 he was sent to the Rock Spring Seminary, a Baptist institution, where his religion was severely tried. Being nearly the only professor among the students, he was made the subject of ridicule. "I was taunted," he said, "with being a professor of religion and a Methodist; and was hissed and hooted out of company." But through all he stood firm, until two or three other professors came into the vicinity, with whom he met once or twice a week for prayer and mutual instruction. He received license to exhort in 1832 from John Dew. March 10, 1833, he was married to Martha B. Scarritt, daughter of Isaac Scarritt, by A. E. Phelps. His license to preach dates from June 30, 1833, signed by Simon Peter, presiding elder. Surely he received authority from a high source! In September he was admitted into the Illinois Conference, and sent to Carlinville. In 1834 he was appointed to Iroquois Mission, and in 1835 to Deplane. This year his health failed, and in 1836 he located, in which relation he remained until 1838, when he was readmitted, and appointed to Somonauk Circuit. His appointments after this were: 1839–40, Milford; 1841, Lockport; 1842, Joliet; 1843, Dupage; 1844, St. Charles; 1845, Mineral Point, Wisconsin; 1846, Hazel Green; 1847–50, presiding elder on Milwaukee District, where, in the midst of labors and usefulness, he died of cholera. He had been making a tour of his district, and returned home worn with labor and care. On the 20th of August, 1850, closing his quarterly-meeting for the Watertown charge, he took dinner with David Brooks and S. R. Thorp, appearing as well as usual. In the afternoon he rode on to Oconomowoc, where his next quarterly-meeting was to be held. He put up for the night at the house of a Brother Worthington, took tea with usual relish, and retired in good season. In the evening devotions, which he led, he manifested unusual earnestness, especially in praying for the Church and his family. At three o'clock in the morning he was taken with cholera. Medical aid was quickly called. He requested J. W. Wood, who was with him, to call in the friends and have a season of prayer. In the devotions he was much interested, and responded with great feeling. He lingered until six in the evening, and then died.

He was a man of robust form, strong muscle,

and capable of enduring fatigue, and had more than usual strength of mind. As a preacher he was solid rather than brilliant, and well versed in theology. As an elder he was very popular. He was a live Illinoisian, a bold veteran, a hard worker, a strict disciplinarian, and a beautiful singer of the old Methodist hymns—a very common accomplishment, by the way, of the old preachers. He had a good stock of assurance, which led him into opposition to error and evil; and at one time he published a series of articles in a Chicago Universalist paper opposing Universalism. There was a speck of confidence in his nature which bordered on self-esteem. The writer well remembers his reading very complacently one of the articles above mentioned at our breakfast-table at George F. Foster's, in 1844, which he had written the evening before. He was not aware of the hurry of Chicago people, and did not realize the uneasiness with which his host sat during the reading of the polemical effort, waiting for its close that he might go to his daily business.

ISAAC SCARRITT never in reality traveled a circuit in the Rock River Conference, nor was he ever a member, save the last nine months of his life; but his connection with the work is such he deserves honorable mention. He was born in Connecticut, June 3, 1775. Receiving the common-school education of that day, he grew up to manhood ignorant of experimental religion, but possessed correct and industrious habits. He had been in the habit of attending the Baptist Church regularly, but he knew nothing of conversion as it is now taught and understood. He had never heard a relation of the rich experiences of grace that are so frequently heard nowadays. One day, while in the sugar-bush alone, at work making sugar, there came upon him a deep sense of his sinfulness. God met him there in the woods, and he felt fully his need of a Savior. Full of distress, he knelt at the foot of a tree to pray, and suddenly a strange peace and joy floated through every avenue of his soul. The days passed on, and he continued in the same happy frame of mind. He concluded to join the Baptist Church; but before an opportunity offered, he heard a sermon from E. H. Sabin, a Methodist presiding elder. Its unction and living spirit chimed with the new experiences of his life. That sermon was the turning-point in his history. The elder was invited home to his father's house, and his conversation was more profitable than the sermon. Young Scarritt soon united with the Methodist Church, and Brother Sabin became his religious teacher. Buying a farm, he prepared to settle in business; but soon felt that he must preach the gospel. Preparing himself, he accompanied Elder Sabin in his travels; and at the second quarterly-meeting after he thus set out with the elder he preached his first sermon. At every quarterly-meeting for weeks after that he took turns with the elder in preaching. Having received license to preach, he was admitted to the New England Conference, held in Boston, June 3,

1807, and appointed as junior preacher on Needham Circuit; and in 1808 he went to Durham Circuit. During this year he was attacked with asthma, and rendered incapable of ministerial labor. In hope that the softer, sunny air of a Southern climate would improve his health, Bishop Asbury proposed to send him south of Baltimore; but he was unable to travel so far. He tried medical skill; he tried the seashore; but, disheartened, he returned home "to die under his mother's care." He labored a little about the farm, and his health improved somewhat.

Thus ten years passed; and in 1818 he married, and removed to Illinois, settling near Edwardsville. Another ten years passed, and in 1828 he joined the Illinois Conference, and was sent to Salem to take charge of the Pottawatomie Mission. While here he preached the first sermon ever preached in Chicago. He afterward traveled Kaskaskia Circuit and Fort Clark Mission, and in 1831 located and settled on a claim in Dupage County. The year being ended on Fort Clark Mission, in October, 1831, he left Sandy Creek, where he was living, and went to the forks of Dupage River to provide a home for his family. He had been there before, selected his claim, and preached the first sermon ever preached in the settlement. On arriving at the place, six miles southeast of Naperville, he went to work alone to build a log-cabin. He also had grass to cut for wintering the horses and cow he was so fortunate as to own. One man, who commenced work in the spring, had raised some potatoes, some of which Mr. Scarritt bought; on which, and some pork he was so fortunate as to obtain, they were obliged to subsist. Bread was out of the question. The potatoes froze, and at one time the family had nothing to eat but frozen potatoes. By the time the logs of the house were up, and the roof on, winter set in, and about the first of January they moved into their log-house, without floor, chinking, or chimney. In one corner the bed was made on a pile of straw, with blankets hung around to make a bedroom. The Indian War commenced in the spring, and times were trying. Through such privations did our early settlers pass. There Isaac Scarritt remained until about 1858 or 1859, when he removed to the home of his son at Joliet. In 1860, old and ready to depart, he came up for admission to the Rock River Conference, desiring to die with his name on the records. In May, 1861, he finally departed this life, being just eighty-six years of age. He had been a member of the Methodist Church about fifty-six years. His daughter became the wife of Elihu Springer in 1831, and the family have done noble work for the Church.

Speaking of his going home to die in 1809, over fifty years before his death, reminds us of an instance or two, which we relate to encourage invalids. We saw in the hands of Rev. W. H. Smith, in April, 1865, a letter written by Bishop Morris in 1826, when he was a Kentucky presiding elder, to a brother preacher, in which the elder complained of disease, and said he was looking for a speedy departure. He had but one thing to give him trouble in view of death, and that was a "want of the blessing of perfect love." The bishop lived about forty years after that letter was written. Isaac Scarritt went home to die in 1808, but lived till 1861—fifty-three years. Luke Hitchcock, in his early ministerial life, was afflicted with disease of the lungs. In 1838, when on a circuit, his health so failed he was about to give up his work, and he expected soon to close his career. One day he was riding on horseback along a lonely, unfrequented way in New York; and as he rode along he was sighing over the gloomy prospects of his failure as a minister. He looked solemn as the grave. He passed by an old, dilapidated house, in front of which a ragged urchin sat on the fence. As Mr. Hitchcock passed this close observer, he gave one of those sighs which come of the heart-ache. Just as he had passed by, the boy exclaimed, in a slow drawl: "Say, Mister, when you die will you let me have your old hat?" Luke Hitchcock did n't die, as the Church he has served so faithfully the last sixty-two years can testify.

MRS. WILLIAM WHEELER was a faithful member of the great Chicago Methodist family from 1838 on, for nearly forty years. She was born in Canada, November 19, 1814, and was married to William Wheeler in 1833. In 1838 the couple removed to Chicago; and thence on, William Wheeler and wife were among the main supports of Clark Street Church. Late in life, when Trinity Church was organized, made up mostly of up-town members of the old Clark Street Church, the Wheelers united there. During all these years she found time to lend her aid to every good work. She was for some time president of the City Missionary Society of the Methodist Episcopal Church. During her term of service, Grant Place, Park Avenue, and Simpson Churches were established as missions. When Southern secession came, she took an active part in the sanitary fairs which originated with the women of Chicago. She was also connected with the Soldiers' Aid Society, and after the war was one of the managers of the Soldiers' Home. She was also for several years president of the Board of Managers of the Old Ladies' Home, with which she was connected from its foundation. In the centennial year of Methodist history (1866), Mrs. Wheeler was one of the most efficient members of the association which undertook to build Heck Hall, the boarding-room of Garrett Biblical Institute. When the Woman's Temperance Movement began, about 1874, she took hold of the work in Chicago, and during the heat of July and August, with a few other faithful ones, kept the temperance prayer-meeting from dying out. Friends in her last sickness sang, prayed, read the Book of Life. "I just leave my soul to the mercy of God through Jesus Christ my Savior." These were her last words. She died in 1875.

ABSALOM WOOLISCROFT was, perhaps, a man of more notoriety than any member of the Conference at the time of his death. He was an Englishman, who, in early life, as we have been informed, was a play-actor. Being converted, he became a thoroughgoing revivalist, and published a small volume of revival songs, which he sold and used in his meetings. He joined the Kentucky Conference in 1828, and continued to travel important Kentucky Circuits until 1841, when he obtained leave of absence and visited England. In 1842 he located, and turned up at Lynchburg, Virginia, in 1844 in a great revival-meeting. In 1845 he came North to escape a slaveholding Church, and, uniting with the Rock River Conference, was appointed to Lewistown. In 1846 he was at Plattville, Wisconsin; in 1847, at Milford, on Fox River; in 1848–49, at Lafayette; in 1850–51, on Knoxville Circuit; and in 1852 went to Washington Circuit. When appointed to Milford, in 1847, he made hasty inquiries for his work, and learned that Milford was in Iroquois County. He hurried away south a hundred miles from Conference, which had been at Chicago, and the same distance from the true Milford, and arrived at a little burg on Sugar Creek to mystify the people by his inquiries. He went over to Ash Grove and spent the Sabbath, and after a time found that *his* Milford was on Fox River. Milford Circuit was all this impulsive man ever traveled in our limits. In the spring of 1853 he went down from Washington to Peoria on business, and put up at the house of a friend. Being slightly ill, he called for magnesia, and took a moderate dose. By mistake he had taken arsenic! A few hours passed, and this live, whole-souled English worker was no more!

JOSIAH W. WHIPPLE, in 1839, was appointed preacher in charge of Sycamore Circuit, with Leonard F. Molthrop as a supply. Brother Whipple was from near Roscoe, and had just received license to preach. He preached his first sermon on the circuit in the house of Elias Crary, at Chicken Grove. His soul was on fire for the work; and what Peter Borein (who had just died) was at Chicago, such was Josiah Whipple on Sycamore Circuit. Revivals spread everywhere, and the preacher's influence was so telling he was remembered for years after. In 1841 he went with John Clark to Texas to carr on the work in that new country. On the division of the Church, in 1844, Mr. Clark and others returned North, leaving Mr. Whipple behind. In 1841 he was stationed in Austin; in 1842 at Bastrop; and in 1843 and 1844 at Houston. From the beginning he has been one of the most successful men in the Methodist work in that hard field, filling the place of presiding elder on some of the toughest of Texas districts. He had the respect of every one, gangs of rowdy rangers at times riding with him to his appointments to protect him from the Indians. At one time, when the Indians were troublesome, no white man dared to pass through certain portions of Northern Texas. Mr. Whipple had an appointment for a quarterly-meeting at a place beyond the country infested by hostile Indians. The notice of the meeting had been seen

by some men who were having a jolly time at a
tavern. One of them asked: "But Whipple will
not be fool enough to go, will he?" To which another, who knew the man, replied: "You may be
sure that if Whipple has an appointment he will
go to it." Whipple came along. The company
strove to persuade him to postpone the perilous
journey. But he would go on. "Then," said the
crowd of rough riders, "you shall not go alone;"
and a party of twenty volunteered as his escort.
The meeting was thirty miles or more away, and
these men escorted him to the place and back.
Such is the tribute paid almost always to true
heroism. It resulted in gaining him an invitation
to preach at a new point, where his preaching resulted in a good revival. Josiah Whipple, like
many others, married a wife who brought him
slaves. These he held (before the Union War)
nominally; but they were really free to do as they
pleased, and were treated as brethren and sisters
in the Lord. He was still living in Texas in 1894.

DAVID M. BRADLEY.

When the writer of these pages—in November,
1842—first entered the Clark Street Methodist Sunday-school in Chicago, he found in the corner pews
north of the pulpit two classes of boys. The one
nearest the pulpit was taught by Robinson Tripp;
the one back of it was a class of boys about seventeen years of age, taught by D. M. Bradley. Into
this he was placed. Soon after, when he joined the
Church, he was put into Mr. Bradley's Church

class; and from that on for four years the teacher and class-leader molded his life more than any other influence.

In the Church-class I met in closest fellowship my dear schoolmate, Charles A. Stowell, and there I found Mrs. Eliza Garrett. The class met at four o'clock Sunday afternoon. In four years I was absent about four times, and I can not remember being absent when Mrs. Garrett was not there. She was a quiet, reliable, noble Christian woman. Of D. M. Bradley I dare not begin to write! He made me. I loved him as I have never loved any other man. There were times in my wayward boyhood when nearly everything around the Church would lose its hold upon me; but at such times Brother Bradley and his class was the golden chain to bind me until the days of wandering were past. This was particularly true of the first year or two. That leader's photograph hangs framed on the wall in my room before me now as I write, and the joyous eyes yet speak to me words of cheer, and bid me rise, and on!

D. M. Bradley came to Chicago in 1837. He was a printer, and entering the office of the Chicago *Democrat*, edited by John Wentworth, he was the main manager of that office for twenty years. At once, on coming to the city, he became an efficient class-leader, and continued to perform the duties of that office until his death in 1857, keeping, if we mistake not, the same class the whole time. He was a native of Concord, New Hampshire; was raised by a pious mother, and experienced religion under the labors of George Storrs at the age of eighteen. Among his last utterances were: "This is all my hope and all my plea—for me the Savior died;" "It is all through Christ." He died September 8, 1857, and his funeral discourse was preached at the Clark Street Church by Hooper Crews. Text, James iv, 14: "For what is your life?"

After his conversion he sought an education to prepare himself for the ministry; but not having good health, he gave up all efforts in that direction. His quiet yet pathetic voice, uttering melodious strains in speech and song, is yet in its tenderness vibrating upon my ears. He lives in influences untold. He lives and speaks through his son, Professor C. F. Bradley, of the Biblical Institute. He lives in the institutions which were, in unison with Grant Goodrich and others, molded by his hand.

JOEL MANNING.

In most of the prominent Methodist Churches there will generally be found leading laymen, who become, through a sort of necessity, and by common consent, a sort of sub-angels of the Churches. Various circumstances give these men these positions. They were first on the ground, or are liberal in their means; but, in most instances, they have gained these positions because of their wisdom or character, and the deep interest they have taken in all of the matters of the Church. They are not usurpers, but hold their places by general consent of the people, who feel that they can hardly do without them. There have been so many of these men in Rock River Conference it is difficult to enumerate them. There were N. E. Lyman and Judge William Brown, of Rockford; Henry Sherman, of Elgin; Samuel McCarty, of Aurora; A. R. Scranton, George C. Cook, and Grant Goodrich, of Chicago; Otis Hardy, of Joliet; and not least among them, Joel Manning, of Lockport. Mr. Manning filled this position more than most because he happened to be a leader in a small place, never strong, where a man like him was indispensable. Lockport was too near Joliet to prosper; and as the town had hard struggling to maintain position, so the Methodist Church struggled through years of weakness. It is not too much to say that for years, had Joel Manning been absent, Lockport Methodism would have had a hard time to maintain an existence. But for thirty years he was there holding the position.

There is another fact worthy of note. It is said that when a Vermonter was asked what they could raise in Vermont, he answered: "We raise men." This has been curiously illustrated. In several instances, when touring in the East, and writing up local histories, they had to look West for some of their brightest sons to give special luster to their pages. A book on Maine Methodism finds two of its chief characters in O. Lunt and William Deering, citizens of Evanston. A certain town in New Hampshire did the same by John Wentworth. So when the sparsely-settled town of Andover, Vermont, wrote up its history it found one of its leading notables in Joel Manning, of Illinois. And it is curious how many notable men went out from that obscure town. There were William S. Balch, one of the most prominent Universalist preachers; Alvin Adams, originator of Adams Express Company; Austin Adams, a supreme judge of Iowa; and Joel Manning, business manager of the Illinois Canal.

Three brothers, Manning by name, natives of Townsend, Massachusetts, settled in Andover in an early day. The families of Joel and Samuel went up with their families in an ox-cart in 1789. After going to Andover, both of these brothers became converted, and joined the Baptist Church. Joel became a preacher, and in after years was the pastor of the Baptist Church. Joseph Manning about the same time became a Methodist class-leader. The Baptist preacher was one of the most rigid and severe Calvinists, while the class-leader was a severe stickler for Methodist doctrine and discipline. This brought the brothers into frequent conflict. If our subject had any fault, it was a disposition to apply the Methodist discipline too severely, and it would seem, by the above facts, that it ran in the blood.

Joel Manning, of Illinois, was the son of Joel Manning, the preacher mentioned above. He was born at Andover, October 9, 1793. He appears to have been a student from childhood. The Andover history mentioned is made up with contributions from old settlers. One of these, writing to Rev. W. S. Balch, says: "I think your father's children and Joel Manning's children the ablest and most talented of any ever raised in Andover. I think Leland Balch and his brother William, and Joel and John B. Manning, four of the smartest boys ever raised in Andover."

Joel Manning graduated from Union College, Schenectady, New York, in 1818, with many notable men, among whom was Sidney Breeze, judge of the Supreme Court of Illinois, who always spoke of Manning as the mathematician of the class. After graduation, he took charge of Chester Academy in his native town. It is probable that when he settled at Lockport he was about the only graduate among Methodists in the Rock River Conference. In 1819, Joel set out on foot for the West. On the way he followed an Indian trail from Fort Wayne to St. Louis. Often his only stopping-place would be the camp of friendly Indians, whose parched corn and venison would be his only fare.

On arriving at St. Louis, he entered the law-office of Judge Carr, where he commenced the study of law. Illinois had just entered the Union as a State, and Manning located in Brownsville, Jackson County, where he practiced law for a number of years. Here, in 1823, he married Diza Jenkins, a daughter of Solomon Jenkins, who had come, in an early day, from North Carolina. Elizabeth Jenkins, a sister of Mrs. Manning, married Dr. John Logan, the father of General John A. Logan.

When the canal from Chicago to Ottawa was projected, Governor Duncan appointed Joel Manning secretary of the Board of Commissioners. On receiving this appointment, he went at once with his family to Chicago. This was in 1836. In 1838 the office of the board was removed to Lockport, and Mr. Manning at once removed to the new location. From that time until his death, January 8, 1869, for thirty-one years he was the life of the town, and especially of the Methodism of Lockport. The members of the Board were men in other secular employment, and only met occasionally; so it will be seen that Secretary Manning was, during all these years, the real manager of the whole business of the canal. He combined in himself the real work of an executive committee, and no safer, surer man could have been found.

Joel Manning's children have all partaken of his enterprising spirit. Especially is this true of his daughter, Mrs. Cornelia Miller, of Joliet, who is noted for her munificent gifts to Evanston and dozens of other institutions.

Rev. S. F. Denning, who was for a long time Mr. Manning's pastor, says of him: "I regard him as a typical man. As a business man and citizen, he was one who always minded his own business, and yet always found time to lend a helping hand to others. As a Methodist, he was always true as the needle to the pole—always at the place of worship, and always on time. His faith was founded on the Bible and the Methodist Discipline. He believed in the spirit and power of a full salvation. He was always prompt in financial support, and a true Christian to the best of his ability." Another account says he adopted the old Biblical rule of giving one-tenth of his income.

SAMUEL McCARTY.

BY REV. A. W. PATTEN, D. D.

Special honor is due the memory of Christian men who have aided to lay good foundations in the West and elsewhere. It is hard to realize that the man who first settled a city, now large as Aurora is, has but just gone to his rest. Mr. Samuel McCarty, whose death we have recorded recently, was born in Morristown, N. J., March 9, 1810. His parents were descended from old Protestant native families that had been for generations in the State, dating prior to the Revolution, and of Scotch and English extraction. In 1812 his parents went to Elmira, N. Y., where they resided for years on a farm. Samuel received a good common-school education, and later learned the trade of millwright. He reached the site of Aurora, Ill., November 6, 1834, preceded a few months by his brother Joseph. Aurora at that time was in the Pottawatomie Indian Reservation, and the site of the village presided over by Chief Waubansie. There were but seven white residents. Joseph and Samuel McCarty were founders of Aurora. In the fall of 1835 the original plat of the city was laid out by the McCarty brothers. Samuel continued through his long life to take pride in the development of the city, donating to it the beautiful Lincoln Park and many church sites. He lived to see the seven increase to twenty-five thousand, and a splendid municipality, with the hum of its factories, the religious power of twenty-one Churches, the machinery of its well-equipped seminary and fine graded schools—one of the most thriving and beautiful communities in the West.

An earnest and devoted Christian, he was the oldest member of the first Methodist Episcopal Church in Aurora. From the first he carried this Church near to his heart. He donated the land on which are the church and parsonage. He has for more than half a century served as trustee, steward, and class-leader. To his foresight is due the flourishing Seminary Avenue Mission, to which he gave a large share of its funds. Especially was he interested in Jennings Seminary. Daniel McCarty was one of the charter trustees of Clark Seminary, and at great personal sacrifice stood by the institution. Samuel was a charter trustee when the new charter was obtained, and the name was changed to "Jennings Seminary." In every time of need he was an unfailing friend to this institution For many years he has been a trustee, and long president of the trustees. He also served for some time as trustee of Northwestern University. He was an uncompromising friend of temperance in theory and practice, and always refused to sell a lot on any terms when he knew it would be occupied for the sale of liquor. There was, consequently, for a long time very little if any of this traffic in Aurora. In his personal religious life he was exceedingly simple and childlike, and a man of unflinching integrity and steady faith. His last sickness was progressive paralysis. One by one the avenues connecting him with the world were closed. Gradually the power of speech failed; but he continued to manifest by signs that he knew the end was approaching, and was trusting his Savior. He entered into heavenly rest March 30, 1889. The funeral services in the First Methodist Episcopal Church, attended by a vast concourse of citizens and by ministers of all denominations, were conducted by pastor A. W. Patten, assisted by Drs. Axtell, Goodfellow, and Mandeville, and Messrs. Lovejoy, Earngey, and Heidner. The official members of the Church and the trustees of Jennings Seminary attended in a body.

Mr. McCarty was married March 26, 1837, to Miss Phœbe Stolp, who died in May, 1839. January, 1847, he was married to Miss Emily Wheeler, of Chicago, and by this union there were two children. His wife died in September, 1850. In April, 1853, he was married to Mrs. Emily A. Davis, formerly Miss Swayzee, of Chicago. Their children are Eva Dent, now Mrs. N. H. Johnson, of Aurora; Sidney George, married, and a resident of Chicago; and Charles S., born in 1863, residing in Chicago. One brother—Daniel—survives, a resident of Chicago, and for many years a trustee and one of the original founders of Clark Seminary. Mr. McCarty was a prominent figure in Western Methodism. He will be long remembered as an invaluable citizen, and by the many who have enjoyed the generous hospitality of his lovely home, and have honored him for devotion to the Church.

OTIS HARDY.

BY REV. N. H. AXTELL, D. D.

Otis Hardy, third son of Lyman Hardy and Sarah Merrill Hardy, was born near Windsor, Vt., September 23, 1810. When he was in his third year (1813), his parents, with eight young children, came West by team, and by descending the Allegheny and Ohio Rivers upon rafts. They settled near Marietta, Ohio, living for five years upon a rented farm. Because of this early emigration but little is known of his ancestry. His mother was a Methodist, and his father was a Christian, but not a member of any Church, because none was accessible. In 1818 the family moved to Meigs County, Ohio, took up a quarter-section of land, and built a cabin in the forest. In 1824 the three older boys were apprenticed to trades—Otis to David Young, a carpenter. He served six years, receiving his clothes, his board, and eighteen pence, and then left because of the intemperance of his employer. A year before this his father had died. Otis provided for his mother until her death in 1831, and for his younger sisters. In 1832 occurred the event that gave character and success to his life. A slave—yet a local preacher—was accustomed to come over from Virginia and hold prayer-meetings. Sometimes his master came; but the slave was preferred, as more talented and more pious. Otis had joined the Church as a seeker—had sought peace at camp-meeting and at quarterly-meeting; but now, at this weekly prayer-meeting at Graham's Station, on the banks of the Ohio, the slave led the meeting, and Otis came to a full and firm decision under his instrumentality and found salvation. The next four years he wrought at his trade in Francisville, La. In May, 1836, he returned to Ohio; and in June he came to Illinois on horseback, alone, with $1,500 of savings, and on August 30th went to work in Joliet, Ill. His tools and clothing, worth $800, were lost in transit. He spent twelve years as contractor and builder.

In October, 1838, he married Miss Angelia Hopkins, who has been a blessed life companion and the mother of his six children, and is his survivor. Two children died in early life, and one— Mrs. Dyer—since. In building his second house, in 1845, Mr. Hardy ran in debt $200, and the embarrassment continued two years, whereupon he resolved that he would henceforth never incur a debt that he could not pay in ninety days. Fortunate, in 1847, in making $700 in a canal contract, he entered with this capital into the lumber business, in which he continued twenty years, and acquired a competence. In 1862 he became a partner in a gas company. In 1868 he retired from business, taking an interest in the First National Bank, and determining to live both prudently and modestly, and give all his income, except his necessary family expenses, to the claims of benevolence and religion.

He had been all along the foremost giver in his Church, and first in all temperance work and in kindness to the poor; but for these twenty years last past he had been agent and treasurer for every good enterprise. The first church in Joliet was on the ground where now stands the Chicago and Rock Island Depot, and was built the first year Mr. Hardy was in Joliet. A brick church followed, which was soon burned down (fired from the shavings of a just-finished adjoining parsonage); but Brother Hardy rallied the people, and under his supervision a new and better one was completed. The Richards Street Church was erected, and its parsonage, at his cost. The enlargement was also largely through him. The Irving Street Church and the parsonage were due to him. He was anxious to live to build a new Richards Street Church, to which he had made the first subscription, $4,500. Churches elsewhere have found in him a helper—in Peru, La Salle, Chicago, Colorado, and California.

His largest contributions have been the quiet, constant, and discriminate droppings into the palms of the toiling poor of Joliet. "I tell you," said a meat-market man, "Mr. Hardy's death means a loss to me of $40 a month. He used to come to the market or send orders to deliver a chicken, a turkey, meat or something to this or that poor person. Of course, they never knew who sent it." Two shoe-dealers standing near said their experience was the same. "Many times Mr. Hardy has brought two or three children into my store, and had me fit them out with shoes." The other dealer said: "Yes, many times has he paid me as high as $20 a month for boots and shoes that he had supplied poor people with."

Not himself having extended education, he has yet been a donor to our schools; Garrett Biblical Institute and Northwestern University have received largely. To give comfort to our soldiers, Brother Hardy, with his daughters, visited hospitals at the front. He went to work as soon as he arrived at Belmont. He was busily scrubbing, when an officer came up rudely, and said: "What are you doing here?" Mr. Hardy, without looking up, answered: "Trying to find a floor here—they say there used to be one." Another said: "You seem to be boss. What office have you?" "Corporal of the scrubbing brigade," was the answer. At Shiloh he found his improvements had been adopted.

For fifty-five years Mr. Hardy has been a member of the Methodist Episcopal Church; for fifty-two years a member of the Quarterly Conference; for forty years president of the Will County Bible Society, and, since its formation, president of the Joliet District Camp-meeting Association. He was lay delegate to the General Conferences of 1876 and 1884. The friends of Otis Hardy have felt assured during the past year that the end was coming. A month ago he himself acknowledged it.

He met the great fact with resignation first, and then with cheerfulness. "This is a strange kind of sickness," said he; "no disease; but I do not get strength." He became very fond of songs of heaven. Frequently they sang a favorite—"I am going home to die no more." To the last he expressed firm trust, saying: "I would like to have seen the church built and a few things done, but the will of the Lord be done." After great solicitude for nine weeks, the intelligence went forth that the most benignant citizen of Joliet was dying. To the last the patient watched his own symptoms, and knew their fullest indications. He carefully made all temporal arrangements. His last words, after making arrangements for the payment of quarterly amounts to the Church, Young Men's Christian Association, and the Woman's Temperance Union, were: "Think of others"—words characteristic of his whole life. The last moment came at twenty minutes to noon, November 7, 1889. Brother Hardy looked up in a surprise, which changed to a gaze or glow of delight; his countenance became fixed, and his spirit was gone. The hero-Christian was asleep in Jesus; but by a fitting close to his noble life, a precious foretaste of the real realm, he had waked—

"Where every power finds glad employ
In that eternal realm of joy."

GEORGE C. COOK.

From 1843 until 1884 there were few more prominent men in Chicago business and Church life than Mr. George C. Cook. His character and life were so exalted, and his labors in connection with the Methodist Church for forty years so efficient, he deserves more than common space in our pages. With all his purity of intention, there was in him, as in many others, a little pride of ancestry that caused him to trace his ancestry back to the early periods of English history. The family had early representatives in New England history. Mr. Cook's great grandfather, Gideon Cook, settled in Berkshire County, Massachusetts, in 1748. His grandfather was a captain in the War for Independence, and was with Ethan Allen when he demanded the surrender of Ticonderoga.

Mr. Cook was born March 10, 1811, in Berkshire, Tioga County, New York. By 1825 his father and mother were both dead; and thus at fourteen years of age he was an orphan, struggling with the world alone. He went to live with an uncle, where he became familiar with the details of business life. He married, in 1834, Miss Lucy Williams, and at once moved to Newark Valley, where he resided until he came to Chicago in 1843. After a somewhat protracted and distressing illness, he departed from earth in April, 1884.

Mr. Cook, on coming to Chicago, like many others, tried different plans of business. He was for a time in a hotel, but finally he became a partner in a retail grocery under the firm name of Satterlee & Cook. This establishment grew on their hands until, after change of name to George C. Cook & Co., it became one of the largest wholesale grocery stores in the West. This continued until the fire of 1871, when the whole was swept away, and Mr. Cook was left penniless. Shortly after he became manager of the Safe Deposit Company, and by this means obtained a comfortable support until death.

From his first coming to the city he became an active member of the Clark Street Church. He was soon appointed leader, and thence on he bore an active part in all the works of that Church, until his interests became involved in Wabash Avenue. When this new Church enterprise was undertaken it became his chief interest, and while he lived his favorite "Wabash Avenue" was his greatest joy. He was of Presbyterian stock, but was converted and joined the Methodist Church in 1833, when twenty-two years of age. He served as church trustee, as class-leader, as Sunday-school superintendent. George F. Foster, who stood with Mr. Cook in early Church-work, was spasmodic. Mr. Cook was ever and always at his post. As a man, he was a model for rising business men. Soon after the great fire, one of Mr. Cook's personal friends was riding in a street-car in New York City, and overheard this conversation by gentlemen who were discussing the effects of the fire. Among others they mentioned Mr. Cook. One of them said: "George C. Cook is an honest man, and of the strictest integrity, and any statement of his may be received with the utmost confidence." One who, years before, was an employee and business associate, wrote him: "I shall never forget the Christian example you set before me during the sixteen years I was favored to be with you, and I may well say they were the happiest days of my life." One who met him in social life said: "I wish I were half as good as he was." Another wrote him: "Next to our Heavenly Father, I am indebted to you, my dear sir. You took me up when a stranger, and also led me, in a measure, to him." Another says: "I believe

Brother Cook took more young men into the Church, and led them to Christ, than most ministers are able to do." If there is any reader of these pages who thinks religion is for the poor or illiterate or old, let him ponder the above concerning the head of the largest business house in its line in the Northwest.

And what is peculiar in a business man, he had a touch of the artist about him. He was wont to sketch little birthday greetings. His love for art and for the beautiful may be seen in some forty large, handsome scrap-books filled with wood-cuts and engravings, artistically arranged, and set in beautiful borders. The pictures illustrate all manners and all customs of the whole world. Some of them are humorous. He had also scrap-books devoted to Methodist ideas. Here are the homes and faces of the Wesleys; the first Methodist preaching-places in England and America; pictures of early preachers and men of to-day. These collections were put together in hours of recreation and rest from business life.

Mr. Cook's home was a paradise. He loved to make it beautiful. Sunshine and gladness seemed ever present. When the weary day was over, how he loved to sit down and sing the old familiar hymns in this quiet home refuge! The first day of wedded life the family altar was erected, and all through his life incense went up from the home altar to God. When the spirit left the house of clay, the remains were deposited in Graceland Cemetery to rest till the Morning!

ERASMUS QUINCY FULLER.

Mr. Fuller was born in Orleans County, New York, April 15, 1828, and in early boyhood removed to Michigan with his father's family. He became J. V. Watson's helper in the publishing business in 1847, went to Chicago as assistant in the *Northwestern* office, and at the death of his friend Watson in 1856, entered the regular work. He was on districts in the Conference from 1863 till he left in 1868, and was more than commonly efficient in that capacity. Few presiding elders have done more to build up the work in all that was permanent than Elder E. Q. Fuller when on Mendota and Dixon Districts.

When the war had subsided and our Church began to be planted in the South the Western Book Agents resolved to start an *Advocate* at Atlanta, Georgia, and Mr. Fuller was selected as editor. This was in 1868. He continued to conduct the *Methodist Advocate* until 1882, when the paper was discontinued for want of support. Brother Fuller became for the time pastor of the Church in Atlanta, and on October 16, 1883, while going home from an errand down in town, in a fit of apoplexy, fell in the streets dead. The years of this noble man in the South, from various causes, are unsatisfactory. The great work he laid out for himself he failed to accomplish, and it is sad to think of the life of one so worthy embittered and disappointed by untoward circumstances. We have no space here to unravel the tangled thread. It will suffice to say here that there was a white interest and a Negro interest in the South, and that Brother Fuller wished to do justice to both. But his intense love of manhood, without distinction of color, forbade that he should, to serve the white interest, abate one item of effort for the freedmen, and between these two interests he was disabled. Had he been editor of a paper devoted exclusively to either class, his would have been a far more joyful career.

It is probable we do the other men of the Conference no injury when we assert that up to 1868 no member of the Conference ever arose with the business capacity of E. Q. Fuller. He never commanded attention on the Conference floor; he was too modest for that, but in the details of Conference business he did not have his superior. While others talked he acted. Something of this may be seen by a recital of one or two of his proceedings. In the centenary year 1866 the four Methodist Conferences of Illinois met at Bloomington for a reunion. A committee to prepare a program for the great day was chosen, made up of an equal number from each Conference. E. Q. Fuller was among the Rock River members of the committee. The committee met in the evening. They had never been together before, and everything was in chaos. E. Q. Fuller was chosen secretary. The secretary took little part in the discussions, but took notes. The propositions and suggestions poured in in floods. Everybody had a plan. Every one had his men to speak. Every one had an idea of the right course to be pursued at the grand meeting that was to come off next day. Matters went on for an hour with nothing accomplished. There was a chaos of suggestions, and nothing more. All this time the quiet secretary had been jotting down ideas from the plans offered, modeling them now and then to suit his own views, and when at last the committee was in confusion for want of some definite action, the secretary observed that he had been taking notes of the suggestions that had been made, and if they pleased he would read his notes. The notes were read. As the reading proceeded the reader heard expressions like these: "That is it." "That is just the thing!" In a very short time the committee was ready to adjourn; for one man who had a "level" head had brought order out of chaos and confusion.

I was once stationed at Earl, a place where the society was small but earnest. To help matters, the outsiders were, as they ought to be always, ready to help. There was a seven-hundred-dollar debt that it was very desirable should be removed. E. Q. Fuller, who was presiding elder, had much influence in the place, and came to the pastor's aid. We went around among members and friends, and by a free discussion of matters secured pledges nearly covering the amount. We took no subscriptions, but simply asked what help they would be able to give. The following Sunday the pastor told the people he wished in twenty minutes to raise $700. The people generally did not know of the canvass that had been made. The day was damp, and the congregation unusually small. The people laughed to themselves at my bold request. They knew, of course, the thing would be a failure. They said afterwards they thought it one of the most extravagant undertakings. Quickly the persons who had been spoken to gave in their names, and many we had not counted on, seeing the thing going so lively, came in to our aid, so that in just twenty minutes the whole was on paper; and Elder Fuller's previous management was what accomplished the deed. That was only a small specimen of the ways in which he pushed the work on Mendota District from 1863 to 1867. He caused, by his inspiration and aid, churches to be built, debts to be paid, and the general interests of the work to go on.

Mr. Fuller was an ardent admirer of J. H. Vincent's new Sunday-school moves, and all these years he was pushing them on his district. By Sunday-school institutes, and other measures, he was ever pushing upward the Sunday-school interests.

He was eminently a man of great foresight and sagacity. At the opening of the Secession War he was pastor at Elgin. He was enthusiastically for the Union. When President Lincoln made a call for seventy-five thousand men, Mr. Fuller remarked to a congregation that they had undertaken a great work. "Why," said he, "I shall not be surprised yet to know that Illinois alone is called upon to raise seventy-five thousand men." All thought this expression preposterous, extravagant; but E. Q. Fuller remained at Elgin till he was called upon to preach the funeral of a member of the 127th Illinois!

The writer spent hours and days in his company,

and never went to him with any question to which he was not ready to give a clear answer.

Rev. J. E. Roy, a Congregationalist minister, writing from Atlanta, says: " And Dr. Fuller, too,—braver man your Church never sent down to stand in that breach. Of massive physique, of boundless health, not knowing fear, but gentle and loving, he endured such hardships as no man knows; bearing reproach with a spirit of charity. He was not vindictive. He loved his Church with a high ardor; he loved the work his Church had set him to do with a consuming zeal. Dropping, as I did often, into his office, the last time I saw him I remember how I admired his brawn of brain, heart, and health, only to learn in a few weeks of his death. When he and his son returned from the Conference in Cincinnati, it was touching to hear the young man, who had grown up seeing his father slighted on the streets of his adopted city, speak of his father being treated in that Northern city like a man!"

That is a faithful picture of the dearest friend of my life.

A sentiment prevails among a large class of Methodist people that the greater profligate a person has been while unconverted, the better preacher he will be. My observation of Rock River men contradicts this. We would not limit the power of grace to save the hardest; but the history of Rock River men convinces me that the true, noble, reliable men are generally those who are raised in Christian families. I can hardly recall a man of continued pre-eminence who did not either come from a Christian family, or was brought into the Church before he was led far into sin. It is a difficult thing to make a permanent, reliable Christian of a profligate man. E. Q. Fuller, in purity, in nobleness, in integrity, was a fair sample of the men who from childhood have been raised in the way of truth. When he was a presiding elder, he told me a thing that was difficult for me to believe. He said that up to that time he did not know how intoxicating liquors tasted. This was in 1867. He died in fifteen years after, and it is very likely he never knew the taste of liquor. Mr. Fuller in boyhood was large and stout; but being a Christian, at school he minded his own business; and because he always avoided quarrels, was sometimes accused of being a coward. At one time there was a rough fellow who began picking a quarrel with E. Q. He would knock off his hat, and in various ways annoy the peaceable lad. And because young "Rasmus" would not resent these things, the fellow began to call him a coward and became more abusive. But one day he carried the joke too far. He came up, and with an upward stroke gave E. Q.'s nose a stinging blow. "Then," said Fuller, relating it, "that fellow got the awfulest licking any rascal ever got; and from that time he became the butt of ridicule."

Up to the year 1859 the statistics were taken in open Conference. This was generally done at an afternoon session. The committees would seat themselves at tables, with blank sheets ruled and prepared by themselves; and then each pastor, as his name was called, would rise and give his reports, members, collections, etc., as the items were called one by one. In 1859 all this bungling business was done away with. The Book Agents had printed blanks for statistics; and by some one's plan, the whole work was to be committed to a *statistical secretary*, who should have the whole week of the Conference session to do his work in. In that year, the Conference being at Galena, the writer undertook to go up to Conference from Fulton by steamboat. The Conference was to meet Wednesday morning. I arrived at Fulton by sunrise Tuesday morning, and by Wednesday afternoon a company of us found ourselves just starting from the wharf of that place. Such are the beauties of waiting for a steamboat. On Thursday morning we awoke in Dubuque. It was the second time I had ever been absent from an opening session. Taking cars, by eight o'clock I was over in Galena, and on hand for the Thursday morning session. My companions in travel arrived toward night on Thursday. When Conference opened, I was informed that the morning before I was elected statistical secretary, with E. Q. Fuller as assistant. So that we two have the credit of being the first to fill those arduous and thankless positions. Fuller and I worked together until E. Q. was made Conference secretary in 1862.

I may add here that I filled the position of statistical secretary until 1871, for thirteen years. The experiences of those figuring years might be introduced as studies in a class in mental philosophy. But I have introduced this matter to say that while Brother Fuller and myself were friends before, this work bound us still closer. I know not how it may be with others, but for myself, from a child I have had my special chosen friend, and that one must be alone my confidant. So ardent was the love between E. Q. Fuller and myself we could not allow any one else to be so near. If Fuller had any rival in my affections it was J. H. Vincent.

I went into Elder Fuller's Mendota District in 1864. J. H. Vincent and his admirers had begun to hold Sunday-school Institutes. Half a dozen, or ten perhaps, younger members of the Conference had entered earnestly into the Vincent schemes; among the most earnest of these were Mr. Fuller and the writer. When I took work in the Mendota District a *District Sunday-school Institute* was organized, with the writer as president. The president's duty, so far as practical, was to hold a local Institute on every prominent charge during each summer. For three summers this scheme was pretty well carried out. But such schemes fail if there is not some outside party to introduce and back up the leader. Even J. H. Vincent in all his movements has to get others to lead the way. The instigator of this work on Mendota District was the presiding elder. Without his backing and aid the whole would have been a failure; with his aid any laudable undertaking was a success. When attending quarterly-meetings at proper places the elder would arrange with the pastor an Institute, and after the president had prepared program and sent proper notices, the elder would go with him to the place, ready to do any work he was called upon to do. He always filled some of the most important places on the program, and took the place of the delinquents. For, with kindness be it said, many of the preachers could not be induced to take part; they saw no good in the new notions. But every neighboring preacher was put on the program, while E. Q. Fuller and the president were often left to fill the places. I remember this as an instance: A would-be prominent man was on the program to direct a superintendent's review lesson on Solomon. He (the man, not Solomon) was present, and had given no intimation that he would not do the work which for weeks had been assigned him. When the subject was called, the man arose and said: "Well, all I have to say about this matter is, that Solomon was a 'brick;' and that is all I know about it." Well, after all these hindrances, with many grand helpers, these Institutes were generally grand successes. The aid rendered by D. T. Wilson, Dr. Quereau, William H. Haight, Fisher, Nichols, Pomeroy, Axtel, Hartman, and others, will not soon be forgotten.

All these days and weeks Fuller and myself were together, and in my sixty years I have never associated with a nobler, a more unselfish soul. There was no subject beyond his reach; no matters concerning which he was ignorant. Particularly was he enthusiastic on the beauties of nature. In those days (1866) there were no more beautiful country residences anywhere than skirted the road up Fox River on the west side. One calm June day we were walking across from the cars at Batavia, to the cars at Geneva. We had plenty of time, and so we sauntered. I shall never forget our explorations that forenoon among the lawns and shrubbery and flowers that skirted our way.

Sometimes these enthusiasms led Fuller into foolish predicaments. Once Fuller and I had dined at a mansion in Belvidere, whose occupant was a lover of all that was curious in nature. After dinner, in rambling in a wood near by, we came across a young owl. After studying awhile the curious, wise, grave thing, Fuller observed that Mr. M. would be so glad to have it, and we started back to the house. The lady of the house, on seeing the owl, said: "O there is that dirty owl that has been bothering us; I got some boys to carry it off to get rid of it." Foolish enough we felt as we took the owlet back to the woods.

When the Doctor started for Georgia some of his anticipations were concerning the pleasures he should enjoy among the fruits and flowers of that State. It seemed to me, then, the most natural thing when the news came that Fuller had gone to a florist for flowers, and was returning with his treasure in hand when he fell in the street to rise no more. It was the most fitting thing that was ever done when that same bouquet was placed on his breast when his great, honest body was laid in the grave.

When I learned in 1868 that he was going to Georgia, I wrote:

> "We two are so joined
> You'll not go to Georgia and leave me behind."

His answer was that his whole trip was an experiment, and he did not know whether it would pay for himself to go. There was never anything in Georgia but Fuller to call me there, and so I never went; but through all the long fourteen weary years that passed I longed to see my friend once more. We had been in harmony in all things before, and I wished so much to compare views with him after he had had so much actual experience in the old slave-land. One of the bitterest strokes of my life was to learn that he was dead, and that I should see him no more! There were so many momentous matters that I wished to talk over with him.

There are two kinds of presiding elders. Men of one sort simply follow a routine. If they fill the duties commonly expected of elders, they are content. They go to the quarterly-meetings, hold the usual services in a perfunctory way, hold the Quarterly Conference, and go home. The other sort may best be described by saying they literally fulfill the saying, "Whatsoever thy hand findeth to do, do it with thy might." Such men bear a helping hand wherever there are efforts put forth on the charges of the district to accomplish any worthy object. Such a man was E. Q. Fuller. The first class always give arguments to the anti-elder people, while men of the Fuller stamp, who are a help in every good work, are those who make the eldership a thing not to be dispensed with. Besides his regular district work, Elder Fuller found three things to engage his attention. There was Clark Seminary in danger of being sold, to which he gave his heartiest endeavors, even being one of the chief instruments in saving it to the Church; there were the new churches being built, and old debts that were being paid to which he gave his nights and days; and the Sunday-school Institutes, of which mention has already been made. He was the most tireless Church worker I ever knew!

When E. Q. Fuller went South in 1868, he went full of indignation at the Rebellion and its authors, and a spirit of enthusiasm for the old flag. He went full of sympathy, as a life-long Abolitionist, for the freedmen. He went with admiration of the Union spirit of those whites who had resisted the Rebellion, and as a consequence had sought a home in the Methodist Episcopal Church. No man had more indignation of soul against wrong of every kind. He went to find the Kuklux Klans at their murderous work. He went to find the Negroes so weakened by immoral ideas and the oppressions of years, that it seemed impossible to get into their heads ideas of thrift or of success in life. He went to find the Union whites an unlearned and unambitious people, who were impatient of Yankee innovations. He went with high thoughts concerning how, by his paper, he was to lift up and enlighten all these; to find peoples that could not read, and did not care to read, and could not raise spare money enough to pay for a paper. He went to find whisky and tobacco supreme, with little love for intelligence or of the beautiful. One can easily imagine how so lofty a spirit would chafe in such surroundings! He found the whites and the Negroes for whom he went to labor, in antagonism; and, worst of all, he was soon to find himself misunderstood and unsupported; sometimes indignantly treated by many of the leaders of his own Church in the North. A man unused to anything of this kind was out of place in the South, unless he was willing to make a complete sacrifice of himself; and this last is really what Dr. Fuller did. He ought to have quit the field and returned to Rock River when he found how things were; but instead, he labored on, and hoped for a better day. He labored on until, in the prime of manhood, he died, leaving a very unsatisfactory result of the sacrifice. The Rock River Conference did a just thing when it placed his widow on its list of claimants, and it is hoped the whole Church will yet do justice to his memory. He went South, by appointment of agents and bishops, to establish and edit the *Methodist Advocate* at Atlanta; but for reasons given above, the paper never obtained a support. Its friends pleaded that it was worthy of aid from the Church as a missionary agency; but these died, or went out of position, and those who thought differently came into power. Other influences prevailed; and lacking proper backing from the Church, the paper failed, and was suspended. Thus Fuller's chief mission to the South came to an end. But surely such sacrifice and isolation can not be without fruit. Surely the great Head of the Church, who sees as we do not, will grant that seed of E. Q. Fuller's sowing in the South will produce a hundred-fold!

Appointments: 1857, Peru; 1858-59, Lee Center; 1860-61, Elgin; 1862, Aurora; 1863, '64, '65, '66, Mendota District; 1867, Dixon District. In 1868 he went to Georgia; in 1883 he died.

E. Q. Fuller was delegate to General Conference from Rock River Conference in 1868, and I believe was a member of every General Conference till his death, from the Georgia Conference.

PHILO JUDSON.

A new circuit and a new preacher appeared together in 1840. It was Savannah Circuit, with Philo Judson as preacher. In the winter of 1843, when the writer was a member of Clark Street Church, N. P. Cunningham, the pastor, passed up the aisle of that church one morning with three dignified strangers, all of whom went into the box of a pulpit. This was a thing to open the eyes of the congregation; for visitors were like angels' visits in those days. One of them arose to preach, taking as his text, " To the Greeks foolishness; to them that are called, the power of God,"—and spoke in such eloquent strains as had never fallen upon our ears before. Never shall we forget that morning sermon! In the afternoon another one preached; for there were three sermons a day in those days. The afternoon text was: "Are there few that be saved?" The sermon was not eloquent—rather dry, after the morning sermon—but full of argument and fine thought. In the evening the third one preached. Altogether, it was a feast-day for the Church. The morning preacher was Professor D. J. Pinckney; the afternoon one, Professor Lyman Catlin; the evening one, Philo Judson. This was our first sight of those three men, who at that time were pushing the interests of the Rock River Seminary. Philo Judson had been a tavern-keeper in De Ruyter, New York; and December, 1836, when Luke Hitchcock was on the Cazenovia Circuit, he was led to Christ through Mr. Hitchcock's influence. He came West soon after, and was admitted to the Rock River Conference in 1840, at its first session, and at once took rank as a clear-sighted man of business tact. He was chosen secretary of the Conference in 1845, in which capacity he served until 1859, when he handed over the secretarial pen to J. H. Vincent. He was appointed to Clark Street in 1847, to Mount Morris District in 1848, and was once or twice chosen delegate to General Conference. He early became agent of Rock River Seminary, and until his retirement from Church service in 1859 was the leader in every educational movement. Evanston was founded and cultured by his care, and the marks of his wise footsteps will not be obliterated from our Methodism. While the Church has a being, our literary institutions will stand as monuments of his energy. As a member of Conference, he seldom spoke; but when he did speak, he always managed to be on the right side, and said something to the purpose. A want of success in some of his business arrangements, especially in the dry-goods establishment which he purchased in Chicago in 1859, caused him to go under a cloud, and in great measure out of sight of the Conference, which had greater things in store for him had his health permitted active service. A great misunderstanding arose between him and a man from whom he purchased the Chicago establishment, in which Judson's friends deem him, and the other also, simply mistaken, and nothing more. His leading trait, while in Conference, was clear-headedness; but in a time when the attention of the preachers was drawn to planting of Churches, the impetuous bent of Brother Judson toward education caused him to lose to a great extent the sympathy he deserved. During the last years of his effective service in the Conference he looked to a great degree through Evanston spectacles. Until his death he was the chief moving spirit in all the progressive movements of Evanston and its stupendous institutions—the agent, the actor, the doer! He passed away quietly from life March 23, 1876, aged about seventy years.

He was born in Otsego County, New York, March 1, 1807. He was married July 28, 1828, to Eliza Huddleston, in Albany, and remained in the vicinity of that city several years. About 1838 he removed to Stephenson County, Illinois, and, as we have seen, joined the Rock River Conference in 1840.

1840, Rock River Conference, Savannah; 1841–42, Dixon; 1843–44–45, agent Rock River Seminary;

1846, Galena; 1847, Clark Street; 1848-49, Mount Morris District; 1850, superannuated.

MRS. ELIZA HUDDLESTON JUDSON'S name appears here, partly because an account of her life supplements that of her husband, Rev. Philo Judson, and also because of some peculiar aids she rendered the Methodist cause. She was born in Catskill, New York, November 11, 1811. Her father was murdered when she was a child. Her widowed mother at once removed to Albany, where Eliza had more than the common-school advantages of that day. When seventeen years of age she was married to Philo Judson, who was himself but twenty-one, in Albany, where Helen (afterward Mrs. Governor Beveridge) was born. In 1830, Mr. Judson and family removed to Central New York, residing at New Berlin and De Ruyter, and in 1836 removed to Cazenovia. Here Luke Hitchcock was pastor, and under his influence a revival of religion occurred. Mrs. Judson was among the first who started, and in December, 1836, both husband and wife were converted, and both joined the Methodist Episcopal Church. The decided stand taken by Mrs. Judson in the family and the community had a remarkable influence upon the people, among whom were the students of the seminary and citizens of the place. Mrs. Judson was particularly influential with the young ladies of the seminary. Many, who at that time were brought into the Church, will never forget her kind and decided efforts to bring them to the Savior.

In 1837 the family started West, spending some time in Ontario County. In 1839 they landed in Stephenson County, Illinois, and in 1840 Mr. Judson took work in the Rock River Conference. From that time, Mrs. Judson was always in sympathy with the work of her husband; and amid the trials incident to a new country she was brave, patient, and cheerful. During her residence at Mount Morris, where for several years her husband was agent, and at Evanston, their home for the last twenty years of her life, her house was often the resort of students who were away from home and friends, and from her many found comfort and counsel. Her piety was uniform and consistent to the last.

She enjoyed good health until near the close of life. When at last the summons came, she was fully prepared. She quietly passed away December 23, 1884, aged seventy-three years. The funeral services were conducted by Luke Hitchcock, who had taken her into the Church just forty-eight years before.

LUKE HITCHCOCK

When I attended the Rock River Conference for the first time, this being at Rockford in 1849, there were four men who were leaders on the Conference floor and in business. These were Richard Haney, A. E. Phelps, Philo Judson, and Luke Hitchcock; and when I attended last, at Joliet in 1891, Luke Hitchcock was a leader still. Through all these forty-four years, leaders one after another have arisen and gone down or out, while Dr. Hitchcock has all the time held the floor. This is a distinction that I have never known any other man to attain unto. Always wise, always discreet, always a man to whom all look with respect, he has always been heard with deference. For forty or more years he has been the Gladstone of the Conference.

Dr. Hitchcock was raised in Madison County, New York, being born in 1813, and was admitted into the Oneida Conference in 1834, when but twenty-one years of age, and was appointed junior preacher at Marcellus. In 1835 he was appointed to Franklin, and, at once making his mark, he was sent, in 1836, to Cazenovia, the seat of the old and famous Oneida Conference Seminary, at a time when George Peck was principal of that institution. In 1837 he went to Ithaca, and in 1838 located on account of lung difficulty, and in 1839 moved to the West for sanitary purposes. "On a beautiful summer morning, August 28, 1839, our boat," says Dr. Hitchcock, "landed at Chicago, coming from Buffalo. This was my first arrival in the city. I found my way to the old Saganash Hotel, at the corner of Lake and Market Streets. It was Sunday morning. In a short time Grant Goodrich called to pilot me across the prairie from the hotel to Clark Street Church. I then preached my first sermon in the West on this spot. Peter Borein had just died (August 15), and it was then intended that I should fill his place. I found the pulpit draped in mourning, and a congregation who gave unmistakable evidence of their great sorrow at the loss of one who had led so many of them to the Savior."

It was expected that Luke Hitchcock would fill the Clark Street appointment; but finding that the cold, damp breezes of the Lake were severe on him, he was allowed to go into the country on to the Dixon Circuit as a supply. The Western climate invigorated him so that, while for years he remained a feeble man, he did efficient work. In 1840 he was made agent of the Rock River Seminary, and in 1841 was readmitted to Conference. It is from this cause that, while of it, he was not a member of the Conference at its first session. He continued in the agency of the seminary till 1842, when he was appointed to Ottawa and Peru. In 1843 he was stationed in Chicago, but was compelled to leave the work early in the spring of 1844. At the Conference of 1844 he was made presiding elder of the Ottawa District. From that time till 1846 he was on a district, and then till 1850 he was on the superannuated list. He was elected to General Conference in 1852.

At the General Conference of 1856 he received eighty-two votes for the office of Assistant Book Agent, against the one hundred and sixteen given to Adam Poe, who, of course, was elected. This was a premonition of what was to follow, and in 1860, when Adam Poe became Agent, Dr. Hitchcock was elected Assistant Book Agent at Cincinnati, to which office he was returned in 1864, and in 1868 was chosen principal Agent, in which position he continued till 1880. He was the second man the Rock River Conference has furnished to that important post; John T. Mitchell, in 1844, being the first. After the General Conference of 1864, William M. Doughty, who had ably managed the Book-room at Chicago for ten years, retired to more lucrative private engagements, and Dr. Hitchcock moved to Chicago to look after the publishing interests of the Northwest.

The following is a photograph taken in 1856 by another hand: "In person he is slender," says J. V. Watson, "and constitutionally somewhat frail. The color of his skin would indicate some severe but successful battles with inceptive chronic disease. . . . His phiz does not do justice to his mind. He is evidently a good-looking man, and does not impress you with any marked mental characteristics, unless it be that of great modesty. . . . His modesty, however, never shakes his firmness. When he is sure he is right, he goes ahead." Sometimes showing a will of his own, however. "Amiability, the handmaid of modesty, constitutes his prominent social quality. To see him, and converse with him, is to wish to do so again; and if good manners consist in the art of pleasing, he is emphatically an agreeable gentleman. As a Church officer he excels in the financial and the administrative. As a presiding elder he 'magnifies his office,' and were the office *always magnified with such men*, we should hear *fewer calls for its abolishment*. . . . As a preacher . . . he gives evidence of an acute understanding of the theology of Methodism," with a leaning toward the progressive. "Sound sense, great but chaste plainness, with a spirit which seems to be perfectly self-forgetting, are the chief characteristics of his sermons. His only object seems to be to do the people good. . . . Take him all in all, he is a preacher that everybody will love to hear, and may always hear with profit. . . . He sits directly before us at this moment, with hair tinged a little with iron-gray, leaning forward upon his left hand, and giving, as is his wont when a little excited, a nondescript nervous snap of his eyes."

This is a correct portraiture, only that it needs to be said that, with the acute depth of thought worthy a Dempster, there is in him, unusual with most clear-thoughted men, a womanly tenderness that often sets his audience weeping, and melts himself to tears. And by occupying responsible stations he has come to feel his position until he will carry his point if it is a possible thing. Peter Cartwright was never, so far as we have heard, headed off but twice; once by Bishop Ames, and again by Dr. Hitchcock. At the General Conference of 1852, Cartwright wished to take a portion of territory from the Rock River Conference to make up a snug district for himself in the Illinois Conference. The mattter was left to the delegates of the two Conferences. Cartwright made a pettifogging speech before the committee, asserting in a very emphatic way that the Rock River Conference had three hundred square miles of territory more than the Illinois Conference. Brother Hitchcock arose, and the following colloquy ensued:

"Brother Cartwright, you are acquainted with the territory along the line between the two Conferences?"

"I was all over it before you was born!"

"Well, how far is it across the State on the line?"

"One hundred and sixty miles."

"We have three hundred miles more than our share," said Hitchcock demurely. "It is a hundred and sixty miles across the State; I suggest that we move the line three-quarters of a mile north, which will make us equal!" The pith of the matter lies in the fact that a Conference line is indefinable, varying from six to ten miles. Cartwright acknowledged himself beaten, and, with a significant nod, exclaimed: "Luke, I will pay you for that sometime!"

Among the Rock River Conference's most honored names, Luke Hitchcock's stands not least. Between the years 1850 and 1860 he was pre-eminently the Conference "leader," and when the Agency took him in some measure off the floor, the business suffered for want of a leader.

MRS. ELIZA GARRETT.

"Fifty years ago (in 1834) Mr. Augustus Garrett came a stranger to my study in infant Chicago to tell me of his plans. Having failed as an auctioneer in New Orleans and Cincinnati, he wished to start anew in Chicago, hoping, if now successful, to induce the parents of his wife to permit her to join him at Chicago. His wife, he said, was a member of the Presbyterian Church in Newburg, on the Hudson River. I was happy to learn from him this fact, and to introduce him to the Christian business men of my Church, and to see him at our prayer-meeting and Church services. When his business proved very prosperous it became so absorbing as to draw him away from these influences. He had said I should find his wife a help to us in our Church-work, and so when, as a crown to his prosperity; she came to gladden his Chicago home, I found her a very valuable accession to our noble band of Christian women." The foregoing I quote from a letter written to me by Rev. Jeremiah Porter in 1887. Mr. Porter was the pastor of the Presbyterian Church in Chicago from 1833 to 1835. But Mr. Porter is not quite correct. There is an ancient tradition at Newburg that Mrs. Garrett was at one time a probationer in the Methodist Church at Newburg. Her parents lived in North Newburg, and were prominent members of a Presbyterian Church two miles away. This was a reason why Eliza, the daughter, was often an attendant at the Methodist Church in town. And when Mrs. Garrett came to Chicago, the Presbyterian Church was the ruling Church in town. She was introduced among the ladies of that Church, and soon joined them in their benevolent and other society work, but there is the best of evidence that she was never a member of that Church in Chicago.

In the winter of 1836 the best place that we boys could find to amuse ourselves through the long winter evenings in Chicago was at an auction-room on the corner of Dearborn and South Water Streets. A jolly man, full of wit and curious pranks, there kept throngs in giddy merriment as he cried off his goods with his euphonious, "Going, going, going!" Each day a black man, George White by name, dressed fantastically, riding an old gray horse and ringing a bell, promenaded the streets crying "Auction," and at night the fluent auctioneer would gather in the golden coins from the highest bidders. This auctioneer was Augustus Garrett, who thus made money which, being invested in town property, became the foundation of Garrett Biblical Institute. Mr. Garrett afterward became the richest man in Chicago, and was several times mayor of the city.

In 1829, Augustus Garrett and Eliza Clark were married. They at once started West to seek their fortunes. They stopped at Cincinnati, then went to New Orleans, then to Nacogdoches, Texas. While going down the Mississippi to New Orleans they were called to the sad duty of landing for the purpose of burying their first born, a daughter of four years of age, who died of cholera. At Nacogdoches they lost a son, which was their only surviving child. After this we believe they had no children. In 1834 they came North, and settled in Chicago. At those glorious revival-meetings held at Clark Street Church by Peter R. Borein, in 1839, Mr. Garrett and his wife were converted, and immediately joined the Methodist Church. Mrs. Garrett remained a faithful member until her death in 1855. Mr. Garrett returned to the world in a year or two, and became prodigiously wicked. Under the labors of W. M. D. Ryan, in 1846, he professed religion again, and frequently, in the basement of the old brick church, he would give simple, childlike recitals that would melt the whole congregation to tears. One evening, when raising money to finish the basement, he offered to cover every five dollars given with another five, and in this way he gave that night seventy-five dollars. He had vicious habits the most unconquerable, and in a few months again fell away, and in 1848 died, leaving no word of encouragement to those left behind him.

Mrs. Garrett was born near Newburg, New York, March 5, 1805, and was raised in one of the finest Presbyterian families. After joining the Church in 1839, she became a noble, consistent Christian, and though living in the best house in the city, and moving in the highest circles, she was ever faithful in attendance at Church, and was scarcely ever absent from her class. For years she was a member of D. M. Bradley's class, which met at four o'clock on Sunday afternoon. The writer for four years was a member of that class, and never remembers the absence of Mrs. Garrett. At Mr. Garrett's death, Mrs. Garrett became possessed of one-half of the property, and from time to time was solicitous that her means should serve the best ends. Grant Goodrich had been the attorney of the family, and to him Mrs. Garrett made application for aid in making a will. From the first she was inclined to the founding of an educational institution of some sort. Mr. Goodrich suggested the founding of a school for the education of ministers. When spoken to on the subject, she said that such a purpose had for some time been the subject of her thoughts. Wishing the judgment of others she consulted her pastor, John Clark. He, not knowing her views, advised the same thing. A few days after, Dr. D. P. Kidder, being in the city, expressed a desire for a Biblical school in the West, and wondered if Mrs. Garrett could be induced to found such a school. Her intention being made known, he visited her to encourage her in the great purpose. Her old pastor, Hooper Crews, whom she greatly respected, also gave the same advice. Thus, led by these united opinions, she concluded that Providence indicated such a disposition of her property, and accordingly her will was prepared, devoting two-thirds of her means to a Biblical Institute. At her death the property, which consisted of lots and buildings in Chicago, was worth three hundred thousand dollars. In January, 1854, a few months after Mrs. Garrett made her will, Dr. John Dempster visited the West with the intention of planting here an institution akin to the Biblical school in the East. On arriving at Chicago he found his way had been mysteriously prepared before him. While Mrs. Garrett lived she would accept only four hundred dollars a year for her own support, wishing to leave all for so noble a purpose.

On the 23d of November, 1855, Mrs. Garrett passed away from this world. After a short sickness of but a day or two she died. In dying she lifted up her hands in holy triumph, exclaiming, "Bless the Lord, O my soul!" and without a struggle, slept! On Sunday she was in her place at Church, on Thursday gone!

For the further and full history of the Garrett Biblical Institute, see the writer's History of Rock River Conference.

It seems a most fitting thing that this writer, who, a timid boy, met Mrs. Garrett in the class-meeting for four years, should write and publish her life. O the sacred memories of those old Clark Street Methodist days!

GRANT GOODRICH.

In all great enterprises there are so many hands that take a part, it becomes difficult to select any special workers and give them special credit; but I presume I will not be doing great violence to the truth or injustice to others, if I say that in the earlier days, in laying the foundations of Methodist institutions in Chicago and Evanston, there are four men—two ministers and two laymen—that deserve fuller credit than others. These are, of ministers, Philo Judson and Luke Hitchcock; of laymen, Grant Goodrich and Orrington Lunt.

Grant Goodrich joined the Methodist Church in Chicago in 1834, and until his death, in 1889, was always a leader in Church matters. He was a shrewd, wise man, often persistent, and to him all paid deference. Through nearly all the years from its beginning he was chairman and chief adviser of the trustees of Evanston institutions.

Grant Goodrich was born in Milton, New York, August 7, 1811, and died in Chicago, March 15, 1889.

He arrived in Chicago May 14, 1834. From the day of his coming he saw the future development of the marvelous land of which the young Chicago was then the center. He was converted in 1832, when twenty-one years of age, and came West in time to witness the erection of the first Methodist church in Chicago. He early gave his influence to education, and was among the first school directors. He was among the first to lay the foundations of the Northwest University, and joined in the long tramps to inspect the offered or suggested sites. The institution was planned in his office. He drew the will of Mrs. Garrett, whose property founded the Garrett Biblical Institute. The Church property plans of Clark Street Church owe much to this Methodist lawyer, who saw the beginning of all Methodist things in the great city. He gave conscientious care to each and every Methodist interest in the city. If the united Methodist forces in and about the city survive to mold the future, those coming consequences will owe a continual debt to Grant Goodrich. The pastor of a pioneer Church may be heroic and persistent, and all that; but, after all, only Heaven knows how much the fathers of Methodism owe to the zeal and support of sturdy laymen like Mr. Goodrich and a long file of others, who held up the hands of the early itinerants.

Mr. Goodrich is the author of one of the most interesting chapters in Sprague's "Annals of the American Pulpit," wherein he tells the story of Peter R. Borein, that brilliant apostle of Chicago

Methodism, who died in 1839. He was remarkable, not so much for any one trait of character that lifted him to eminence, as for that general knowledge and uniformly accurate judgment that made his presence indispensable in every board of officials with which he was connected. He was for years the legal adviser of Mrs. Garrett. She was a woman of strong character and excellent judgment. She was not easily turned from her determinations; and yet there is reason to know that such was her confidence in the judgment and integrity of Judge Goodrich as a Christian counselor, his opinions on matters of education had great weight with her when she made her final decision to found a school for the education of ministers. In the financial crash of 1837, Mr. Goodrich, like nearly every other property-holder in Chicago, became involved in debt. The debt was the appalling amount of sixty thousand dollars. But he held lofty conceptions as to moral obligations; and at a time when the laws gave a bankrupt release from obligations, he insisted, in the face of offers to compromise, upon paying the utmost dollar. But it took a struggle of twenty years to do this.

In 1836, Grant Goodrich returned to Westfield, New York, where he had been converted in 1832, and was married to Miss Juliet Atwater. This union continued until his death, fifty-three years.

Mr. Goodrich was not heartily in favor of the lay delegation movement of 1870; but after the adoption of that measure, he was one of the first lay delegates from the Rock River Conference. He was a prominent and successful lawyer, and at one time a Judge of the Superior Court.

During the days of the writer's membership at Clark Street Church (1842–46), Grant Goodrich was class-leader and assistant Sunday-school superintendent. He moved about among the doings of the Church as a sort of overseer; never obtrusive, but always intent on seeing that all things were moving in order. Here is a man that, from its beginning, had an active part in all that pertained to Methodism in Chicago and Evanston for fifty-five years. Surely that is an honor that falls to very few persons in this world.

ORRINGTON LUNT.

It will perhaps surprise some modern people to learn that Orrington Lunt won his first favors in old Clark Street Church by the power of song. When I first entered that Church, in the fall of 1842, and during the following winter, one of the things that most attracted and charmed me was the solos of Brother Lunt. He had a sub-alto voice that sounded rich in solo. I never heard him sing in any other way, except that sometimes he sung at Abolition meetings in a quartet club. There were two or three pieces that were his favorites. Among them were, "When for eternal worlds we steer," and "The morning light is breaking." In those days, too, Brother Lunt used to pray at the altar in times of revival. But these practices, I think, he entirely dropped as he grew older. In writing of Joel Manning, I wrote of leaders in local Church affairs.

Now, Orrington Lunt was never one of these, I think, in any Church. He acted as an official member; took great interest in all liberalities; but never acted as a class-leader or worked in Sunday-school or revivals. He was too modest for all this. Grant Goodrich gave his time to Church work and to Church extension as much as to college matters, while Orrington Lunt was more conspicuous in educational lines. This is no place for comparisons; but it is perhaps true that while Judge Goodrich was abundant in influence and counsel, Mr. Lunt was really more active in pushing things to final completion. Goodrich planned; Lunt executed. Witness his efforts in securing a location for the Northwestern University. I think it is true that, till 1880, no layman had so much to do in founding Evanston institutions as Orrington Lunt.

Our subject was the son of William Lunt, a prominent citizen of Maine, who for some time was a member of the State Legislature. The family came in a direct line from Henry Lunt, who settled at Newburyport, Mass., in 1635.

Orrington was born at Bowdoinham, Maine, in 1815. In January, 1842, he was married to Miss Cornelia Grey, who for over fifty years was loved and honored as one of the noblest of women. In 1845, at a revival in Clark Street Church, I have seen her at the altar praying for penitents.

Soon after his marriage, in 1842, Mr. Lunt set out for Chicago. He came West to seek his fortune, and found it. From 1842 till 1845 he was engaged in small trade, getting an insight into the business of the future city. But there never was a deader town than Chicago was from 1837 to 1845. The reasons are given in the chapter on *Chicago*. In 1844, Mr. Lunt returned to Maine for his wife, whom he had left behind. From that time, their home has been in Chicago and Evanston. Mr. Lunt was a Methodist when he came, and at once identified himself with Clark Street Church.

In 1845 he began to buy wheat. At that time there was no public conveyance, save the old stage-coach, west of Chicago. Farmers from all the country for a hundred miles around came flocking, with their two-horse team-loads of wheat, into the city. The streets were filled with buyers; and in the fall of those years, till 1850, South Water Street would be so crowded with these teams, waiting their turns to unload, that one could hardly pass along. Orrington Lunt began business in earnest among these buyers. I was with George F. Foster, and we filled two large storehouses with Mr. Lunt's wheat. Besides these, he filled a large elevator. In November, on the very day of the dedication of the new brick Clark Street Church, Mr. Lunt sold out all the wheat he had. The profits were such that he gave a large thank-offering to the Church that evening. That sale gave him a standing; and from that time until now he has been in the lead among the business men of the city. He was a projector and vice-president of the old Galena Railroad, the first railroad ever built from Chicago, which run its first cars from Chicago to the Des Plaines in the fall of 1849.

I never knew so thoughtful, so safe, so shrewd, so wise a business man in Chicago as Orrington Lunt. Always thoughtful, he said but little; in a grand enterprise, enthusiastic, but never carried away by visions. I can best illustrate his pertinacity—*pertinacity*, that is the word—and the in interest he took in great enterprises, by giving the account of the "discovery" of Evanston.

The first meeting of persons favorable to the establishment of a Methodist College at Chicago met at the office of Grant Goodrich, May 31, 1850. There were present Revs. Zadoc Hall, Richard Haney, R. A. Blanchard, and laymen G. Goodrich, O. Lunt, H. W. Clark, John Evans, J. K. Bottsford, and A. J. Brown. Resolutions were passed in favor of the immediate establishment of a university. A committee was appointed to secure a charter. The charter was secured in 1851, and accepted by the trustees at a meeting held June 15, 1851; and A. S. Sherman, G. Goodrich, J. K. Bottsford, John Evans, O. Lunt, A. J. Brown, Geo. F. Foster, J. M. Arnold, E. B. Kingsley, James Kettlestrings, N. S. Davis, and A. Funk were elected trustees. A preparatory department was recommended, and the Executive Committee was authorized to raise $20,000 for its beginning, and also report a site and plan of building. A lot east of Clark Street Church was offered for $4,800, but not accepted, it being thought too dear; worth now half a million, or more. Orrington Lunt and Dr. Evans were appointed a committee to examine other lots. At the annual meeting, September, 1852, the president reported receipts of $1,193 towards the university. The committee on lots reported that lots on the corner of Jackson Street, owned by P. F. W. Peck, could be had for $8,000, and they recommended their purchase for the site of the preparatory school. The committee was ordered to purchase the lots. The committee (Lunt and Dr. Evans) gave their personal guarantee for the payment. Mr. Lunt now says the sharpest thing the trustees ever did was the holding on to those lots. It is the site of the Pacific Hotel, and the land is still owned by the university, and yields a very large sum for rentals.

Orrington Lunt, Dr. N. S. Davis, Rev. S. P. Keyes, and Dr. John Evans were appointed a committee to look up a site for the university. This committee made little progress. At the meeting of trustees, June 22, 1853, the Executive Committee was authorized to select a site. The committee took excursions to Rose Hill, to Winetka and Glencoe, and finally to a point in the town of Jefferson, twelve miles from Chicago, and about eight west of the lake. The high price asked for land, and the difficulty of finding a large enough tract in one place, hindered the selection. Through their agent, Rev. Philo Judson, they bargained for a large tract at Jefferson, and were about closing the bargain when Mr. Lunt, who pleaded for a site on the lake, asked for a little delay. He went north on a ride with a Mr. Benson. There was no railroad north in that day. The stage-road took dry ridges a mile or so west of the lake. All along between this road and the lake there lay a dreary swamp, which caused all to suppose there was no suitable place there. Mr. Benson stopped for business for a while. Mr. Lunt struck out across the bogs toward the lake. He made his way, stepping on fallen logs and grassy projections, until he came out in sight of the beautiful ridges of Evanston. He returned to the city. But the impression made by the beautiful situation so enthused our adventurer that he dreamed through the night of the beautiful future of the university. It was difficult to get the committee to go north again. The Jefferson parties were pressing for an immediate decision. But Mr. Lunt determined that he would not vote for the Jefferson site until the lake-shore was examined. This settled the matter; and the committee, consisting of O. Lunt, Rev. Philo Judson, Dr. Evans, and George F. Foster, on a beautiful summer day in August, took carriages and rode northward. On reaching a point on the road opposite the present Evanston, they struck across for the lake. They came out upon the present university campus. At once, the lake, the trees, the ground, the beautiful location, enchanted them. The noble-souled, enthusiastic George F. Foster swung his hat, and they all exclaimed, as if in one voice, "We have found it!" No doubting or discussion was heard from that moment. The committee reclined under the noble oaks, and entered upon a discussion of ways and means. They returned to the city. O. Lunt and Dr. Evans were appointed a committee to negotiate for the land. They found Dr. Foster the owner. He at first thought the land worth fifteen dollars per acre; but as he looked into the matter, he demanded seventy dollars per acre, what was then deemed an exorbitant price. But looking at the future, the committee concluded to buy, and immediately three hundred acres of land was secured. The place was called Evanston, from Dr. John Evans, the president of the Board of Trustees. From that time Evanston has been going upward; and now for forty-three years Orrington Lunt has been the chief soul of the place.

GEORGE FRANKLIN FOSTER.

When the writer of these pages entered the old Clark Street Church, in Chicago, in 1842, there was no more prominent person in that Church than Mr. Foster. Grant Goodrich was no doubt the most influential member, but certainly George F. Foster was the most conspicuous. His noble form, his exultant, manly utterances, attracted attention, and no one could have been an attendant and not observed the pushing, high-spirited Foster.

He was born in Maine about the year 1812, and while a young man was converted under the labors of Samuel Jewett, the father of S. A. W. Jewett. He learned the sailmaker's trade, and with his nephew, George A. Robb, came empty-handed to Chicago in 1837, to grow up with the new West. The two opened a sailmakers' shop in an old warehouse on the river's bank, North Side, between Clark and Dearborn Streets. They were out of means, and had to wait for work. They were so hard-pressed they picked up wood along the river to cook their food; and for meat they were glad to get some rusty pork from a barrel that a captain had put ashore as too poor for his crew to eat. They were living in this condition, almost ready to abandon their enterprise, when, on a stormy day, a vessel came booming in with her mainsail badly torn. The vessel went up to a dock at the point. The young sailmakers hastened after her, and secured the job of repairing the torn sail. This gave them a start, and from that time, through many hard times, George F. Foster prospered as a business man; and when the writer went into the establishment in 1844, Mr. Foster was one of the thriving business men of the city. Until his death he was engaged in various business enterprises, and generally prospered.

He came to Chicago a Methodist; but being one of those persons who are up and down, he soon lost his zeal and came near giving up. But during the summer of 1837 he attended a camp-meeting, held by John Clark on Fox River, where, after hours of struggle through darkness, he passed into renewed light; and from that time his voice was ever heard in the Church. The Borein revivals of 1838–39 were glorious days to him; and the revivals of Hooper Crews, of 1840–41, found no better worker than he. From those days on he was always a leader in every Church work. His experiences and his nature made him a camp-meeting man, and old Des Plaines always found in Mr. Foster an ardent supporter. When the Indiana Street Church was organized in 1847, he was the leader.

In the years 1846–49 the Chicago people were having much trouble with the presiding elder, James Mitchell. Indiana Street and Canal Street Churches were for him, Clark Street against, and George F. Foster was the leader of the Mitchell people. And there appeared a strange freak of human nature here. Mr. Mitchell, for one thing, was accused of being a slaveholder. Mr. Foster was an anti-slavery man. But he had taken a great liking to Mr. Mitchell because he went in for all the free, enthusiastic measures of the Southern type of Methodists. When the Rock River Conference met at Canton in 1848, Mr. Mitchell was to be put on trial. Mr. Foster went down there, and among the pro-slavery people of Canton called and held a popular indignation meeting to overawe the Conference. An anti-slavery man working for a man who was being tried, in part, for holding slaves! When the Methodist Church in Chicago held its even course in spite of faction, Mr. Foster and a party of like feeling withdrew from the Church and undertook to set up for themselves. After a time better counsels prevailed, and nearly all came back to the Church, and lived to rue the day and to confess their error.

Mr. Foster's greatest interest lay in the direction of revival work. He never went to Sunday-school, and did not take a very active part in outside measures; and yet, with his intimate friend, Orrington Lunt, he had a hand in many of the Evanston movements. He was a member of the first Board of Trustees of the university elected in

1853; and when the trustees were looking for a site, Mr. Foster had a part in the selection.

At one time the schooner *Vermont,* owned by the firm, missed the pier, and was in danger of driving down on to the south shore. Mr. Foster, in his excitement, manned a boat, took lots of rope, and was putting out into the lake towards the vessel, where he could have been of no earthly good. The boat had not gone far till the crew were well sprinkled by a dashing wave. That brought Mr. Foster to his senses, and he exclaimed: "What are we going out here for?" He put back, and sent a steamer for the vessel. At another time, about midnight, there was a cry of fire. Mr. Foster and myself arrived at the store at about the same time. The fire was away up the river a quarter of a mile. The clerk had left the store and locked the door. Mr. Foster was ready to go to carrying out his goods, and began kicking at the door and berating the clerk, who had abandoned the warehouse. I remarked that I would go and hunt the clerk and get the keys, and started on my errand. Mr. Foster followed, and arriving at the fire took his place at the engine, and forgot his store. It was far away, and safe. This indicates the whole character of the man, and his Church work was for the greater part done in this way. And yet he had a great, loyal, loving soul, and, with all his faults, I loved him then, and cherish his memory as old-time stories.

Mr. Foster was so much in his element in revivals he was always prone to underrate all work that was not done in a revival furore. If the Church was not in revival it was amounting to nothing, and when the revival was on hand he was a host. He was a man of the "glory hallelujah" stamp. The tendency led him greatly to undervalue all Church work that was not done in that style, and also he was of but little service when he was not in a "glory hallelujah" spirit. And yet this sort of man had his place. Such men as Orrington Lunt, Grant Goodrich, and George C. Cook, when wanted, were always there; but being always the same cool, reliable men in a revival that they were in everyday Church work, they did not always—in those old days—rally with victory shouts to urge on the battle. But when there were signs of an engagement, the voice of G. F. Foster was sure to be heard in the din of battle. He was a man that could do but one thing at a time, but that one thing he did with all his might. It was from this cause that, when he was pushing worldly matters, he forgot the Church, and when he took hold of the Church he forgot all else. This made him through all his life peculiarly uneven in his course, and it brought much severe criticism on himself. But better all this than a symmetrical statue of marble, or column of ice! And, as may well be seen, such a nature was often given to despondency; sometimes so deep he could not pray at his family altar, and called upon any one that happened to be near to help him out.

In all my observation I have never met a finer instance of a Christian business house than that of Mr. Foster in 1845. At one time every person from kitchen-girl to clerk, from foreman to boss, was a members of the old Clark Street Church. Those were halcyon days when Eben Gustine, Cyrus F. Tarbox, J. K. Webster, Abner Scranton, Mark Merritt, O. Lunt, and A. D. F. mingled together in business life about the old establishment on South Water Street! Often in revival times, when some sailor or other person of our acquaintance was among the penitents, when Church would close, Mr. Foster would take these seekers and some of us over to his own house, and there, for an hour or two, engage in prayer for their conversion.

Mr. Foster's first wife, described as a noble Christian woman, died in the early part of 1842, leaving a noble child, Orrington Crews Foster by name. He married again at the close of 1842, Miss Saville Loring, of Naperville. This was a high-minded, intelligent woman, who added grace to the Christian companies in Chicago for over thirty years. No woman besides my mother has left such impressions for good on my soul as this woman. I shall never forget her kind words and acts toward me in my youthful days.

For some reason Mr. Foster spent his last years in connection with Centenary Church, where, as everywhere else, he was a Church power. I have heard it stated that he went to Centenary simply because they needed help. He is remembered by the Centenary people as one of their most worthy workers. He died, and left his last record with them about 1880.

Surely no work on Worthies and Workers of the Rock River Conference by the writer can afford to leave out the name of G. F. Foster, for forty-three years a Chicago Methodist.

Mr. Abner Reeve Scranton died in Chicago in 1885. He was a layman that filled emphatically our standard of admission to these pages as given in the Preface.

In 1843 the writer of these pages resided in Chicago, on the West Side, but had frequent occasion to pass to the lake on the North Side. At this time Noah Scranton—father of Abner—and his sons were block and spar makers in an old frame that served as shop and residence, on the north side of the river on State Street. Mr. Scranton also owned a rope ferry that crossed the river at that place. I never passed that way but my attention was called to a sailboat belonging to the Scrantons (the finest in the city in that day, and one in which of evenings, a year or so after, Abner, my friend Charles A. Stowell, and myself took evening rides on the lake), which was manned by three or four urchins under command of a small, stern, curly-headed boy of fifteen years, who as captain was doing a wonderful sight of play-business about the river. This was Abner Scranton, the youngest son. Bold, stern, imperious, this lad of fifteen was born to command. I never could pass without loitering awhile to admire the skill of the captain and his crew. In the spring of 1844 I went into George F. Foster's ship-furnishing establishment. The concern had much dealing with the blockmakers over the river, and it fell to my lot as errand-boy to do the business transpiring between the establishments. This drew me nearer to Abner. Finally, in the spring of 1845, he came into the Foster establishment as youngest apprentice, and from that day until Abner's death we were bound friends. Abner was a young Grant. I had a will of my own, and sometimes we were in conflict; but, on the whole, from the first we loved one another.

Abner was born in the city of New York in 1828, and came to Chicago with his father's family in 1839. His father was a wicked man; but his mother in their old home had been a member of some Christian Church, and now was one of the best of women. In a letter to me, written in 1847, Abner says he should, he feared, have been borne down by the temptations of Chicago life if it had not been for one of the best of mothers. A mother's hand hath molded the lives of so many men who have done work for the Church.

Previous to coming into the Foster establishment, Abner hardly ever went to Church; but when he came to us he came into a company of Christians. A great revival at Clark Street had brought our whole company into the Church. I myself had been a member for three years. From clerk to kitchen girl, from foreman to boss, every one of us was a member of Clark Street Church. Abner at first (as he confessed to me afterwards) held himself in reserve. He expected such a lot of Methodists would "preach him to death," and so he was prepared to act on the defensive; but as he found little of this, but instead a cheerfulness and high hopes and thoughts, he was gradually drawn into the influence, and began with the rest of us to attend Church and Sunday-school. It was not long till he asked me of his own accord how he might become a Christian.

During the summer of 1845 the old frame church was removed to a lot on Madison Street, to make way for the new brick that Wm. M. D. Ryan was building. The first quarterly-meeting of the year was held so soon after Conference the presiding elder did not get moved in time to hold it. C. B. Tippett, one of the Book Agents at New York, who had been in attendance at the Western Conferences, on his way East was detained by the pastor to hold the quarterly-meeting. Mr. Tippett had spent a Sunday at Clark Street in the summer, and now all people sought to hear him again. There was preaching Saturday evening. As youngest apprentice, it was Abner's business to stay in the store, and my privilege to go to the meeting. With deep, strange interest I took the place in the store while young Scranton went to the church. About nine o'clock, I closed up and went to the church, hoping, at least, to be in at the last song. It was a dull Saturday evening service—not a large congregation; but it seems some one had taken a notion to call for seekers. When I entered they were holding a prayer-meeting. One lone mourner was at the altar. It was a small thing, and the only mourner a small boy; but that boy was A. R.

Scranton, who thus began a life that was for just forty years a power in Chicago Methodism! He was the last seeker ever at the altar of that old church, where hundreds had been converted. In a month the building was abandoned, and we were worshiping in the new brick house. That night Abner went to sleep in our room. The moon made it almost as light as day. I was watching at the bedside of a sick captain in a house near by. At midnight I stole into the room where Abner slept, and, kneeling by his bedside, prayed for the sleeping boy. From that time till his death I loved him as David loved Jonathan.

Abner joined the Church, attended class, and entered upon all the duties of membership. At night, previous to retiring, one of us would read a chapter, and then we would kneel in silent prayer. The finishing of the new church was on hand, and Abner never missed a chance to have his pittance among the gifts. It is said that he paid to the Church ten dollars out of his salary as apprentice of thirty-five dollars a year. He did not immediately experience religion. When I was at school at Mt. Morris he wrote me a letter, dated March 8, 1847, saying that there had been many conversions at the church, and that he himself had been so happily converted that he was induced to shout "Glory to God!" His letters to me at that time were filled with descriptions of grand religious experiences.

In 1847, Indiana Street Church was organized on the North Side. G. F. Foster and most of his company became members there. Young Scranton was one of the number. But just then the Church was being rent by the trouble James Mitchell was giving; and when finally, in 1848, Mr. Mitchell was condemned by the Conference, both Indiana Street and Canal Street (now Centenary) Churches were near secession. G. F. Foster and many others withdrew, and set up for themselves. Young Scranton was one of these. Before a year, however, about all returned to the Church. I mention this to relate an incident. In 1857, Jefferson Street Church received as pastor a transfer, who proved very unsuccessful. At the close of his year the parsonage was mortgaged to raise money to pay the preacher's salary. There was great opposition to the preacher's return, and when he was reappointed there was almost a rebellion among many. I stopped on a visit to Mr. Scranton on my way down from the Conference at Waukegan, and while walking with him he told me of the difficulty, and said he must go up and have a talk with D., one of the prominent members of Jefferson Street, who was about to withdraw. We went up together. The two talked awhile. D. said finally, in so many words, that he should leave the Church. "You had better not do it," said Scranton. "I tried that once, and have never ceased to regret it!"

Mr. Scranton became G. F. Foster's foreman while yet an apprentice. Soon after, he bought an interest in the concern, and finally, with George Purrington, he became owner of the business, which he continued until the fire of 1871. His profits, beyond the needs of the business, for many years were invested in lots, on which he erected buildings; so that by the time of the fire he was a man of quite large property. About the year 1850 he was married to Miss Elizabeth Hoyt, that estimable lady who shed thenceforth such a gentle light along his pathway.

All these years his chiefest joy and care was his beloved Church; and when at last old Indiana Street Church began to build Grace Church, Mr. Scranton was almost the sole superintendent of the building. He cared for Grace Church as much as for his own business. Indeed, the care for this Church was a part of his business. The first church was built in the form of a T. The cross was built first, to be used as a vestry when the main part was erected. Mr. Scranton put $5,000 into this vestry alone, besides superintending its entire construction. It was richly adorned with frescoes and painted windows, with emblems of his own devising. One of these was the beautiful arrangement of the anchor, the cross, and the crown. This vestry, which was erected in 1864, was used for a time as a church, and then, by the hardest efforts, the beautiful front went up. The Church had few wealthy members. The task of building so costly a church was too hard for any people to undertake. During its erection the contractor became alarmed concerning his pay, and was only induced to go on when A. R. Scranton pledged his individual name. Several times he paid as much as $10,000 beyond the moneys in hand. This church had been finished but a year or two when the great fire came—that direst calamity for mortal to look upon. Mr. Scranton saw the fire slowly advancing from the south. It destroyed his store on the South Side, and then leaped across the river and began to devour all before it on the North. He worked bravely, like a man, and quailed not. His buildings went down, one after another. With brave soul he took his family from their beautiful, newly-erected residence to a place of safety. He said afterwards all these things failed to move him; but when some one came and related how the flames had laid hold of Grace Church, then he broke down and wept.

The fire left him with limited means; but after, in various ways, with his old-time energy he kept himself and family afloat, and was the same ardent supporter of Methodism as in the past. During the last year of his life he acted as superintendent of the Assembly grounds at Lake Bluff. He died of a long and painful disease, caused by cancer, August 6, 1885.

It comes home to this writer as a sad thought that I shall see Hooper Crews, E. Q. Fuller, and A. R. Scranton no more on earth.

A. D. FIELD.

It is probable that there are few members of the Rock River Conference that have so much pure American blood in their veins as A. D. Field. His father was from old Massachusetts stock, and his mother from the first families of Connecticut.

His father, John Field, a son of Captain Field, a soldier in the Revolution, and his brothers, about 1819, left their home in Belchertown, Massachusetts, to seek their fortune in the West. The West was then in the State of New York. They cut themselves farms out of the forests of Central New York, in Ontario County, and began life as farmers. John Field soon married Charity Damon. From this union were born four children, of whom A. D. was the youngest. He was born in Ontario County, in the town of Bristol, October 22, 1827. At the time of his birth one or two maiden aunts were visitors in the family. These, having the New England proclivity, were great readers. Just then they were reading some Spanish story or history, and they protested that, since the family had Joseph, John, Peter, etc., it was time to bring in something new in the line of names; and so, from some Spanish notable or other, the new-born nephew had Alvaro fastened upon him as a name—a name that ever to him proved a burden, for it was always a matter of burlesque to his friends. From this, and the name of his maternal grandmother, we have Alvaro Dickenson Field. But he himself always prefers to obscure the long cognomen by the simpler A. D.

About the year 1829, when Alvaro was past two years old, his father died. In the spring of 1831 his mother married Isaac Hale, and moved with him into the neighborhood of Warsaw, in Genesee County. Here, when A. D. was three and a half years old, he began attending school, and learned the alphabet, if no more. From this time until he was twenty, most of the time he was in the best schools to be had.

In the spring of 1832, Mr. Hale moved the family into the wilds of Chautauqua County, where, first in the town of Stockton and then in Portland, the family resided on farms until the spring of 1835. During this time Alvaro attended his first Sunday-school all the summer of 1834 in sight of Chautauqua Lake, thus becoming a Chautauquan forty-six years before his friend J. H. Vincent ever saw the place.

In the fall of 1834, Mr. Hale, with a two-horse wagon-load of passengers, set out for Illinois. In the spring he sent for the family. The mother, with her children, took passage on the steamboat *Thomas Jefferson* at Erie, Pennsylvania, and on June 8, 1835, they were landed at Chicago, the new town with which our subject has been quite closely connected until the present time.

Mr. Hale became a contractor, furnishing brick and timber to the various improvements going on in the city. This caused him to move about considerably, and this is why A. D. came to reside at Hammond, at Hegewisch, South Chicago, and other places. But much of this time for eleven years he was more or less in the select and public schools of Chicago. As a matter of interest we quote an item or two from Mr. Field's notes:

"The first free public school in the State of Illinois was begun in Chicago in 1834. In 1835 I attended that school. Nothing but paid schools had been in existence before. The school referred to was held in the Presbyterian Church. This building was built on west side Clark Street, between Lake and Randolph, and fronted on the alley. Mr. McCord was teacher. In the summer of 1836 I attended school in a frame building at The Point, at the junction of Lake and West Water Streets. Mr. Wakeman was teacher. In 1843 the one West Side school was in an old dwelling from which the partitions had been removed, fronting on Monroe Street, between Canal and Clinton Streets. In 1845 I was in school on the North Side, taught in one of George W. Dole's vacant store buildings. In 1846 we went into a fine two-story brick building erected for school purposes. When I was at school on Clark Street in 1835, it was the only school of any sort in the town. I have attended schools on the South, West, and North Sides, when the school I attended was the only school at the time in that part of the town. School-books were scarce, and the scholars used any book they could pick up at home. At the school on the West Side, in 1836, the New Testament was the only reader."

In 1839, Mr. Hale settled on a claim a half mile south of the present Plato Center Station, in Kane County. He settled there, within forty miles of Chicago, three years before the land was even surveyed by the Government.

In the fall of 1842, Alvaro was living at home, and at that time became a Christian. This occurred in October, and in a week he returned to Chicago, and put himself under the care of his two brothers, who were older, and were living in the city. The fact of his becoming a Christian may be thus stated:

"During the time that I had been at home, I often attended the Methodist meetings held in that part of the country. It was there I saw and heard first a Methodist preacher; this first preacher being Josiah W. Whipple, then on the old Sycamore Circuit. I was particularly impressed by a quarterly-meeting held at Elias Crary's, in 1840, and by a camp-meeting held under the care of John T. Mitchell on the ground of Stephen Archer, in 1841; but I never felt any disposition to become a Christian. There were three boys then in the neighborhood who were afterwards heard from. These were M. V. Burdick, afterwards a prominent judge in Iowa, and George W. Perry and A. D. Field, of the Rock River Conference. In the fall of 1842 a few young men, mainly Baptists, who attended Church in Elgin on Sunday morning, began a four-o'clock prayer-meeting at the house of Benjamin Hall, five miles west of Elgin. Soon there began to be converts at these meetings. I attended the meetings out of curiosity frequently. At length my nearest friend, M. V. Burdick, became a Christian, and as soon as he reported this to me I at once surrendered, and began a Christian life. It was the first time I ever felt that I ought to be a Christian. I can never look back on those momentous days without thrills of deepest emotion. There has nothing happened in my life the memory of which stirs me so! In a week after, I returned to Chicago to attend school, and to engage in some life business. In one day after I became a Christian I knew that my destiny was to preach. In going to Chicago I had concluded to join no Church, but to be a free Commoner. My older brother, Joseph, was an officer in the Presbyterian Sunday-school, and as he was my chief mentor, I joined the Presbyterian Sunday-school, a school I had first attended in 1836. There were one or two circumstances that led me over to the Methodist Church. First, the Methodist meetings at Plato had charmed me. I loved the free way of the Methodists, especially their rapturous songs. Besides, I could not endure the dry sermons read by the Presbyterian ministers. Second, at the select school I was attending, there was a young Methodist, Charles A. Stowell by name, whom I learned to love because he was a devout Methodist Christian. I was constrained to follow him. And third, there was at this time a glorious revival of religion going on at the Methodist Church which I delighted to attend. It must have been near Christmas when, feeling that I was a stray sheep whom nobody owned, I joined the old Clark Street Methodist Church. I entered the Sunday-school, and joined a class of boys taught by David M. Bradley (the father of Professor C. F. Bradley). I remained in that school for four years, becoming a teacher in 1844. I was placed in the Church class led by Mr. Bradley. In that class I met in the closest fellowship my dear schoolmate, C. A. Stowell, and Mrs. Eliza Garrett, founder of Garrett Biblical Institute. Our class met at four o'clock Sunday afternoon. In four years I was absent about four times, and I can not remember being present when Mrs. Garrett was not there. Of D. M. Bradley I dare not begin to write. He made me! I loved him as I have never loved any other man. There were times in my wayward boyhood when nearly everything around the Church would lose its hold upon me; but at such times the Sunday-school and Brother Bradley and his class were the golden chain to bind me until the days of wandering were past. That leader's photograph hangs framed on the wall in my room before me now as I write, and the joyous eyes yet speak to me words of cheer, and bid me rise and on.

"When I joined the Church, we worshiped in the old wooden frame built on the North Side by Henry Whitehead in 1834, moved to Clark Street and twice enlarged, so that the original frame was but a quarter of the frame of 1842. We worshiped there until November, 1845, when we entered the splendid brick church built by W. M. D. Ryan. I worshiped in after years, as a visitor, in the block built in 1857, that went down in the fire of 1871. The fourth building stands now on the old corner.

"The pastor of the Church when I joined was N. P. Cunningham; the presiding elder was Hooper Crews. The pastor and elder lived in the city. Besides them, there was no other Methodist preacher nearer than Naperville, Elgin, and Waukegan. It was the only Methodist Church in Chicago. The leading members were: Grant Goodrich, George F. Foster, Orrington Lunt, Robinson Tripp, William

Wheeler, S. H. Gilbert, D. M. Bradley, J. B. Mitchell, James Robinson, A. S. Sherman, Thomas George, Isaiah Shaw, Christopher Metz, Ira Reynolds, M. B. Clancy, J. K. Bottsford, and S. W. Talmadge. Afterwards, while I was a member, came G. C. Cook, J. W. Waughop, Dr. Banks, J. A. Hoisington, and A. Biglow.

"In 1846 there were fourteen classes, holding sessions every week. There was not a prominent lawyer or merchant or doctor in the Church but was an earnest class-leader.

"I am convinced that all I have ever been that amounts to anything, all I hope to do, all I hope to be, I owe to the fact that in my early boyhood, before I was fifteen, more than fifty momentous years ago, I became a Christian and joined that old Clark Street Methodist Church. The greatest desire I have to live is the hope that I shall yet be able to do something that shall be a worthy service to the dear old Church and the Rock River Conference and her crowned workers."

This wish is in some measure fulfilled in the publication of this volume.

In the spring of 1844, young Field became a member of George F. Foster's family. There, in that Methodist home and that Methodist business-house, he spent two most joyous years; and to-day, after fifty years, he remembers with gratitude all the kindness of Mr. and Mrs. Foster.

In May, 1846, Alvaro, by the advice of the presiding elder, James Mitchell, started for the Rock River Seminary, at Mount Morris. While there, he was licensed to exhort, and he preached his first sermon in a school-house in the Gappin neighborhood, six miles north. In the spring of 1848, while living for a time at Mineral Point, Wisconsin, he received license to preach, and a recommend for admission into the Rock River Conference, both papers signed by the presiding elder, Henry Summers. In July, 1848, when he was somewhat past twenty years of age, he was received into the Conference, and sent as junior preacher to Hennepin Circuit, with William C. Cumming as preacher in charge. From that on, for twenty-three years, he never failed to report at Conference for duty. Most of his first circuits—Iroquois, La Harpe, Momence, Mazon, etc.,—were in the bounds of what, on division of the Conference in 1855, became the Central Illinois Conference. On some of these early circuits there was wilder, newer country than can be found anywhere now. He traveled five years before there was a railroad in Northern Illinois. His first and second years he received eighty-six dollars a year; his third, fifty-five dollars; his fourth year (this being his first married year), he received eighty-five dollars. Being poorly clad, and riding over the houseless prairies in coldest winter weather, he suffered more than people of this day know of; and by this means his health was so injured that he suffers to-day the effects of those perilous days. If he cared to write out tales of frontier-life and endurance, he could do so; but he looks back upon all those days with joy upon any memories of good, and sorrows only over his many mistakes and the poor work he has done. The failures arising from the inexperience of youth give him many a pang of grief. His loudest declaration to-day is, that the biggest thing in the world is the religion of the Lord Jesus Christ; and the strongest efforts he still makes are to aid in the promulgating this uplifting religion of the Cross.

For various reasons, we record some facts here that will afford an explanation of some things to the friends that remain. Mr. Field always took high rank in the Conference and at the public gatherings of the preachers; and it was always a wonder to many, why the disparity between his Conference standing and the grade of his appointments. The secret is revealed here for the first time. In the Conference he stood high. We will only cite one or two particulars. He was statistical secretary, and a ruling man among the secretaries for thirteen years. When the grand centenary year closed with a centenary meeting at the Conference at Dixon in 1867, the two speakers appointed six months before were A. D. Field and Dr. T. M. Eddy. Two or three times he was united with Dr. Eddy in dedicating churches; and yet in his appointments he did not rate so high. Why? This is the fact: Mr. Field, from his earliest years, was a student, and had a passion for writing; and when he joined the Conference he saw, among writers, many prominent men. He admired Abel Stevens, Edward Thomson, and other noted writers in the Church, and he resolved to be one of these. He made the mistake of giving his right hand power to the pen, and his left to the ministerial work. With the pen his success was considerable, if not great. He has in his scrapbook perhaps a thousand columns of his productions, clipped from newspapers. He was for some time American correspondent of the London *Watchman*. The *National Magazine* and *Ladies' Repository*, from 1855 to 1865, contain columns from his pen. He attained a Church-wide reputation, and was better known in New England than in his own Conference. When Gilbert Haven, in company with G. M. Steele, met him, Haven swung his arms about so as to embrace the two, and exclaimed, *"Par nobile fratrum!"* He was in conversation one day with Dr. Vincent, when circumstances induced Vincent to remark: "Field, I suppose you know that you are considered one of the finest magazine writers in the Church." In 1866 a committee from a town of ten thousand inhabitants waited upon him, offering him a position as editor of a political paper at fifteen hundred dollars a year. His inveterate love for the Methodist Church, a love which is his very life and being to-day, caused him to turn aside from such an offer. His ambition was to rise to some position in the Church, where his pen might find full employment in a way for which he always felt that he had a natural calling. All this, so seemingly out of place, has been recounted to make known the secret of the disparity named above. He gave himself all through his ministerial life to writing. This made him a recluse. He was naturally diffident, and his scholarly habits shut him away from the people, giving him a cold reserve which resulted in years of partial failure. And yet there are compensations. His History of Methodism in the Rock River Conference has had the highest praise from secular men in the highest position in civil life. John Wentworth, for so long a Chicago editor, and a member of Congress from Northern Illinois, thought so much of the book that he prepared a minute index of the work for his own use. As the years go by, and Methodism and the Northwest rises in importance, that book is becoming more and more a fountain of facts, and the men of the future will be glad that such a painstaking writer ever happened into Northern Illinois. He lost passing success for long and permanent good. He has two ambitions left. One is to get this present showing of Worthies and Workers published; and the other is to found at Evanston a permanent Methodist Historical Society, with an open Library and Depository of facts and things. As an addition to the above, it may be said that Mr. Field put in as much as a solid year's work on the Standard Dictionary; his work being the selection of quotations from authors.

In 1871 he superannuated, and removed to Indianola, Iowa, where at present he is active in Church-work.

It is a question worthy of the notice of the curious whether there ever was a person that felt a literary propensity that did not at some time try his pen at rhyme. The new soul feels the literary inspiration, but does not seem to know what peculiar gifts or faculties it may possess; and so must needs try, if but for experiment, to shape the comely rhyme. The subject of this sketch is no exception. All along his life he has felt the desire to do something in the poetic line, and has printed enough lines to make a book. The following is appended to illustrate two things: First, the failure of one who lacks the true poetic afflatus; and, second, the peculiar *outre* nature of much of the performances of our subject, both in the pulpit and in literature. The main lines of this piece are common enough; but in the refrains there is a weird, doleful undertone, that will be found on closest examination to have a more terrible truth in them than appears on the surface:

THE VIOLIN.

'T was midnight in the spacious hall,
Where music ruled the gorgeous ball,
And swiftly sped the dancers' feet,
As the pace of a deer, so wild and fleet;
But the violin shrieks like a dying soul,
That has reached at last its dismal goal!

Then loud and wild is the dancers' cry,
As over the floor they swiftly fly.
The mirth runs high, the wine flows free
As the hours of night so merrily flee;
But the violin wails in wild despair,
As if tortured souls were imprisoned there!

There is joy 'mid the waltzers on the floor,
As they trip so gayly the figures o'er;
And the murky lamps gleam more dim,
As pleasure's cup is filled to the brim;
But the souls of the dancers speak in the strains,
As the violin shrieks in its deathly pains!

The call of the leader is loud and clear,
As tripping feet keep time like a cheer.
Bright and sparkling are the dancers' eyes
As the stars that shimmer in the evening skes;
While the strings of the violin shiver and shriek,
As the souls of the dancers through them speak!

Nothing on earth can so entrance
The trifling crowd as the jovial dance;
The graceful move of the tripping feet
Is to the gay a bliss complete;
But the violin shivers as if in pain,
Like the wail of souls in every strain!

Hastening on are the morning hours,
While o'er the scene the darkness lowers.
In the gloom of morn the tired feet
Plod homeward o'er the frosty street;
While the violin trembles as if in pain
As the souls of the dancers close the strain!

OTIS HENRY TIFFANY, D. D.,

May be called, I think, the "bright particular star" of the Rock River Conference previous to 1880, and was nearly the first of the special transfers. I have been listening to Methodist preachers for over fifty years, and in that time have heard but two preachers that could raise a tumult of noise with sermons delivered from manuscript. Both of these men turned leaf after leaf, and read closely. One of these men was Bishop D. W. Clark. At the Conference at Freeport in 1869 the bishop read a sermon on prayer that raised such a tumult of weeping and shouts that at times he could hardly go on. The other man was Dr. Tiffany. I heard him preach a great many times, and always he read closely; and always he raised a tumult of shouts.

Perhaps one of the highest points Dr. Tiffany ever reached was at Joliet in 1862. He was pastor at Clark Street, Chicago. He had been there two years. He and C. H. Fowler, above all Chicago preachers, inspired the Union cause in the city. Tiffany was cradled in Baltimorean patriotism. When a boy, once on a time he was wrapped in the very flag that floated over Fort McHenry when Key

"Saw through the night that our flag was still there."

So ardent was Dr. Tiffany's leadership in the Union cause that he was put in charge of large sanitary stores, to be transported under his care to the armies in Tennessee. When on a steamboat on the Tennessee River he was taken dangerously sick with the prevailing malady, resulting from drinking the impure river water. The physician administered burnt brandy. From the effects of this the Doctor became oblivious of all things. For a day or two, to him, life was a blank. Reason was dethroned. In this delirium he helped himself to the wines of his sanitary stores. When he returned home he was suspended from the ministry until the meeting of Conference. Four months passed, and Conference met at Joliet in September, 1862. The Doctor had been appointed the year before to preach the missionary sermon. The appointment for this discourse stood on the program for Friday afternoon. The case was, as usual, referred to a trial committee. After two days, on account of deep contrition and a general renovation of religious life, the ban was taken off, and Tiffany was restored to the pulpit once more.

Two carloads of Chicago friends came down to hear the sermon. The Juliet Church was packed. It was to be the sermon of the Conference. It was the first preaching of the man for four months. It was the signal-day of restoration to Conference confidence, and to his old place of pulpit power. It was the coming of the eagle out of the murky storm into the sunlight. The occasion was great, and on that day the preacher was great. He read closely, as was his custom; but in the delivery it was the victor riding on his triumphs. He had not proceeded far till a tumult arose. Shouts of praises, mingled with the voice of weeping, became so loud at times the preacher's voice was nearly drowned. As he pictured the victorious, conquering progress of the glorious gospel of the kingdom he carried all hearts with him on the tide of exultant triumph. I remember that Laird Collier, who sat in the pulpit to assist in the services, was so elated that as he sat on the sofa he would raise his foot and bring it down with a stamp and the shout of hallelujah!

It was a wonderful scene, that rejoicing company shouting over the mellifluous flow of words read page by page from manuscript! I think Dr. Tiffany never preached without full manuscript, but in all his public addresses he spoke without a scrap of paper. On such occasions he was always grand. I will recite an instance. The four Conferences of Illinois met in September, 1866, at Bloomington, for a reunion. Just before, the mob at New Orleans had driven out the Union Legislature of Louisiana from its halls with bloodshed and murder. A deputation of Union men was sent North to arouse the Union people. Among these was Dr. J. P. Newman, then a Methodist pastor at New Orleans. Dr. Newman was going through the North like a flaming spirit of doom, crazing the vast crowds by his momentous theme. Remember that C. H. Fowler and Dr. Tiffany were the brightest flaming torches of freedom in Chicago and the regions about. The Union meeting of the Conferences was to be held on Wednesday. On Tuesday evening there was to be a great mass-meeting of citizens to hear Dr. Newman. I was quartered with J. H. Vincent. We were seated together in the center of the hall amid a crowd of two thousand people. By our side sat David Teed, another Rock River man. We were all three city boys that were used to the way crowds are managed, and, feeling a little mischievous, we were disposed to run things a little. Somebody put up a well-meaning, prosy man to kill time till the crowd was settled. But this man, like all prosy men, when he got to going did not know when to stop, and so when we thought it was time for a change, we three began calling, "Newman," "Newman." It was some time before the crowd saw what we were up to, but soon joined their voices and helped to change the program. Then Dr. Newman came. For two hours he entranced us. It was the one greatest occasion of my life. No tongue or pen can describe the matchless eloquence of that hour. The effect of the speech was such that, instead of being tired when it was done, the appetites of the people were whetted for more. Besides, the trio of us wanted to see how some of our favorites would compare with Newman. So, when we saw that the Doctor was about to conclude, Teed said, "Let us try Fowler;" and the moment Dr. Newman closed we raised the cry of "Fowler." But we made a mistake. Fowler was but yet a beginner, and besides, till this day, Bishop Fowler needs time to get started. He could never dash off like a flash as some men can. Fowler failed to get the crowd, and soon gave it up. Dr. Newman had gone too high for common men to follow. As Brother Fowler was about to close we said: "Let us try Tiffany." We raised the "Tiffany" cry. The crowd joined us, and out from behind the scenes Dr. Tiffany came and conquered. He came upon the stage with a sort of stride, pulling off his overcoat as he came. All could see at a glance that there was "blood in his eye." As he came he exclaimed (and every appearance showed that he was not shamming): "I am mad! I am mad! To think that I have lived to see this day, when rebels have been paroled and pardoned, only to strike down the generous hands that have been reached out to lift them up," etc. It is not necessary to say anything further. The reader can see what sort of a speech followed from such a begining. From the first the vast concourse was wild with cries of terrible assent. Tiffany talked in this strain for a few minutes until he held the people in magnetic control, and then he put the audience to the severest test I ever witnessed. If I remember correctly, no State at that time had given the Negro the right to vote. That was one of the burning questions. And we were, in Central Illinois, not far from the line where secession sympathies began to be common. In such a crowd as that was raised this most delicate of questions. The Doctor was carrying the people away with applause over Lincoln and emancipation and Negro rights, when he turned upon the crowd with bitter sarcasm and threw into their faces, almost tauntingly, this: "Yes, you shout at emancipation and the cry of freedom, but you won't give the Negro his rights! You won't allow him to exercise his manhood! You won't give him his rights! You will not allow him to vote!" Then arose all over the house the cry, "We will!" "We will!" "No you won't!" said Tiffany. "When it comes to the test, you will not do him justice." Then louder than ever rose the cry, "We will!" "We will!"

"Will you?" exclaimed the Doctor. "Will you? Well, then, I'll give you a chance to utter your will. Those in this audience who are willing to grant the Negro the right to vote say aye." And strange to say, like the swaying of wind arose, as if but one voice, the loud "aye!" from those thousand voices. Dr. Tiffany was amazed.

Newman and Tiffany held that assembly in their hands, and could have led them at will.

If I am asked in what did the eloquence of Dr. Tiffany consist, my answer would be: His eloquence consisted in an elegant diction, a rich flow of words uttered in rich musical tones. His voice was his chief power. Add to this a noble, fraternal, kindly soul, and a most beautiful face and form, neatly clad, and perhaps you have the whole answer. During the War there was always a Conference Committee on the State of the Country. Dr. Tiffany was generally made chairman of the committee, that the people and preachers might be inspired by his exultant Union utterances. He read one of these reports at Rockford in 1863. Some one moved that the report be printed in certain papers named. Dr. Dempster, immediately on the utterance of the resolution, added: "And that it glow in every sunbeam that greets the sight!"

With such a personage as this I choose to let some of the ablest pens record their thoughts. And first we add the following from Prof. George R. Crooks:

"I doubt if a preacher precisely like Dr. Tiffany has appeared in our Church. Reared in the enjoyment of all that wealth, one might say luxury, could give, it would scarcely have been imagined that he would accept for his portion in this world the Methodist itinerancy. His father's house, on the outskirts of Baltimore, was hospitably opened to the Methodist worthies of fifty years ago. There Bascom was entertained during the General Conference of 1840. I have seen, too, sitting at his table men whose memories are very precious to us now. Comfort Tiffany was a genial host, who enjoyed the enjoyment of his guests, and delighted to share the pleasures of his beautiful home with Methodist ministers. His son, Otis Henry, appeared among us at Carlisle [Dickinson College], a beaming young fellow, full of spirit, yet in dead earnest for study. He entered junior, was graduated in two years, and quickly made known his conviction that his life career was to be in the Christian ministry. I think—but I am not sure—that I heard his first sermon. A Sunday appointment was to be filled in Shippensburg, hard by Carlisle, and we went together. We divided the work of the day, he taking the second sermon. . . . It was a most modest sermon, but displayed some of the characteristics which throughout life distinguished him: carefulness of preparation, sweetness of voice, grace, without superfluity, of gesture, and a smooth diction. Indeed, I never knew the time when he was not an accomplished declaimer. One of his college declamations has clung to my memory for fifty years. Its clear, outringing tones, and his matchless action, are as vividly present now to my mind's eye as if he were speaking before me this moment. Much of his grace he had learned in his father's drawing-room; it was simply the bearing of a gentleman occupied in meeting the requirements of a public occasion. He had, however, a large share of the oratorical temperament. He was a born rhetorician. What strange providence made him a professor of Mathematics I never could conjecture. The figures nature intended him to deal with were figures of speech, and he could, with quicker instinct, define the just limits of hyperbole than trace the extensions of the hyperbola. He had in him the elements of a brilliant professor of Belles-Lettres and English Literature; but there were no such chairs in our Methodist schools in that day. College tradition credits him with entire success in his mathematical professorship. Any one who knew him would have expected as much, for he had the ambition to do thoroughly well whatever he undertook to do. Like many other students of Dickinson in that period, he came under the spell of the power of John P. Durbin, John McClintock, and Robert Emory. These men he knew not distantly, but familiarly. With Dr. McClintock he was intimate. What young man could resist the charm of McClintock's cordiality? . . . When he joined the Baltimore Conference, he took horse and saddle in the good old style. I do not think he had many privations to bear, for he was not far from his home; but it was the time of the 'hundred-dollar' dispensation. . . . I declare, unhesitatingly, that if Otis Henry Tiffany had been called on to meet such experiences for a series of years, he would have met them without a murmur; for he was manly to the core! Though bred in affluence, he accepted the itinerant's lot with entire cheerfulness. It was his joy and his pride, under all circumstances, to be known as a Methodist preacher."

About the year 1868, William Morley Punshon was known as the greatest orator of the Wesleyan Church in England. With us over here, who only knew Mr. Punshon by what we read, this was his only prominent quality. In the year named above, Mr. Punshon came over to our General Conference, which met at Chicago, as the Wesleyan delegate. We were all anxious to hear him, to take a measure of English oratory. It was the writer's privilege to hear both his formal address to the Conference and his sermon before that body. During the time I was in conference with some of the best members of the Conference, and among all I met, there was a general disappointment. The exclamation of nearly all was that we could readily pick out numbers of our own men who excelled the eloquent delegate. And almost every one turned instinctively to Dr. Tiffany. He was fit in every way and circumstance to be compared with Punshon. Their careers and characters were very much alike. None of us had any hesitation in putting Dr. Tiffany at the head.

And, curiously enough, they were brought into active and actual comparison. Dr. Punshon remained in Canada for a year or two. The story of their meeting I will condense from Dr. Crooks. Dr. Tiffany was sent for to speak at an anniversary, in company with Mr. Punshon, in Toronto or Montreal. Mr. Punshon had made little special preparation. Dr. Tiffany thrilled and enraptured the Canadians. The encomiums of the Canada papers were such as are seldom bestowed on any speaker. Mr. Punshon was so dissatisfied with his own performance that he begged the managers to invite Dr. Tiffany and himself to occupy the same platform the following year. They met the second time with about the same results.

We quote from Dr. Crooks again:

"Like Simpson, like Gough, he died in harness; for the death-stroke fell on him just as he had uttered the first sentence of a sermon in the Presbyterian Church at Red Wing, Minnesota. It was Conference Sunday. He had spoken of the great power of God, when he fainted away. From the time of the first sermon . . . to that last day it was a long interval—forty-six years as I reckon—but it had been filled with a prodigious amount of work."

This is the way he is described by his friend, General Rusling, a student when Tiffany was professor at Dickinson:

"He had little the appearance of a professor or parson in those days, but looked rather as an active lawyer or bustling man of business; rosy-cheeked, clear-eyed, smooth-browed, and appareled like a man of the world, rather than a Dryasdust of the cloister. Athletic and vigorous in build and movement, the youngest member of the faculty, and seeming still almost like a college-boy himself, he was the pride and admiration of the undergraduates, and shared their fun and frolic to the full as far as a professor dared to do. . . . No one was more commanding than he when he drew the reins in the lecture-room or elsewhere. But he kept a warm side to the college lads, and never forgot that he, too, was once a student. It goes without saying that he filled the chair of Mathematics there ably and successfully. . . . We recognized his brilliant genius, and this often stood him in good stead when he came to skating over thin ice where others would have broken through.

In intellect, in voice and speech, he was superb. . . . What a fineness of courtesy he had! What a grace of voice and gesture! What perfection of manners! Not Chesterfield himself at his best could have surpassed this suave Baltimore American. . . . When he was to preach or lecture the churches were always crowded. . . . He was as eloquent as Webster, as fiery as Clay, and as scholarly as Sumner; and at times, in voice, action, and thought, seemed to equal them all."

The geographical outline of Dr. Tiffany's services is thus epitomized: Clark Street, Grace, and Trinity Churches in Chicago, with Evanston near by; Broad, Arch, and Spring Garden Churches in Philadelphia; Fifty-first Street, St. Paul, and St. James in New York City; full terms at St. James, New Brunswick, N. J., and at Metropolitan Church in Washington City. His last pastorate was at Hennepin Avenue, in Minneapolis, which began in October, 1889.

He was born in Baltimore, July 3, 1825, of Puritan ancestry. He entered the junior class in Dickinson College in 1842, and graduated in 1844. He served two years, from 1847, as tutor in Dickinson, and from 1849 to 1858 was professor of Mathematics.

He filled the pulpit of a Baltimore Associate Reformed Church from 1858 until 1860, when he came to Clark Street, Chicago, and joined the Rock River Conference. From here he was transferred to New Jersey in 1867. He returned to Chicago, and served Trinity Church from 1875 till

1878, when he returned to the East to remain until, as noted above, he went to Minneapolis, Minnesota, in 1889, where he died Saturday afternoon, October 24, 1891, aged sixty-six.

Dr. Tiffany joined the Baltimore Conference in 1846, and was appointed junior preacher, at a hundred dollars a year, on Hereford Circuit. In 1848 he married Eliza B. Hamilton, daughter of William Hamilton, a man of note in the Baltimore Conference. In 1847 he went as junior to Great Falls. In 1848 his appointment was as tutor in Dickinson College. His further appointments have been given elsewhere.

After the fainting-spell at Red Wing, noted above, tenderly was he lifted by his friends and borne to his home in Minneapolis. With the shadows gathering all about him, he wearily whispered: "This is the beginning of the end." Day by day his weakness increased. One by one the moorings that held him to the shores of time were broken, and he drifted gently out with the ebbing tide.

THE END.

www.ingramcontent.com/pod-product-compliance
Lightning Source LLC
Chambersburg PA
CBHW020237240426
43672CB00006B/561